THE LIFE
WE CHOSE

THE LIFE WE CHOSE

WILLIAM "BIG BILLY" D'ELIA AND
THE LAST SECRETS OF AMERICA'S
MOST POWERFUL MAFIA FAMILY

MATT BIRKBECK

wm

WILLIAM MORROW
An Imprint of HarperCollinsPublishers

HarperCollins books may be purchased for educational, business, or sales promotional use. For information, please email the Special Markets Department at SPsales@harpercollins.com.

FIRST EDITION

Designed by Nancy Singer

Title page art by Ryan McVay/The Image Bank/Getty Images

Photograph credits for insert: page 1 (top and bottom): Courtesy of the Bufalino estate; page 2 (top): Courtesy of the Bufalino estate; page 2: (bottom left): Courtesy of the D'Elia family; page 2 (bottom right): Courtesy GETTY IMAGES/New York Daily News; page 3 (top and bottom): Courtesy of the D'Elia family; page 3 (middle): Courtesy of the Bufalino estate; page 4 (top and bottom): Courtesy of the Bufalino estate; page 4 (middle): Courtesy of AP Photo/Bill Ingraham; page 5 (top left): Courtesy AP file photo; page 5 (top right): Courtesy AP Photo/Mario Suriani; page 5 (bottom left and right): Courtesy of the D'Elia family; page 6 (top and bottom): Courtesy of the D'Elia family; page 6 (middle): Courtesy of the Bufalino estate; page 7 (all): Courtesy of the D'Elia family; page 8 (top left and middle): Courtesy of the D'Elia family; page 8 (top right): Courtesy of AP Photo/Carolyn Kaster; page 8 (bottom): Courtesy of Matt Birkbeck

Library of Congress Cataloging-in-Publication Data has been applied for.

ISBN 978-0-06-323467-3

23 24 25 26 27 LBC 5 4 3 2 1

For my dad, who is always with me

The impossible we could fix right away.

Miracles take a day or two.

—Russell Bufalino

CONTENTS

Contents

PROLOGUE

It was a late afternoon in October 2006 when a black Lincoln Town Car pulled in front of the modest house on a hill in Hughestown, a borough in northeast Pennsylvania midway between Scranton and Wilkes-Barre.

The driver, a tall, middle-aged man with jet-black hair, was about to open his door when a car abruptly pulled in behind him, blue lights flashing. He looked into the rearview mirror. Behind the blue lights were more vehicles, their lights also flashing. Closing in ahead of him were even more cars and SUVs, filling the normally tranquil street in front of his home.

Above was a loud whirring noise, and he peered up through the front windshield to see a Chinook helicopter overhead.

Within seconds his car was surrounded by frantic men and women, some in uniform, others wearing windbreakers emblazoned with "FBI," "Secret Service," and "Homeland Security." All had their guns drawn and pointed at him. They screamed out directives to put his hands up and to slowly get out of the car. It was all happening so fast, with near-military precision, but he knew the drill.

"Here we go again," he mumbled to himself.

Five and a half years earlier, on May 31, 2001, the FBI, U.S. Secret Service, Pennsylvania State Police, Internal Revenue Service, and U.S. Postal Inspection Service had all raided the same home. He had just driven away but was pulled over on a local road. When they searched his car then, they found several guns in the trunk, including an AK-47 and a shotgun. In the backseat was a suitcase, and inside was a MAC-10 submachine gun. A nine-millimeter Beretta was holstered to his side.

Now, on this late fall afternoon and with the sun already setting, he was again surrounded by an overwhelming show of law enforcement officers and agents. But this time they included the Department of Homeland Security, Border Patrol, and Immigration and Customs Enforcement. Free on bail from an earlier money-laundering charge, he wasn't carrying any weapons. But he did have $38,000 in cash in his inside breast pocket, money he had just collected from a Russian in Hazleton, Pennsylvania.

As he slowly emerged from the car and into the cacophony of chaos and noise, he could decipher the loud, nervous repetitions of *"Hands above your head!"* and *"We'll blow your fucking head off!"*

One young agent pointing a gun at him couldn't keep his hand from shaking.

"Easy with that," he said.

He turned around and was shoved against the car, searched, handcuffed, placed inside an FBI vehicle, and then taken to the local magistrate and charged with trying to hire a hit man to kill a witness in his money-laundering case. After, he was transported to the Lackawanna County Prison in Scranton. His stay there was short but pleasant given all the food—mostly Italian delicacies and desserts—that had been sent to his cell courtesy of friends, local businesses, and restaurants. His jailers didn't mind. Many knew him personally. A few days later he was transferred to the prison in neighboring Pike County, which borders New York State and New Jersey.

It was there, without warning, he was roused from his cell, shackled, and escorted out of the back of the prison and into the rear of an unmarked FBI SUV. Within minutes, a long procession of unmarked law enforcement vehicles sped west along Interstate 84. It looked like a presidential motorcade, but that didn't stop an overzealous state police highway trooper from flagging down the lead vehicle, which he had clocked going over ninety miles per hour.

When the trooper approached, the driver opened his window and confidently flashed his badge and FBI credential.

"License and registration, sir," said the trooper.

The FBI agent, a bit flummoxed, held his identification higher. "FBI, transporting a prisoner to the federal courthouse in Scranton," he said.

The trooper remained undaunted. "License and registration, sir."

"FBI," said the agent, now a bit agitated. "We're transporting a prisoner to the federal courthouse in Scranton."

"I don't care. License and registration," the trooper repeated. He peered into the rear of the truck and immediately recognized the large figure in an orange jumpsuit seated on the passenger side. The trooper's eyes grew wide.

"*Is that Billy D'Elia?!*" he said, gawking.

"Yes," said the FBI agent.

"Well, why didn't you tell me you had Big Billy in here! Then go through!"

• • •

William "Big Billy" D'Elia was the most sought-after organized crime leader in the United States, who had for years been on the radar of federal, state, and local law enforcement agencies.

He was known as the mob's "negotiator," the guy who was summoned to settle problems—or make them go away. New York, Philadelphia, Kansas City, Los Angeles. Wherever there was trouble, the call went out to Big Billy.

But he was more than just the mob's fixer. Billy was Mafia royalty, the so-called son of Russell Bufalino, who was arguably the most powerful and important organized crime figure of the twentieth century. Billy had spent nearly thirty years at Bufalino's side, from the mid-1960s until Bufalino's death in 1994, and subsequently became the unquestioned leader of the Bufalino Family.

Now that he was finally in custody, law enforcement agencies throughout the country were eager to talk with him. Almost every week Billy was transported from the Pike County prison to the William J. Nealon Federal Building and U.S. Courthouse in Scranton to meet with one investigator after another.

There were the detectives from New York City assigned to the FBI/NYPD Joint Terrorism Task Force who quizzed him about money-laundering operations based in the Bronx that allegedly wired tens of millions to Middle Eastern terrorists. Another group of detectives, from New York's organized crime task force, sought information on decades' worth of Mafia activity there with a focus on the hierarchy of the Five Families, while Philadelphia detectives were keenly interested in Billy's firsthand knowledge of their city's once-powerful and violent crime family, which had been through two bloody wars.

More FBI agents arrived looking for information on Mafia families in Chicago, Kansas City, Los Angeles, and elsewhere, while the Secret Service wanted to know about counterfeit-money operations throughout the country. New Jersey investigators wanted to hear about his ties to illegal gambling and money-laundering operations in Atlantic City, which had banned Billy from entering the city in 2003. And in Harrisburg, Pennsylvania, the state capital, Billy was subpoenaed to testify before a grand jury investigating a longtime friend, a Scranton billionaire, who was suspected of lying about his mob ties to gain approval for a casino license.

Every week, there was someone or something new to discuss. And of course, there was Jimmy Hoffa.

That first trip to the Scranton federal courthouse, the one interrupted by a state trooper, was to bring Billy face-to-face with two

FBI agents from Detroit who were part of a new unit assembled to investigate the 1975 disappearance of the former Teamsters leader.

Though Billy was never a suspect himself, Russell Bufalino was among the handful of men the FBI strongly believed had taken part in Hoffa's disappearance and alleged murder. Frank Sheeran, a Bufalino subordinate and Billy confidant, was another suspect, and the FBI was convinced they both had shared details with Billy about their involvement. They must have, the agents reasoned, given how close Billy had been to both men. But when the federal agents announced their intentions, Billy brushed them off, saying only that Hoffa was "not on the farm," a reference to a field in Michigan where investigators were searching for the former Teamsters boss's remains.

The dejected agents flew back to Detroit empty-handed, much like every other federal agent, investigator, detective, and prosecutor who came to speak to Billy then, and over the ensuing years. But Billy did have a story to tell.

He was just waiting for the right time to share it.

CHAPTER 1

Pittston

Blood, brains, and bone were all that was left of Snowball's little furry white head.

Just a few weeks old, the puppy had been playfully prancing in the backyard with the boy. It was a gift from a neighbor who had one too many puppies. When he came by the house to deliver the dog, he delighted the little boy, who held him to his chest and immediately knew what he'd name him.

It was just a couple of days later that the boy took Snowball outside and the white puppy romped from one side of the backyard to the other. But then he wandered among the soon-to-be-ripe tomato plants way in the rear, and the boy watched in horror as a brick suddenly came crashing down on the puppy's head with such force it killed him instantly.

The boy ran to the dead animal and fell to his knees in a state of grief and shock that only a four-year-old could feel. Teary-eyed, he looked up to his father, who was still holding the brick, which dripped red puppy blood and dark brain matter.

The father took pride in his garden, and he didn't appreciate anything, including a puppy, disturbing his tomato plants.

"You wanted a dog. Now clean him up," he said.

The boy, whom everyone called Billy, followed his father's command and put the dead pet, along with its brains, into a bag.

His father, William P. D'Elia, was a plumber by trade, but his day job was driving a rig for the city of Pittston's fire department. He worked a four-days-on schedule, with his three days off split between earning extra cash with the odd plumbing job and drinking beers at Viola's bar, his personal refuge on Main Street.

When his father-in-law died, William P.'s wife, Theresa, knew to call him there.

"Pa died," she cried.

"What are you calling me for!" he shouted. "Call the undertaker."

William P. was the son of Italian immigrants. They had arrived in Pittston around the turn of the century via the same route over the vast ocean that had led many others before them to this little town on the banks of the Susquehanna River in northeast Pennsylvania. It was pretty there, the river slicing through the mountains, which were painted green during the summer and with brilliant brown hues during the fall.

Dozens of communities sprouted up along the river's banks, from Scranton south to Wilkes-Barre, after anthracite coal was discovered in the late 1700s—tons of it. The communities had names such as Port Griffith, which was eight miles downriver from Scranton, and Exeter and Kingston, which were just across from Wilkes-Barre.

By the late 1800s Pittston had become a central coal hub, the brittle black rock mined and shipped through its canals down to Philadelphia and even farther, into Baltimore. Italian immigrants had come in such droves, they eased out the Scots and Irish working the mines and took control of them.

Mining jobs in Pittston were plentiful. An underground river of anthracite called the "Big Vein" stretched through the entire town and under the Susquehanna River into West Pittston. Several mining companies worked the rich vein, much of which was virtually free of impurities. That made the black rock even more valuable. But the work was incredibly dangerous, and injury and death were a way of life.

One early morning in June 1896, the roof of the Red Ash vein of the Twin Shaft mine caved in, killing seventy-five of the one hundred men and boys who were working there, four hundred feet underground. Their bodies were never recovered. In 1905 seven miners working the Clear Spring Coal Company's shaft in West Pittston ended their shift and boarded a cage meant to carry them to the surface. As they were hoisted up, the cable broke and the men plummeted two hundred terrifying feet to their deaths. Rescuers found only body parts.

Despite the dangers, Pittston became one of several final landing spots for the thousands of Italian immigrants who sailed into New York but didn't want to stay in the crowded city. Many traveled even farther west and settled in places like Detroit, Pittsburgh, and Buffalo, while others went no farther than Pittston. Some families even split up, with some members staying in Pittston while brothers, sisters, parents, and cousins continued the journey. Geography didn't matter for Italian immigrants. For them, blood ties were everything, not your location.

The D'Elias lived in a white house on Wilford Street, which wasn't far from the river. Single-family homes with small front gardens and white picket fences lined the street.

After his arrival from Italy, Billy's grandfather had worked underground in the mines for several years but later avoided the drudgery and early death that went with mining when he became the weighmaster for the Pennsylvania Coal Company. His favorite activity was sitting on his front porch every Thursday afternoon slicing up vegetables and fruits from his brother-in-law's grocery store. They were too old to sell but too fresh to throw out, so he cut up the good stuff and canned it.

Billy loved his grandparents, George and Maria, who lived in a separate apartment that was attached to the house. And Billy cherished his mother. Warm and nurturing, Theresa D'Elia was of Irish descent, with a maiden name of Walsh. She worked as a clerk at Kleinrock's Army & Navy downtown. It was Theresa's sister, Aunt Lottie, who watched over Billy and his two older sisters, Margaret, whom everyone called Peggy, and Shirley. A sweetheart of a woman, Lottie had never married, and between her and Theresa they took care of the big house, which had been sold to William P. by his father. George had owned three houses and sold one to his son on the condition that Maria be allowed to stay in the separate apartment when he was gone. Theresa agreed, but only if her sister could live in the house too.

The two-story home had plenty of room with a big kitchen. And of course, there was the backyard with the tomato garden in the back, a place where Billy never ventured after disposing of Snowball.

"What was I going to do?" said Billy, recalling that terrible memory years later. "I was just a little kid. I mean, the puppy just ran into his plants. It wasn't nothing. He could have just told me to pick it up and take it inside, but he was a nasty prick. He just picked up a brick and smashed the dog's head in front of me. That's a tough thing to see for a little kid."

WILLIAM J. D'ELIA WAS BORN in Pittston Hospital on June 24, 1946, and aside from the traumatic experience of witnessing his dog's murder, growing up in Pittston with a vacant father but loving family during the 1950s was fairly idyllic.

Quaint homes, each displaying an American flag, lined every block, and the neighborhood children owned the streets, riding their bikes, playing games. One of them was Sam Marranca, whom everyone called "Kooch." He was a bit of a rascal who at just age ten knew his way around a pool table. One of Billy's best friends, Kooch lived by the firehouse where Billy's dad worked. They got along together,

Kooch and William P., as did William P. and Wally Shandra, another mischievous sort who lived a couple of blocks away on Oak Street. William P. would take them and other neighborhood kids fishing, but never his son.

"It was kind of weird," said Billy. "He was good to the other kids, just not me."

A gifted athlete, Billy played American Legion baseball and was on a team that won a tournament when he was twelve. But unlike many of the other kids, whose parents cheered them on during games, Billy's didn't. His mother worked full-time, and his father took no interest in any of his activities.

The distance and anger between father and son erupted one Christmas when Billy interceded after his father knocked his sister Shirley into the Christmas tree during an argument.

"They were having words and he slapped her in the face," said Billy. "He knocked her down, so I jumped in and said, 'You prick. Don't ever touch her again.' I was just a kid, eleven, twelve years old. He didn't really hit us a lot, only when he had a cocktail before. But after I jumped in he says, 'As long as I live, you'll never get a dime of my money.' What did that mean to a twelve-year-old? Nothing. Like I said, he was just a nasty prick."

When she wasn't working, Theresa devoted much of her time and attention to keeping the peace between her husband and gentle son, who, despite doing little homework, happened to be a good student at Jefferson Elementary School. Theresa adored Billy, and her motherly affection instilled a softness and likability in her only son.

"My mom, she always stood up for me," said Billy.

So long as he avoided his father, the family dynamic remained relatively tranquil. Billy played with his friends after school and by the time he got home, Aunt Lottie usually had dinner on the table for everyone. On Sundays the entire family would dress up and attend the nine A.M. Mass at St. Mary, Help of Christians, with the exception of Grandma Maria. Born a Catholic, she became a Protestant and eventually a "Holy Roller"—part of an Evangelical denomination. Its members would gather on the front porch every Wednesday with other believers and work themselves into a frenzy, rolling across the porch at exactly three P.M.

"It was like God would be coming into them. It went back to the early days when Catholics couldn't get jobs in Pittston," said Billy. "So some people, like my grandparents, who came right from Italy became Presbyterians. My father converted back to Catholicism when my sister Shirley made her confirmation. My grandmother went from Catholic to Presbyterian to becoming a Holy Roller. But she had this other side to her. She used to walk by the shoe store with her shopping bag where they had all the samples out. But they wouldn't put the whole set out, just one shoe. So when she died they found twenty left shoes in her closet. She stole all the samples."

When Mass ended they'd wait in line with the other parishioners to greet the priest and then drive over to Ristagno's bakery in nearby Exeter for warm Italian bread, which they'd bring home and dip into the tomato sauce that Grandma had been simmering all morning. A couple of hours later they'd start on the pasta and meatballs.

When he entered Pittston High School, Billy was thin as a rail but stood well over six feet tall. He had given up sports by then. Sort of. Instead, he and Wally sold football betting sheets, the small, rectangular slivers of paper where bettors would pick the winner of a minimum of four college or NFL games. But each pick had to beat the spread. They'd hand out the sheets at the beginning of the week, then retrieve them and the money before the weekend's games and give them over to the bookie.

"A lot of people in Pittston liked betting football," said Billy.

There were also a lot of kids his age working the sheets, so he and Wally tried some other ways to make money, such as selling newspapers. They weren't employed by the papers. Instead, they'd wait for the delivery trucks to drop the stacks of papers on Main Street, steal them, and resell them at a discount. While they made a few bucks, after a while it wasn't worth the effort. So Billy took a job at his uncle's grocery store, only to soon realize that his customer service abilities were less than ideal.

"I needed to work, so I went there, but I was always getting yelled at," said Billy. "My uncle always told me to be careful with this and that, like be careful with those chocolate éclairs because they cost him a lot of money. But I was real skinny, like ninety-seven pounds, and kind of sensitive to people thinking I was weak. So one day this guy that was bigger than me asked me to carry his groceries to his car. I told him to carry his own fucking bag. My uncle said this wasn't working out."

Another summer he went to work with his father. Their relationship had remained frosty at best, but William P. needed a plumber's assistant and grudgingly offered the job to his son.

"He had a contract to replace all the fire extinguishers in the Pittston public schools," said Billy. "They had those old copper extinguishers, and every year they had to be inspected. You'd go in, twist the top off, and there was a bottle of acid in there. You had to dump that out and put new acid in, and then pump out the water. That was a big contract, and he was getting fifteen dollars a fire extinguisher, and he was going to pay me half. So when the check came I said, 'Where's my half?' and he said, 'You eat here, don't ya? You sleep here, don't ya? That's your half.'"

Billy was still working the football sheets with Wally, and every Monday they'd run up to a printing shop in Clarks Summit and pick them up and distribute them to the regular clientele. If Pittston had a local pastime, it was gambling. And not just football. Bookies lingered at all hours on nearly every street corner and inside the local pool halls, like LaTorre's and the Imperial, their pants pockets usually bulging with cash.

The pool halls were filled day and night, men and boys shooting pool or playing cards or pinball in the dimly lit, smoke-filled quarters. Pool was so popular in Pittston that several local men, such as Lou

Butera, emerged as challengers for world championships. Shooting pool was a serious business in Pittston, with men wagering on every game, and sometimes every shot.

"North Pittston is where I grew up, but south Pittston was where all the action was," said Billy. "You had two, three poolrooms across the street from each other. They were always crowded. We had Pearl's Pizza and another pizza place down the street. On Friday nights you couldn't walk along the sidewalk. That's how crowded with people it was. Gambling was a big deal."

It was at Pittston High School in the early 1960s that a lab teacher asked Billy to go downtown for her and place a bet on a horse. She gave him twenty dollars and a half day off to make the bet. Not long after, Billy and Wally were running bets for all the teachers.

"We had thousands in the bank from the sheets and the teachers' betting," said Billy. "I thought I was a little wise guy with the leather jacket and combat boots. One of the bookies was 'Big Lou' Butera and he was married to Pearl Medico, who owned Pearl's Pizza and was a sister of the Medico brothers, Bill and Phil. They owned this big business in the area making tools and weapons for the government. I didn't really know anything about them until later. But at Pearl's Pizza, they had a divider there between the tables and the front end where they cooked and served takeout. So I'd sit there with a rubber band and matches and shoot them over the divider into the sauce. One day there was a guy in there watching me and he yells out, 'Why don't you kick him in the ass.' I looked at him and said, 'Do you think you're big enough?' and he says, 'Yeah, you want to try me?' Guess what? He kicked my ass out the store and all the way up the street to the bank building. He was a tough little guy. His name was Loquasto."

It was around that time that Billy started dating Ellen Ward. She was a tiny, cute girl who lived nearby and was part of a bigger group of kids that Billy hung out with in the neighborhood or downtown at the pizza parlors. But most of the time they'd be at Ellen's house.

"We became very close. We all went there because her mother would feed everybody," said Billy. "Every kid in the neighborhood ate in that house. Her father worked for the Pennsylvania Power and Light company and when he would come home from work, he'd put on his sweater. They were so nice together it was like the perfect home, like *Father Knows Best*. But at nine o'clock he'd say, 'It's time to fix the furnace,' and that was it. Everyone knew it was time to leave."

Billy and Ellen dated when they were fifteen, but Billy's teenage eyes always roamed, and Ellen found another boyfriend. When he graduated high school in 1964 he had grown to six feet four inches tall and towered over everyone. He had plans to attend college and study accounting, but that following summer he kept running the football sheets with Wally. They'd meet at the Imperial poolroom, in which locals and gangsters were often found together. Aside from coal and the poolrooms, if Pittston had anything, it was gangsters. And a lot of them. They had been there since the late 1800s, and they melded with the community.

It started with Stefano LaTorre, who owned LaTorre's poolroom. He emigrated from the small Sicilian town of Montedoro in the late 1800s. A member of the Mafia there, he was only seventeen when he arrived in Pittston, where he quickly took up extortion, loan-sharking, and murder. Other Montedoro men, such as Calogero Bufalino, whom everyone in America called Charles, and Santo Volpe joined him.

They all worked the mines but quickly settled into their old-world customs, often exploiting their fellow immigrant Italian miners. Together, they were known as the Black Hand.

The police tried to control them. Their first arrests came in 1907, when several Black Hand members were charged with terrorizing the community by demanding payoffs and tribute from fellow Italian miners. Charles Bufalino and LaTorre were convicted and spent a year in prison. Volpe was acquitted and for months after the trial led a bloody vendetta in which local residents who had cooperated with the police were murdered in retribution, their corpses left along Railroad Street in south Pittston.

Despite the unwanted police attention, by 1910 they had control of all underworld activity in Pittston and the surrounding towns and set their sights on expanding their business, buying coal mines and gaining influence over the burgeoning unions. By 1914 many of the two hundred thousand miners in northeast Pennsylvania worked in sites owned by the three men, who also used bribes and other enticements, as well as violence, to rule the new unions representing the miners. Men and boys were required to give up a portion of their net pay every week if they wanted to work in one of their mines.

The power of the Black Hand grew every day. Some resisted, but the weekly bloodletting on the south side along Railroad Street earned Pittston the nickname "Murder Capital of the World."

And since those early days there had remained a formidable group of gangsters who owned many of the businesses that lined Pittston's Main Street and still had direct ties to Charles Bufalino, Santo Volpe, and Stefano LaTorre. One such establishment was the Imperial, where there were four pool tables and six card tables, with a number of pinball machines along the wall. Men with slicked-back hair and gold chains around their necks and wrists would gather in its smoky environs every afternoon and evening. It was there, between games of eight ball and pinball, that Billy and Wally would strategize. They were ready to move on to larger enterprises. One such scheme saw Billy—now eighteen, with a driver's license—venture out to Philadelphia to buy men's high-end suits from a company there called Mini Shade. They paid $80 to $90 for each suit, drove back to Pittston, and sold them for $500 each.

"We made a lot with that, and Wally kept all of our money," said Billy. "I told him to give me a couple of thousand dollars. I'm going to get us more suits. He says, 'I can't.' I asked why and he says, 'I put it all in my sister's safety deposit box at the bank.' I says, 'Are you fucking crazy? Go get me three thousand dollars.' So he took all our money out of the bank, gave me three thousand, and I went back to Philly. But before I left I said, 'Where are you going to put the rest of the money?' and he said somewhere inside his house. I said, 'What happens if the house burns down?' He said the fucking house will never burn down. So I'm coming back from Philadelphia and I see a big glow in the air. Guess what? The fucking house burned to the ground with the money."

They retreated again to the Imperial to gamble away their depression over their financial loss, and it was there that Billy saw the squat guy who'd kicked his ass up and down Main Street outside of Pearl's Pizza. His full name was Modesto Loquasto and he was the bodyguard for the man just behind him, a much older, well-dressed man of medium height with a droopy eyelid and only three fingers on his right hand.

It was Russell Bufalino.

Russell was the nephew of Charles Bufalino; everyone in Pittston either knew him or knew of him. He controlled most everything in Pittston and the region. Loquasto used his thick arms to create a path for him as his admirers sought handshakes or gave him respectful slaps on the back.

Billy had seen him on occasion at the Imperial and knew that Bufalino was the head of the Mafia family that bore his name. Everyone in Pittston did, though no one would ever say it out loud.

Some years earlier, when he was a kid, Billy had stood on a chair here to watch the black-and-white television that was mounted up high in the corner. Bufalino was testifying before a U.S. Senate subcommittee in Washington, DC, that was investigating the influence of organized crime on labor in the United States. Robert Kennedy, the committee's aggressive counsel, was questioning Bufalino and had become increasingly agitated when, after each question, Bufalino claimed his Fifth Amendment right not to speak. He did it over ninety times during the hours-long hearing.

"We all watched and were rooting for Russell," said Billy. "I didn't know why other than everyone was saying he was like this local hero who helped people here. One guy needed a roof and went to Bufalino, another woman needed help with a sick parent, or the church needed money. I'm just a kid, so what do I know?"

Billy stood next to a pool table, his height affording him a clear view as Loquasto and Bufalino made their way through the crowd and headed right toward him. When they reached the tall gangly teenager he'd once beaten to a pulp, Loquasto offered a faint smile of acknowledgment. Bufalino followed, and Billy put out his hand.

"How you doing, Mr. Bufalino?"

The older man looked up, took Billy's hand, and squeezed firmly for an extra second or two.

"I'm doing fine, kid."

Billy's eyes followed Bufalino as he went out the front door and was escorted into the front passenger seat of a shiny black Cadillac.

"You see this guy you really only hear about and he shakes your hand and you're thinking, 'Wow,'" said Billy.

Graduation from Pittston High School in 1964 led to enrollment in a two-year accounting program at Wilkes-Barre Business College. Billy had always been good at math, and the thinking was he could make a career of it, maybe as an accountant. But it wasn't his first career choice. He had thought about becoming a priest when he was younger. He'd even mentioned that to Father Sammon, the parish priest. Father Sammon looked at him, lifted his thick brow, and paused a bit, hoping to draw on all the wisdom he could muster.

"He said he had no problem with me being a priest, but before I do that, why don't I finish high school," said Billy. "He knew that by the time I graduated, being a priest would be the last thing I wanted to do. And he was right."

It only took one semester of college for Billy to recognize that the life of an accountant sitting in an office working numbers wasn't for him either. But he remained in school and got a job at Arrow Distribution, a wholesale dealer of top-of-the-line appliances that served two hundred stores throughout the United States. His sister Peggy introduced him to the owner, Zeke Abraham, an irascible man who, while he didn't show it, took a liking to the tall, affable teenager, even after he tossed the garbage in the oil burner, not the incinerator, and smoked the place out. Not long after, he was promoted to parts manager.

As if college and a job weren't enough, the Vietnam War was surging, and as friends, one by one, were drafted, Billy decided to join the U.S. Army Reserve. The six-year commitment required him to report to Fort Dix in New Jersey for six weeks of basic training. He then had to report one weekend a month and one entire week in February. Upon his return from basic training, Zeke promoted him to salesman. Zeke suffered from diabetes and with his health deteriorating, he was looking ahead for someone to run the store for his wife.

"We became close," said Billy. "He was tough, but I loved the guy. One day he said, 'C'mon, we have to go to New York City,' so I drove him there. I had been doing all right as a salesman, but he wanted more from me. It got to the point where he got really sick and both his legs were amputated and I had to carry him to his appointments. He sort of made me his main man. But I knew it wasn't for me either. And that's when I met Dave Osticco."

James David Osticco was a brute of a man with a fearsome reputation for violence, known as "Dave" for reasons no one knew—or asked. His day job was as traffic manager at Medico Industries, a local defense contractor that supplied weapons to the U.S. Army, among other things.

Balding and in his early fifties, Dave was Russell Bufalino's underboss, and he was among Russell's closest friends.

No one in Pittston or anywhere else missed the newspaper headlines when Russell and Dave were arrested in November 1957 in Apalachin, New York. The state police raided an estate in that small town near Binghamton and surprised over sixty high-level gangsters, who were meeting to iron out a number of issues following the assassination of Albert Anastasia, the leading organized crime figure in New York, who had been murdered in a barbershop just a few weeks earlier.

Russell and Dave were at the meeting, and at their arraignments they smiled for the camera.

Dave's only son, Anthony, was dating Billy's sister Shirley, and it was through their relationship that Billy was introduced to Dave.

"I used to see him at this car wash I hung around at, so he had seen me before," Billy recalled. "His wife, Helen, was like a mother to me, and Dave would give you the shirt off his back. But I also knew who he was. I mean, everyone knew that he was close to Russell Bufalino, that he was Russell's top guy, the underboss. So I already knew Dave was with him. Even as I got closer to Dave—between work and college I was eating lunch at his house every day—I never asked what he did for a living. I knew he had a regular job, but I didn't know what he did in his other life. He was very colorful and looked the part. I'll tell you, he wore some wild fucking outfits. But as nice as he could be, I'd also say he was crazy. I mean, he was not the person you would want mad at you. He'd snap your neck in two seconds."

Dave's quick temper was on display for everyone to see at Anthony and Shirley's wedding in 1966. Word of their quick engagement drew whispers that Shirley was pregnant. She wasn't. They had actually begun dating months earlier than everyone knew, only Shirley had kept it quiet, given her boyfriend's infamous father.

The wedding was a typically large Italian affair, with over three hundred invited guests at the Greenwood Hotel, a popular supper club in Moosic that was filled with well-dressed men in silk suits with pinkie rings. They arrived from places like Philadelphia, Pittsburgh, and New York. During the cocktail hour Billy was standing at the bar with Dave, Dave's daughter Patsy, and several other men and saw Russell Bufalino again. He had arrived with Joe Pepitone, the all-star first baseman for the New York Yankees. The room exploded with oohs and aahs from the men at the sight of Bufalino, while women squealed with delight upon seeing the handsome Yankee.

"Pepitone was a big-time Yankees ballplayer, and he was with two bodyguards. So I'm standing at the bar right next to Dave, and his other daughter, Patsy, was right next to him. She was real gorgeous. One of Pepitone's bodyguards comes to the bar, gets a look at Patsy, and says to me, 'Man, wouldn't you fuck the brains out of that.' I said, '*No, you don't say that,*' but it was too late. *Boom!* Dave took one of those bar stools and almost took the fucking guy's head off."

The wedding reception continued, less one injured guest, and later, after things quieted down, Billy was again standing with Dave and several others when Bufalino walked up to the group. After a few minutes, Dave took Billy by the arm.

"Russ, this is the kid Bill, Shirley's brother."

Billy extended his hand following the unexpected introduction, and Bufalino grabbed it with his.

"Yeah, I've seen you around," said Bufalino. "Nice to see you again."

"Right," said Billy. "The pool hall."

"Don't let my *goombadi* ruin you," said Bufalino, pointing to Dave.

Bufalino left to rejoin the famous guest at his table, and Billy watched as he walked away, like he had when Bufalino left the poolroom. Two other men were with Bufalino. One was Casper Giumento, a small man around fifty whom everyone called "Cappy." The other was a short, thick dolt of a man, Angelo Bufalino. He was Russell's cousin, whom Billy had seen a couple of times at Dave's house. They both trailed Bufalino, who moved fast, with purpose, like someone who knew he was important, and he easily slid into his chair next to Pepitone. Then Billy noticed something odd: Wedding guests, one by one, visited the table, but not to seek out the famous Yankee. Instead, they paid homage to Bufalino, just like at the Imperial.

As a twenty-year-old who knew nothing of the world or his place in it, Billy couldn't help but be impressed.

He completed the two-year accounting program at Wilkes-Barre Business College but put the degree in a drawer at home. He had four years remaining with his army reserve commitment and still had his sales job working for Zeke at Arrow Distribution. But instead of sales, Zeke had him spending most of his time installing eight-track tape players into cars.

Arrow had received its first shipment of the new, wildly popular devices. They played large, rectangular tapes about as big as a hand. Record companies were manufacturing and selling tapes from their artists. Everyone, it seemed, wanted an eight-track tape player in their car.

Dave asked Billy to install one in his big 1966 Chrysler Imperial Crown. When he was finished, Dave asked him to put one in for his pal Phil Medico, one of the brothers who owned Medico Industries. After Billy completed that installation, Dave asked him to do another.

"He said Russell Bufalino wanted one, so I said no problem," Billy recalled. "So I put an eight-track in Russell's Cadillac and Dave tells me to take it to this restaurant, Leo's Lunch in Pittston. He gave me the keys and I took the car over there. I had met him at my sister's wedding, but I was a little nervous, I gotta admit."

Now six feet five inches tall and 190 pounds, Billy had finally filled out. He was handsome, with a baby face exuding the innocence of a young man raised and nurtured by two women—his mother and Aunt Lottie. But his height and dark hair made for an imposing figure, so when he entered the restaurant the men inside sitting at the counter and at the tables turned to inspect the unknown visitor, and their heads followed as he slowly walked toward a table in the rear, where Bufalino was sitting.

Russell was in his early sixties, of medium height, but looked firm and vital for his age. As Billy got closer, Bufalino looked up to welcome his visitor, staring at him with his good left eye. Russell suffered from strabismus, a visual disorder in which one eye is misaligned—in his case, the right eye.

"Leo's Lunch was one of his hangouts, and the guys inside watching me were part of his crew," said Billy. "But I just went in and walked up to him, said hello, and handed him the keys. He was well-built for an old guy. He looked strong. He said, 'What do I owe you, kid?' and I said it was on me. I mean, I knew who he was and I wasn't going to charge him. But he was surprised and said, 'What?' I said that one is on me. So he said, 'Can you be here tomorrow at the same time?' I didn't even think about it. I just said, 'Sure.' So when I walked in the next day he's in the back again and he waves for me to come over. He says, 'You're a pretty big kid. You think you can handle yourself?' I said, 'Yeah.' So he takes off a diamond ring and says, 'If I give this to you, you think someone could take it off of you?' I said, 'No.' He said, 'Okay, come back again tomorrow.' I wasn't sure at first what he wanted but when he asked me to come back again I could have said 'No, I have to work.' But I didn't. There was something about him.

"He wasn't a rough guy, at least not like you'd expect. I mean, I knew *who* he was, but he didn't scare me. I liked him. My own dad always pushed me away, but here was someone, someone big, who asked me to come back. I was curious, and something inside me said yes. I didn't have any second thoughts or anything like that. So I showed up again the next day and the next thing you know I'm spending a lot of time with him. He was at Medico's a lot, and he'd call and say, 'Hey, kid, get me fourteen steak sandwiches,' or 'Go get me twelve hot dogs.' It was lunch for the guys that were there. Dave had his office there too. He actually worked there. So every time I went there it was easy getting to know some of the other guys. I kinda fit right in. This went on for a while and I'd run around for Russell. I loved being around him. I mean, I had my own family, but this was different. Russell was bringing me in closer to him, day by day. There was always something going on. I didn't know what, but it sounded exciting, and there was a lot of money around. He'd ask me to drive him in his Cadillac here or there and everywhere we'd go he had so much respect. He was already in his sixties and people treated him like he was God or something. Pretty soon word got around who I was with and people were treating me differently. I can't say I didn't like it. Even my parents knew, but they didn't say anything. It wouldn't have mattered if they did. I really liked Russell. I liked everything about him.

"When I first stepped into that luncheonette, I was like a million other kids trying to figure out their way ahead. But now, after being with Russell, all I knew was I wanted to be with him. No one ever treated me like he did, and I just wanted to be with him every single day."

CHAPTER 2

Russell

Through the first half of the twentieth century, the Federal Bureau of Investigation ignored the Italian Mafia and its growing influence on American business.

Organized crime dominated life in parts of Italy, particularly in Sicily, and sprinkled among the tens of thousands who sought to escape the corruption, extortion, and even murder in their homeland were the very men who had forced them to leave. And among those were Stefano LaTorre, Calogero "Charles" Bufalino, and Santo Volpe.

They were members of the local Mafia in the north central Sicilian mining town of Montedoro and, for one reason or another, decided to follow the trail of those fleeing Sicily to begin new lives in a new country.

And for LaTorre, Bufalino, and Volpe, that trail passed thousands of miles over the Mediterranean Sea and Atlantic Ocean to New York City and then another 120 miles over land to the northwest, to the lush Wyoming Valley, within whose embrace were Scranton and Wilkes-Barre, and mining towns such as Pittston.

By 1906, the three men had brought their old-world customs to the region, terrorizing the immigrant Italian populace with extortion demands that required Italian miners to pay them tribute from their weekly earnings. Those who resisted, or even worse, squealed to the police, were dealt with through threats, beatings, and murder. One miner who had the audacity to complain to the police moved his family outside the region to escape their reach, but he was found and beheaded.

It wasn't long before LaTorre, Bufalino, and Volpe were leading an organized crime group that not only controlled all the gambling, prostitution, and extortion in the region, but through their own mining companies employed many of the tens of thousands of miners, and they controlled the unions, or bribed the ones they didn't control.

By the 1920s their influence went beyond the confines of the mountains of northeast Pennsylvania to other cities, among them Buffalo and Detroit.

Cousins of the trio and other family members who bypassed Pittston landed in those outposts, and followed the same formula of terror and violence. A loose network developed, connecting the families in those different cities.

Marriages were arranged to cement ties between families, further lessening the importance of geography. Family, not geography, was what mattered. So cities such as Buffalo and Pittston virtually became one, as did Pittsburgh and Youngstown, Ohio, and Pittston and Detroit.

And with the fortunes they earned during Prohibition, the families expanded their reach through the 1930s and 1940s, so much so that they gained the attention of the Kefauver Committee. The U.S. Senate subcommittee initiated an investigation in 1950 into the mob's hold over labor, with a focus on the burgeoning garment industry and the Mafia's stranglehold on unions, particularly the Teamsters.

The subcommittee, headed by Senator Estes Kefauver of Tennessee, spent a considerable amount of time studying several American cities and shocked many with the level of crime and corruption it uncovered. One city especially stood out: Scranton, Pennsylvania.

Scranton and the surrounding region, especially Pittston to the south, were rife with gambling activity, including poker rooms, horse betting, and slot machines. Extortion and loan-sharking were also endemic. Perhaps most shocking, local law enforcement simply looked the other way, as many police chiefs accepted bribes and payoffs and provided cover.

It was just gambling, they reasoned, a harmless activity. But there was more, much more, and with it came violence and often death.

Organized crime controlled most, if not all, of the local dress factories supplying stores across the country with merchandise. When the International Ladies' Garment Workers' Union sought to organize the thousands of local workers in northeastern Pennsylvania beginning in 1945, they were met with a violent reaction that led to the destruction of equipment and property and several murders, including that of the brother of the leading ILGWU organizer, Min Matheson.

So under direct orders from FBI director J. Edgar Hoover, the bureau's Top Hoodlum Program was born in 1953. Agents in field offices throughout the country were ordered to identify and document the activities of the nation's most important organized crime figures, and within the very first reports sent to Hoover was surveillance on a mysterious man identified as the new leader of the Mafia in Pittston, Pennsylvania.

Rosario Alfredo Bufalino was born in September or October of 1903, though his actual birth date and country of origin were questions that would haunt him during the latter years of his life.

What was known was that his father, Angelo, left his pregnant wife, Maria Cristina; daughters Guisseppa, six, and Cristina, two; and son, Calogero, five, in Montedoro, Sicily, in July 1903 and boarded a ship bound for America. An important man and member of the local Mafia in Italy, he envisioned great things in America and left to join his brother Charles and friends Santo Volpe and Stephen LaTorre. But his American experience was brief. Forced to take a job as a coal miner, Angelo was killed in a mine explosion on September 23, 1904. His family and infant son had joined him before his death but returned to Italy. Two years later, they were back in Pittston and remained there until 1910, when Maria became ill and died soon after.

Rosario, whom everyone called Russell, was sent back to Italy. But he returned in 1914 and lived with his uncle Charles, who was now among the most fearsome men in Pittston.

Russell went to elementary school there, a fifth-grade student learning in a third-grade classroom, scoring As and Bs, but he was sent to Buffalo to live with relatives. In 1917 he enrolled in the Elm Vocational School to become an auto mechanic. After graduation he took a job at a local garage and later opened his own shop, the Russell Bufalino Garage. But repairing cars wasn't his life's goal.

His uncle Charles and Santo Volpe introduced Russell to John Montana, the highly respected underboss of Stefano Magaddino, the powerful head of the Buffalo crime family.

Under the tutelage of Montana and Magaddino, Russell ran with the Buffalo mob, taking part in petty thefts and hijackings and selling stolen property, including autos and auto parts through his garage.

He even took out advertisements in the *Buffalo Daily Courier's* classified section in August 1925. "Russell Bufalino Garage—Storage, washing, repairing, ignition work specialists," it said. "293 Franklin St., Tup. 10249."

But his love of cars wasn't confined to engine work. Russell liked to drive fast, and his recklessness led to several speeding tickets and a severe accident. He had returned to Pittston often, and it was in Pittston on March 24, 1924, that he drove a brand-new Dodge sedan over the Water Street Bridge. He attempted to pass two cars, but an oncoming bus forced him to press hard on the brakes. The car swerved onto the sidewalk and lodged between two girders. Bleeding profusely from a large gash over his right eye, Russell had to be extricated from the wreck and was taken to the hospital. He was received in critical condition and treated for deep gashes on his forehead and over the right eye, which had been damaged. His right earlobe was sliced in two.

He recovered, and as he neared his twenty-fifth birthday he was introduced to Carolyn "Carrie" Sciandra. She was a cousin of John Sciandra, who had left Buffalo a few years earlier for Pittston to work with Volpe, Charles Bufalino, and LaTorre. Russell and Carrie's marriage in 1928 unified the Bufalino and Sciandra families. But one tradition they could not fulfill was having children. They tried, but Carrie couldn't conceive. When they traveled to Pittston in April 1930 to attend the wedding of Russell's cousin to Santo Volpe's daughter Gaetana, Carrie's sadness was evident. Everyone told her and Russell to try harder.

The Pittston wedding was such a grand event a special Mass was held at the same time in Montedoro with the entire village of three thousand attending. The feast that followed there was a gift from Volpe and his wife. His daughter and new son-in-law, a Bufalino, also received a cable with the benediction of Pope Pius XI.

By then, Russell had business interests in Buffalo and Pittston. It was in Pittston that Volpe, who had amassed his own fortune mining coal and bootlegging, introduced Russell to two eager, industrious brothers, William and Philip Medico.

The Medicos were young and were developing their own interests in those same endeavors. With them was a wild, short-tempered teenager from Pittston, Dave Osticco, who drove nighttime "beer runs" for the Medicos.

Two years later, in 1932, Carrie's cousin John Sciandra had assumed the leadership of the Pittston family from Santo Volpe, who stepped aside following his acquittal of a murder charge. Charles Bufalino and Stephen LaTorre, both wealthy, preferred to remain in the shadows.

Russell became one of Sciandra's most trusted confidants, and he and Carrie moved to Binghamton, New York, which was only seventy miles from Pittston but allowed for a reunion with Joseph Barbara, whom Russell had known in Buffalo.

A vicious killer and bootlegger, Barbara had been dispatched to Binghamton to oversee Magaddino's operations there, and Russell was brought in to assist him. He and Carrie settled into an apartment in the western suburb of Endicott and Russell took a day job, supposedly as head of maintenance at a Canada Dry bottling plant owned by Barbara, who'd bought the business with a $65,000 loan from Santo Volpe, local Pittston coal baron Louis Pagnotti, and Russell's uncle Charles Bufalino.

Carrie remained at home but received her notary public license from Broome County, which came in handy for Russell.

It was at the Canada Dry plant that Russell lost his thumb and half the forefinger on his right hand. While some whispered it was mob business gone bad, Russell told Carrie it happened in an accident while he was working on machinery.

By the end of World War II, Russell was spending even more time in northeast Pennsylvania and had launched a firm, Famous Coal Co., using funds borrowed from Louis Pagnotti. Famous sold coal from Pagnotti-owned mines to businesses in New York, delivered via Pagnotti-owned trucks. It was during one of his coal trips to New York that Russell met Max Stein, the owner of several dress companies. Stein couldn't find enough dresses to sell, so Russell opened his own manufacturing shops in Pennsylvania with names such as Penn Drape and Curtain, Bonnie Stewart Dress Co., and Claudia Frocks.

He also maintained a position with his friends William and Phillip Medico at their Medico Electric Motor Co. in a role as an engineering consultant. Russell had become so close to the Medico brothers, many believed he was a silent partner in their business.

Of more immediate concern was the coal business. Following the war, the nation had found other energy sources and the demand for anthracite coal plummeted, which led to mine closings throughout the Wyoming Valley. In their place sprang up garment manufacturing shops. Women and children as young as ten worked twelve-hour days stitching together dresses and other clothing, which were then transported to New York City. The nonunion work paid little more than $2 a day.

With Russell's growing business interests, Carrie was left home alone. She attended church every Sunday and served on various committees, including one in which women made clothing for European war refugees. And she became good friends with Barbara's wife, Josephine. But it was the Pittston area where they wanted to make their permanent home, and the opportunity came in September 1949 following the sudden death of John Sciandra, Carrie's cousin. The head of the Pittston crime family, now fifty years old, had been admitted to the hospital with an unknown ailment on a Sunday night and died the following day.

Charles Bufalino, Santo Volpe, and Joseph Barbara served as honorary pallbearers while Russell was among a group of relatives who carried the coffin into St. Cecilia's Church in nearby Exeter. Following the funeral, Russell and Carrie took up residence in a flat above Wyoming Avenue across the river in West Pittston.

At the age of forty-five, and with the support of his uncle Charles and Volpe, Russell Bufalino became the new boss of the Pittston family.

The FBI's Philadelphia field office said just that in its initial report for the Top Hoodlum Program, stating that Russell was "the active leader of the Mafia of the Pittston, Pa. area" and had gained control of the garment industry and gambling in the region, from which he received a "cut" of all proceeds.

Agents subsequently followed Russell to local hangouts such as the Imperial poolroom and on his weekly trips into New York City.

The report linked Russell to other reputed gangsters, including Angelo Bruno in Philadelphia, and said his closest friend was William Medico. Russell, they believed, was a silent partner in Medico Electric Motor Co. Agents also learned from informants that

William Medico was a capo, or captain, within Russell's organized crime family, which the FBI was now calling the Bufalino Family.

His power increasing, Russell expanded his interests into legitimate businesses and obtained his license to promote boxing matches. He also earned attention for his other businesses, particularly his ongoing union battles with Min Matheson.

To soften the negative headlines, he participated in a host of civic and philanthropic efforts. In February 1953 he became chairman of industry for the Greater Pittston Heart Fund. Later that year he was named cochairman of the Miscellaneous Industries Division and worked along with chairman William Medico to raise $100,000 for the region's Community Chest Campaign. But the FBI was always watching, even when he left the country.

Russell routinely trekked to Cuba beginning in the early 1950s, following a route that took him from Florida to the Bahamas and then to Havana. During one visit in 1956, agents followed him, William Medico, and Dave Osticco to the Sans Souci nightclub and casino in Havana, where they met with Santo Trafficante, the head of organized crime in Miami. Russell remained there for a month and returned via the Bahamas, which the FBI confirmed after intercepting a postcard with a postage stamp from the British Empire, which Russell had sent from there in May 1956.

He was later questioned by New York City police investigating the murder of Albert Anastasia, the "boss of bosses." Russell was in New York in October 1957 the day Anastasia was executed in a barber's chair inside the Park Sheraton Hotel in midtown. He appeared before a grand jury investigating the murder, but he invoked his Fifth Amendment right not to incriminate himself. A few weeks later Russell organized a national meeting of mob leaders at Joseph Barbara's estate in Apalachin, New York. Accompanying him were Dave Osticco; Angelo Sciandra, the son of the late John Sciandra; and William Medico.

When the state police inadvertently learned about the meeting, they set up roadblocks, raided the compound, and began to make arrests. They caught Russell trying to escape in a car with Vito Genovese, who was believed to be the mastermind of Anastasia's murder.

The national publicity that followed led the U.S. Immigration and Naturalization Service to begin deportation proceedings against Russell on the grounds that he was an undesirable alien born in Sicily, not Pittston, as Russell always claimed. On January 21, 1958, at a hearing in Philadelphia, Russell's attorney Ettore Angelino admitted that his client was indeed an alien after immigration officials produced records provided by their Italian counterparts confirming he was born Rosario Alfredo Bufalino in Montedoro, Sicily, on September 29, 1903. Russell arrived in New York three months later, on December 21, 1903, on the steamship *Città di Milano*, which had departed from Naples for New York City. According to the ship manifest, the Bufalino family included his mother, Maria Cristina; sisters Guisseppa and Cristina; and brother Calogero. The government also argued that Russell's birth record in the Luzerne County Courthouse had been illegally edited in pencil by someone. All other records had been typed.

Russell was eventually ordered to leave the country, but he appealed.

On May 21, 1959, Russell, Dave Osticco, and Angelo Sciandra were each awakened in their home at six A.M. by police and arrested for conspiracy in connection with the Apalachin meeting. Sciandra's mother, Josephine, later wept as she posted her son's bail.

By then the Senate's McClellan Committee, which had been investigating organized crime's infiltration of U.S. labor unions, particularly the Teamsters, had turned its attention to the stunning raid and subsequent arrests at Apalachin, where the nation saw for the first time the direct and intricate connections linking one family to another, one city to another.

Headed by U.S. senator John McClellan of Arkansas, and with members including Senators John F. Kennedy of Massachusetts and

Barry Goldwater of Arizona, the committee subpoenaed many of the men arrested that day. Sam Giancana from Chicago, Carlos Marcello from New Orleans, Anthony Provenzano from New Jersey, and Vito Genovese from New York were among those who said nothing as they were grilled by the committee's hostile counsel, Robert Kennedy.

The previous year Kennedy had given the same treatment to the newly elected Teamsters leader Jimmy Hoffa during his contentious, nationally televised testimony. And as the nation was getting ready to celebrate the July Fourth holiday, it was Russell's turn.

Over several hours Robert Kennedy mercilessly queried Russell about his role in organizing the Apalachin meeting and his relationships with the men who attended. Russell declined to answer. Kennedy went on to ask Russell about his curious relationship with Jimmy Hoffa. Russell's cousin William Bufalino had become a prominent figure in Detroit as head of Teamsters Local 985. It was Hoffa's local, and William was now Hoffa's attorney. Kennedy also asked about Santo Volpe; Russell's work as an "expediter" at several dress factories, which earned him $100 to $125 per week on the books from each factory; and his interest in sports, particularly basketball, with the implication that Russell was fixing games. He refused to answer, invoking his Fifth Amendment right against self-incrimination. After Kennedy's final question, which also went unanswered, he said of Russell, "We consider that this individual is a very important figure . . . he took part in the labor negotiations that took place at the beginning of the year . . . he made the arrangements and appointments for the meeting at Apalachin. He is a man of considerable importance and a man of great contacts throughout the United States and the underworld."

When the committee completed its final interview a few years later, it described Russell as "one of the most ruthless and powerful leaders of the Mafia in the United States."

CHAPTER 3

Initiation

The two-door jet-black 1968 Pontiac Grand Prix was a thing of beauty.

It had a front grille that opened on each side, exposing the headlights, and it could hit sixty miles per hour in under seven seconds.

Billy loved his car, which was a gift from Aunt Lottie. Where she got the money to buy it he had no idea and didn't care. He loved hearing the engine roar as he sped through the streets of Pittston and beyond. But he'd only have it for a couple of weeks.

Now twenty-two, he had received his certificate in accounting from Wilkes-Barre Business College, yet he'd forgotten where he had put it. It could have been in a drawer at home or a closet. He didn't know. And didn't care.

He had found something else to do.

For two years he answered Russell's calls, anytime, any day, and he loved hearing his old, craggy voice on the other end of the phone: "Hey, kid, get this," or "Hey, kid, I need you to run here."

Other times, when Russell was in town, Billy would usually find him over at the Medicos', who had changed the name of their business to Medico Industries, and Russell would give him the keys to his Cadillac so Billy could drive him to his appointments. It didn't take long for people to identify Billy as "Russ's kid."

Billy had grown on Russell, and as a man who never had children of his own, his developing affection for Billy was real. So much so that after having Billy run errands for him in Pennsylvania, Russell decided it was time to finally bring Billy into his other life in New York.

So in February 1968 he asked Billy what kind of car he drove.

Billy knew what that meant.

"We were getting close," he said. "It got to the point where I was with him more than I was with my own family. I was with him for Christmas, Easter, holidays. I'd be with my family for a little while, then say, 'Gotta go.' I'd get to Russell's house and he was always happy to see me. Carrie was sweet but a bit guarded. They didn't have any kids. She couldn't. I think there was some sadness there about that. But nothing that they talked about. She just made sure I cleaned up after myself. She was a bit of a stickler for that."

For as long as anyone could remember, Russell had kept a regular schedule. He'd start the week on Sunday afternoon by saying good-bye to Carrie and driving to New York City, where he'd stay before returning home to Pennsylvania on Wednesday. Once home, he'd go to dinner with Carrie and then meet friends at the Club C&C, which was owned by one of his associates. Thursday morning he'd go to Medico's and sit down with Dave to discuss what had gone on in New York that week. Sometimes he'd give Dave jewelry he had picked up that had to be fenced. On Fridays, Russell could be anywhere, from Scranton to Philadelphia to Buffalo, to discuss business in those cities. Friday night was usually date night with Carrie at a local restaurant. Saturday he'd be out again and Sunday, after Carrie returned from Mass, it was back to New York.

Billy had no idea what Russell did in New York, and he was smart enough to never ask. During Russell's weekly absences, Billy drove over to Medico's to hang out with the other men who made up the hierarchy of the Bufalino crime family.

He was already close to Dave Osticco. Dave had still been a teenager when he was arrested by the Pittston Police "dry squad" in October 1930, who had stopped Dave during a late-night "beer run" for William Medico. They found five half barrels of beer in the back of his vehicle. Dave paid a hundred-dollar fine and was released. A month later he was charged with assault and battery for attacking a man in a cigar store.

In February 1931, Dave and William Medico faced federal charges for operating a large still, and both men were arrested again in January 1934 for assault. William was part owner of the Barnum colliery in Pittston, and during a regional coal strike, two of his miners went to his Pittston home to confront him over shortages in their pay. Soon after entering the home they were thrown out and Dave pounced on them, sending one to the Pittston hospital with severe head lacerations.

A few years later the Medicos, seeking to expand their political clout, joined the Young Democrats of Greater Pittston. They put the volatile Dave on the ticket for school director, but he lost. They then sought to have him appointed as Pittston's next police chief as part of a deal to support a mayoral candidate, who lost too.

Dave was arrested again with William Medico in November 1947 when agents of the Pennsylvania Liquor Control Board seized $1,200 worth of alcohol that he illegally delivered to William's home. By that time, Dave had a regular job as a driver for what was known then as the Medico Electric Motor Company.

The company was formed in 1938 as a partnership between the five Medico brothers, and by the 1950s it grew into a large concern, fueled by a local congressman, Daniel Flood, who had a gift for theatrics.

Flood had worked as a Shakespearean actor but detested the pauper's wages. After attending Harvard Law School and the Dickinson School of Law near Harrisburg, he took his law degree and acting experience to Wilkes-Barre and opened his own practice. In 1935 he was appointed a Pennsylvania deputy attorney general, and in 1944 the Hazleton native ran as a Democrat for Congress and won, with voters drawn to his handlebar mustache and flamboyant manner, his speeches exercises from his past life onstage. Among his earliest supporters were William and Phillip Medico. Flood showed his gratitude by steering government contracts to what was later renamed Medico Industries.

Dave had been employed there since the beginning, and aside from driving for them, he learned how to operate a crane, which he'd later use to help friends with outdoor projects, such as digging a large hole in a backyard for a swimming pool. Most recently, he'd held the title of traffic manager. But everyone in Pittston knew Dave and the Medicos were close to Russell. Especially Dave.

The newspapers ran front-page stories about them in November 1957 following their arrest with dozens of other men in Apalachin, their names intermixed with others such as Bonanno, Profaci, Scalish, Gambino, Genovese, Castellano, Giancana, and LaRocca. The papers said they were all allegedly involved in organized crime and that Russell ran the rackets in Pittston and Dave was his underboss. But no one really cared about that. Billy didn't. To him, Dave was a funny guy who once in a while flew off the handle.

Edward Sciandra, Carrie's cousin and Russell's consigliere, or counselor, was a different sort.

Born in 1912 into a Mafia family in Montedoro, Sicily, Edward chose a different path after arriving in New York and went east, to Long Island and the small town of Bellmore. It was from there that Eddie handled Russell's business in Manhattan.

"Everyone called him Eddie, and he and Russell were very, very close. They went way back," said Billy. "Eddie was a very serious man. He was Russell's street boss in New York. One time we were out at his house on Long Island eating and someone said to him, 'Eddie, you got something on your shirt.' Eddie asked if it was blood. The guy says, 'No, it's sauce.' Eddie said, 'Then don't worry about it.'"

Cappy Giumento was once one of Russell's "everymen," or guys who did what Billy would later do—run errands. Cappy was from another scrappy Italian enclave, in Dunmore, which was on the fringe of Scranton. Aside from Dave, there was no one closer to Russell. In his midfifties, Cappy was a small, thin man who wore pointy-toed shoes. He had known Lucky Luciano back in the 1930s and introduced him to Russell. Cappy gained notoriety during World War II when he stole over $1 million worth of gas ration stamps and sold them. Everyone thought it was a hell of a score.

It was Dave who introduced Russell to Cappy, who also ran a textile shop and had a hand in card and dice games throughout the region. He was supposed to operate one of those craps games with the bodyguard Modesto Loquasto near Kingston under the protection of the police chief. But the state police got wind of it and stopped it before it started.

Another so-called errand boy was Russell's cousin Angelo Bufalino. A thick, brooding, somewhat dim-witted fellow, he was mainly tasked with driving Russell to New York on Sunday and back to Kingston on Wednesday.

Angelo had been by Russell's side for years, often assigned jobs that did little to raise his profile. His connection to Russell was made public during a 1958 deportation hearing in which Russell testified that he put Angelo in business as proprietor of the Penn Drape store in Pittston. In truth, it was Russell's business, with Angelo serving as a front man. Russell also testified that he had given Angelo power of attorney so he could "pay bills and conduct business."

Like the others, Angelo had his brushes with the law. In 1959, he was indicted along with eight other people for causing a riot during a strike at the plant of a rival sportswear manufacturer. He was acquitted. Angelo was devoted to Russell, and he more than anyone else was taken aback by the attention Russell was giving to Billy.

That wasn't the case with Frank Sheeran. Billy's introduction to the man many spoke of with fear and apprehension was at the Howard Johnson's in Pittston. Louis DelVecchio, an amiable sort with a love for boxing, managed the hotel for Russell, who had secretly owned it for years. It was where he would host his important out-of-town guests.

All Billy knew about Frank was what he'd heard from the others, that he headed a Teamsters local in Delaware, had been accused but not convicted of murdering several people, was very close to Jimmy Hoffa of the Teamsters, and was even closer to Russell, who relied on Sheeran to do his dirtiest work, the kind where people ended up dead, disappeared, or both. Just that morning Russell, Dave, and Cappy had mentioned Frank at the Medico offices. They'd passed around a newspaper story relaying how Frank had just been charged with murder in the shooting of a Teamsters official in Philadelphia. According to the paper, Frank had given a "hand sign" that led to the shooting. He was one of five men arrested, and he was out on bail.

Billy understood all the talk about Frank when he emerged from the hotel's front entrance. He was a large man, around six feet four inches tall and 250 pounds. His sandy-colored hair was slicked straight back, and he wore a beige jacket and beige slacks. When he walked out from the hotel, Billy thought he looked every inch the frightening figure Russell, Dave, and Cappy said he was. Frank opened the door and slid into the backseat of the car. Russell didn't waste time with the introductions.

"Billy, say hello to Frank Sheeran," said Russell. "Frank, say hello to my boy Billy."

"How ya doing, kid, nice to meet ya. Heard a lot of good things about ya," said Frank, stretching out his hand, which was as big as a catcher's mitt.

"Nice to meet you," said Billy, who had never shaken hands with anyone with as strong a grip.

"Frank came up to see Russell a couple of times a week," recalled Billy. "He was a Teamster, and Russell had a big hand in the Teamsters. So I figured they had a lot to talk about. But Frank was a scary guy. Sometimes I'd drive them to Aldino's, which was probably one of the best restaurants in Wilkes-Barre, and then I'd usually wait outside. He always wore Perry Como sweaters and used to keep five thousand in this pocket and five thousand in this pocket. During the times when I was invited inside with them, he sat at a bar and he'd drink champagne with strawberries, Heineken beer, and a shot of sambuca as a wash, then order another and do it again and again. No one, and I mean no one, could outdrink Frank. Other times he'd just meet Russell for lunch at the Howard Johnson's. He was dark and he scared a lot of people, but he was also a funny guy, some of the stuff he did. One time he came out of a hotel in Philly with a hooker and she was just annoying him, so he told her to shut the fuck up. This guy comes over thinking he's going to help her and Frank pulls out two hundred from his pocket and says, 'Here, take her someplace.' The guy said, 'I think he just insulted me,' and Frank goes, 'Yeah,' and then—*boom!*—he knocks the guy out. The guy is laying there and Frank bends down and puts the two hundred in his jacket pocket and says, 'Have a good time.' He was fucking crazy."

It wasn't long after Billy's introduction to Frank that Russell asked what kind of car he drove. Billy said he had a Grand Prix, but it wasn't the one his aunt Lottie had bought the month before. That one was in pieces in a junkyard.

With Russell away in New York half the week, Billy frequented the local strip clubs, of which there were many, including the Baghdad and the Welcome Inn in Wilkes-Barre. He became a regular and was known among his friends as "the King of the Go-Gos." One particularly cold night at the Welcome Inn he got into a dustup with a bouncer, who didn't like how Billy had sat up front with his feet resting atop the edge of the low stage.

"He came over and he hit me with his knees," said Billy. "I almost fell off the chair and then we get into it, that fucker, 'I'll get you, you cocksucker.' So then about a week later someone set fire to the curtains that were set up on the side to let the dancers change in private. They thought I did it, but I didn't. So the next time I go there, I have my new car and I park right in the front. I hang around for a while and leave and get into my car. I start the ignition and—*boom!*—the front hood goes flying upward and I jumped out. I don't know why someone put a bomb in my car, but I didn't have a scratch on me. I go out and the next day got the same exact car."

Cappy had always accompanied Russell to New York in the 1950s, but in recent years it had been Angelo who took him back and forth. So Russell surprised everyone when he decided it was time for Billy to drive him, and when the young apprentice was told to pack a bag, he jumped at the chance.

"I drove him in the worst snowstorm ever," said Billy. "It took us a few hours but we finally get close to the city and he wants to stop at Newark airport. He's got some business there. So we go and there's a truck stuck ahead of us. He says, 'Go around it,' but I said, 'He's stuck.' He yells, '*Go around it, goddamn it!*' But now *I* was stuck and we couldn't move, the wheels just spinning every time I tried to gun it out of there. I was so nervous. His voice, when he yelled, it just went through you. It wasn't the last time I heard him like that."

Unable to move the car, Billy jumped out to call a relative, his uncle Lewis, who had a limousine service at the airport. Billy told him he was stuck and had to get to New York. Lewis offered a limousine to take them there and a truck to tow the car to a local mechanic.

"I tell Russell and he says, 'Are you stupid or something? This brand-new car, you're going to leave it on the road? Tell him to keep his limousine.'

"There were two colored guys sitting on the guardrail. He opens the window and says, 'You guys want to make one hundred each to get us out of here?' They almost picked up the car to get us out."

After finally making it to Manhattan, Russell directed Billy straight to midtown and to the front of Johnny D's, a popular saloon off Broadway, owned by a restaurateur everyone knew as—what else—Johnny D.

"It was Russell's hangout for like one hundred years," said Billy.

"I walked inside behind Russ and it's got a small bar that would fit maybe ten people and behind the bar were about a hundred pictures of Russell with different celebrities, all on the wall. He had a private room in the back that served about twenty people. We walk in and the place is crowded and everyone comes over to greet Russ. I mean *everyone*. And this wasn't Pennsylvania, it was New York. I'm thinking, 'What the fuck?' We go in the back and Russ introduces me to his friends as 'the kid, Billy.' It's my first time with him in New York and all these guys are grabbing my hand. We're just sitting there and I have no idea what I'm supposed to do. Then Russell says, 'Hey, Johnny, who's at the Copa tonight?' He says, 'Al Martino.' Russell is close to Martino. Russell says, 'Let's go,' so him, Johnny D, and me and a couple of other guys go to the Copacabana. It's this famous club on the Upper East Side. We walk in and Russell introduces me to Jules Podell, who ran the Copa since the nineteen forties. It's packed, jammed with people. But Jules takes us through the crowd and sets us up right in front, two tables. I couldn't believe it. And as we walk through everyone wants a piece of Russell. They want to say hello, shake his hand. He's treated like a movie star. My eyes are wide open. It's one thing to be treated like a king in Pittston, but in New York? We sit down and the waiter comes with two setups of Dewar's and water. I ordered a screwdriver. Russell looks at me and says, 'What the fuck? You want to let everyone here know you're a farmer from Pittston? Drink Dewar's like a man.' I've drank Dewar's ever since.

"Later when we get back to the hotel I'm still in a daze. I was just in the Copa, in New York, driving a man I knew was important and powerful, but never fucking realized just *how* important. He *owned* the Copa. Who was this guy? I was still asking myself that question when we got back to the hotel and I saw I lost a cuff link. I go, 'Russ, I lost a cuff link.' He says, 'Let me see that.' He studies the other one I have and then goes, 'It's not worth the cab fare.'"

Billy remained in New York with Russell through Wednesday, and just like in Pennsylvania, where Russell had his two or three favorite restaurants and clubs, he was a creature of routine in New York, where life centered around his suite at the Consulate Hotel on Forty-Ninth Street and Broadway. It was large, with a living room and television, kitchen, guest bedroom, and master bedroom. He had lived there since the 1940s. Rent-controlled, it cost him only $438 a month. And it wasn't just a place for Russell to hang his hat. It served as a base of operations for the various businesses Russell was involved in. And there were a lot. Billy knew about Russell's dress factories in Pennsylvania, but he quickly realized that New York City was the center of Russell's world.

"I knew Russell was big in a lot of things, especially the garment industry," said Billy. "He worked with a guy named Max Stein at Fairfrox, or at least that's what everyone was told. But Russ got his W-2 and health benefits there. He needed them."

Billy had also gleaned from the visits by Frank Sheeran that Russell had a hand in the powerful Teamsters union. He heard them talk about Jimmy Hoffa, the head of the Teamsters who had been in prison since 1967 for jury tampering, fraud, and conspiracy.

"People kept asking him, 'How's Jimmy?'" said Billy. "When Russell talked about him you could tell he loved Hoffa. He always said good things about him, thought he was tough and honest. It didn't take long to figure that Russell was close to Hoffa and had something going on with the Teamsters. I'd hear him talking about who wanted a loan and what for. I didn't ask then. I would never ask, about anything. If I needed to know something, Russell would tell me. Besides, it would all come out later. Guys were coming in from all over the country to see him and discuss Teamster business: who had to go on strike, who controlled what local, who needed a loan."

Billy had been to New York a couple of times before with Zeke from Arrow Distribution, but he wasn't familiar with the streets and traffic. Russell was, and as they drove from one meeting to the next, he sat in the front passenger seat with his hands on his lap directing Billy.

"He'd sit there and point his good thumb this way, then that way, and if I missed a turn he'd say, 'No, you fuckin' dummy. I said *that* way.' He could sometimes be rough, but I didn't care. I loved being around him. But no matter what we were doing, we'd stop and go eat at Vesuvio on Forty-Eighth Street or Johnny D's. Russell loved to eat, and those were his two favorite hangouts. Vesuvio had a lot of screenwriters and TV producers, and Russell had been going there for years. People would come in just to see him. Everyone said Russell owned the Vesuvio but I don't think so. Maybe he should have. He could be rough on the waiters. Wherever we went to eat the one thing about Russell I quickly learned is he didn't care what you charged him. You just had to give him what he wanted. When he ordered something, he wanted it cooked this way, like don't mix onions and garlic in his sauce. And when he didn't get what he wanted, look out.

"One time we go into the Vesuvio with some guys and sit down and Russell said he wasn't that hungry and just wanted a veal parmigiana hero. But the waiter—his name was Fiori—he goes, 'Mr. Russ, Mr. Russ, I have a special for you, two-a lamb chops, cooked perfectly for you.' Russ says again he's not that hungry, he just wants the veal hero. Fiori goes, 'Oh, Mr. Russ, you'll love these chops. It's our Sunday special.' Russ again says he's not that hungry but Fiori won't quit. 'Mr. Russ, I assure you they are delicious,' he says. So Russ goes, 'Okay, just bring me one chop,' and he waves him away. Fiori doesn't get the hint. 'But, Mr. Russ,' he says. 'It's-a two lamb chops. That's the special.' Russ fucking explodes. '*I don't give a shit if it's two or ten fucking chops! I told you I'm not that hungry. Now go back there and get me one fucking lamb chop!!*' Fiori couldn't stop shaking. 'Yes, Mr. Russ. Of course, Mr. Russ,' he says as he runs back into the kitchen. When Russell yelled, people moved."

On the drive back to Pennsylvania that Wednesday afternoon, Russell talked about his love of sports, particularly boxing, and his cooking. He said he had his own culinary tools at home with which he prepared gourmet meals, and he shared several of his favorite recipes. Russell's interests also extended to world events and books. He could quote Shakespeare, he said. Billy took it all in, and Russell could see the kid was no dummy. He listened and was astute, which was something he couldn't say about the guys who had been with him for years. If they didn't talk business, there was nothing to discuss. They would go silent. But not Billy.

He had been hanging around with Russell for two years, but their connection was galvanized during their first time together in New York. By the time they returned home, Billy felt closer to Russell than he did to his own father.

"He was so smart, by far the smartest man I ever met in my life, and he could talk about anything, from boxing to art," said Billy. "He knew stuff I never even heard of. He told me a story about when he was twelve and he built a car and drove it by himself to Buffalo. Everybody in Pittston had family in Buffalo, and he told me how he grew up there. So all the way back from New York, we just talked."

Once in Kingston, Billy pulled the car into the garage of Russell's ranch-style home. It was off the corner of East Dorrance Street in a quiet neighborhood just a few blocks away from the Susquehanna River. The neighborhood was filled with similar ranches and two-story homes with small gardens in the front. Billy had been to the house many times before. He had envisioned Russell living in a larger, gaudier home with lion sculptures guarding the short driveway. But Russell had explained it several times, telling Billy to never forget it: don't ever draw attention to yourself.

"We go inside the house and he tells me to stay put, runs downstairs, and comes back up with a pair of sapphire cuff links and a sapphire ring," said Billy. "Russell was an expert in jewelry. He'd carry a magnifying glass with him all the time, and he remembered I lost the cuff link at the Copa. He gives me the sapphires, which had to be really expensive, and says, 'Now you have real jewelry.'"

CHAPTER 4

Learning the Ropes

Following their return from New York, Russell had Dave gather Cappy and Angelo for a meeting at his home. He had an announcement to make, and they'd all go downstairs to his personal sanctum.

The color scheme was right out of the sixties. He had a bar with five bar stools with cantaloupe-colored upholstery; a card table with a chessboard and four chairs, two with yellow upholstery and two with orange; and in the rear three green felt sofas arranged in a U, with one against the back wall and the other two facing each other. A round table with ornamental legs was in the middle.

The room was finished from floor to ceiling in deep brown wood paneling. A pair of red boxing gloves hung on one side, and several picture frames were on the other side, one with a flyer advertising a performance by Al Martino at a local club. The room was comfortable, simple, which suited Russell perfectly. It was also where he kept his money, important papers, and jewelry, all in three safes, one of them inside a wall.

Carrie fixed a meal for Billy in the kitchen while Russell went downstairs with Dave, Cappy, and Angelo to discuss business. Unlike Russell, Carrie had yet to warm up to her husband's young protégé.

It wasn't that she didn't like him; she really didn't know what to do with him besides feed him.

Billy knew it would take a while for Carrie to come around, and he didn't push it. She wasn't the warmest, fuzziest person in the world. Carrie was stern and meticulous, especially with her house, which was organized and clean. She didn't allow a mess of any kind. Whenever Billy finished a meal, he knew to clean the table and put his dish in the sink.

It wasn't long after the men disappeared downstairs before Angelo poked his big head up from the stairwell and told Billy he was needed. Russell had an announcement.

"Russ said he gave Angelo nosebleeds," said Billy. "If he'd need to go somewhere and Angelo wasn't around he'd be screaming, '*Where the fuck is he!*' And when he found him he'd yell, '*What the fuck are you doing?*' So he said that from now on, I was going to be his driver. He liked having me around. I was punctual, and we'd talk about stuff outside of business and he seemed to enjoy my company. I think I even made him laugh a couple of times. So he finally had enough with Angelo and said I was going to drive him."

When informed of the change, Angelo protested meekly. The insult hurt, even after Russell explained he needed him to spend more time in Pennsylvania with the dress factories and gambling operations. It was a lie, but Angelo knew that when Russell made up his mind, that was it and there wasn't anything he could do about it.

Dave and Cappy also couldn't help but notice Russell's growing reliance on and affection for Billy. Russell was a careful man who had always maintained a very tight circle around him, yet Billy had pierced it.

"Don't let my *goombadi* ruin you!" said Dave with a smile.

Billy took up the routine of driving Russell back and forth to New York. The rest of the week Billy would take Russell wherever he had to go. But in April 1968, Russell told Billy to bring a bag. He was going to stay with him in New York that week. He had several meetings planned, only Russell didn't tell Billy their locations.

"We get to New York, and then the next day he says we're going to Philadelphia and a bar he called Skinny Razor's, where a lot of guys hung out. He introduced me to Angelo Bruno there, the head of the Philadelphia family. Russell and Angelo went way back together. Angelo and Russ were so much alike. Pretty similar personalities, quiet and soft-spoken. They were old-timers, old-school, and there was something about coming from that time where they grew up and learning how to keep your thoughts to yourself or share them with just a very few around you. Russell introduced me as '[his] boy' and I sat off to the side with some of Bruno's guys while Bruno and Russell talked. When they're done we get into the car and I'm figuring we're going back to New York but he says, 'Let's go, we're going up to Buffalo.' Fucking Buffalo? So we drive all the way up to Buffalo and he introduces me again as his boy to Stefano Magaddino. He'd been the boss in Buffalo and upstate New York since the 1920s and was pretty old. He wasn't like Bruno in Philly, who was like Russell, more personable. But Russell knew Magaddino for a long time. And he knew Buffalo really well. Russell grew up there, and when we get there it was like everywhere else, they're all fawning over him.

"He has his meeting with Magaddino and a few others and when that's done I'm figuring it's back to Pennsylvania. But he says, 'Let's go, back to New York.' I have no idea what's so important that we have to drive to Philly, Buffalo, and then back to New York in one day, but we drive all the way back to the city and go straight to Johnny D's, and he goes in the back to have another meeting. There were guys waiting for him. Now I'm beat. I drove all day. When that meeting is finally over and we get in the car it's gotta be close to midnight and I'm thinking it's back to the hotel, but he tells me to go to the Copa. *What?* He said Peggy Lee was there and he wanted to see her. He apparently knew her. She had that hit song 'Fever.' So we go to the Copa. The place is packed but of course Russell walks in like he owns the joint and they put us right up front again, the setup with the Dewar's, the whole routine. But when Peggy Lee finally comes on he falls asleep. She's singing and then looks at us and stops. She puts her hand out for the band to stop. Russell has his arms out on the table but is out cold. She points to him and says, 'Russell, you're snoring! Wake up!' He opens his eyes and waves his hands, no, no, like he wasn't sleeping. Everybody is clapping and laughing. Peggy Lee is laughing.

"That was unusual because Russell was a night bird. He'd always stay out till late. One night at the Copa we were still at the bar upstairs and it was closing time, so Jules Podell gave Russell the keys and asked him to lock up. But that night after driving all day, Russell was tired. I didn't know why we traveled so far to those cities, and I never asked Russell why he did anything. But he needed to see all those people—Bruno in Philadelphia and Stefano Magaddino in Buffalo, and then the people in New York—and the only thing I could tell that was bothering him at the time was Bobby Kennedy. He had just announced he was running for president, and one thing I did know then was that Russell hated the Kennedys. They all did. But Russell *especially* hated Bobby.

"Russell said he had testified before this committee in Washington, the one I saw on TV when I was a kid, and that Bobby had tried to embarrass him with all kinds of questions about his business, who he knew, and said that he was a gangster. But Russell said he didn't take the bait. He just sat there and took the Fifth all day and they went back and forth. He had no respect for the Kennedys. There was a lot of tension there. So he said when the hearing was over and he was leaving the Senate building, Bobby came running out and said, 'Mr. Bufalino, maybe we need to sit down and have lunch together.' And Russell said he turned to him and said, 'Why would I have lunch with a faggot like you?' Bobby said, 'Mr. Bufalino, you will regret that statement for the rest of your life.' Like I said, Russell hated the Kennedys, especially Bobby."

THROUGHOUT HIS LIFE RUSSELL HAD an affinity for jewelry. Good jewelry. He considered himself a master jeweler and carried a solid-gold single-eye magnifying glass, or jeweler's loupe, to gauge the quality of jewels. Whenever someone brought him a "piece," he'd whip it out and press his one good eye against the lens to analyze it.

For years, going back to the 1940s, Russell was a fixture in the Diamond District, a stretch of jewelry stores near Rockefeller Center on West Forty-Seventh Street, flanked by Avenue of the Americas and Fifth Avenue.

Behind the windowed storefronts were diamond bracelets and rings, gold and silver chains, engagement rings and gems, and just about any other kind of jewelry sought by potential customers. Inside, men and women manned the counters, while outside, passersby were harassed along the sidewalk with the promise that every day was a special sale day.

Along with his interests in the garment industry, jewelry was perhaps Russell's biggest business in New York. His bread and butter. And each time he received a new jewel or diamond, he'd hand the loupe to Billy and tutor him on the fine points of examination, such as looking for chips or black dots—carbon flaws—in diamonds, or glass replicas of precious gems, otherwise known as "fugazies."

Stolen gems from the tristate area usually ended up here, in the Diamond District. And Russell got his hands on a lot of them through Herbie Jacobs, a diamond dealer and jeweler Russell had known and done business with for years.

For Billy, visits to the Diamond District were akin to attending school, and class was always in session.

"Russell had all the connections on Forty-Seventh Street," said Billy. "We could get anything you wanted. He knew everyone. We even had a New York cop that worked that beat. A kid would come there with a bunch of stolen gold chains and the cop would grab him and let him go, but now he's got the chains and gives them to Russell. He got all the good stuff, and he got it all."

The business was relatively easy. Collect the merchandise from wherever it came from and sell it at cut-rate prices. Since they got it for "free," any price was pure profit.

Billy followed Russell's lead and kept a briefcase full of stolen jewelry at home and sold it to friends and acquaintances in Pittston, especially around Christmas.

"Every November I'd get like ten to twenty thousand worth of jewelry. Somebody might want a watch or something, or an engagement ring or diamond," Billy said of what would become an annual and lucrative enterprise.

When they weren't in the Diamond District, Russell liked to go downtown to visit with his friends and business associates in the garment industry. For years he made a living selling overcuts: he took extra material from dress orders for his factories in Pennsylvania and manufactured more dresses, or overcuts, which he'd sell at a discount to willing buyers.

"Russell's factories did all the cutting," said Billy. "What I mean by 'cutting' is that one of his factories would have a contract for, say, six hundred dresses, right? They'd fulfill that contract but we'd take the extra material and make more dresses, put the tags on them, and we'd sell those for ourselves. The first time I was involved my cut was around eighteen hundred dollars. So there was a lot of money in that. But clothing and jewelry were just a few of the things Russell was involved in.

"Being with Russell wasn't like having a regular job. He wasn't paying me, he was teaching me. I was learning how to make money, and I learned pretty quickly there were many ways to make money, and a lot of it. And I think the greatest thing he ever taught me was how to negotiate. That's what made him who he was. I saw early on that he was always getting called in to resolve disputes. He was like a rabbi. A lot of people, especially in New York, would have problems, and they'd come in and he'd straighten it out. His voice was the last on a subject. He had that power, and no one questioned it. He wanted me to have that power one day.

"But I think the night where I really realized the power of Russell was when he decided we'd have dinner at Jilly's. It was on Fifty-

Second Street and was owned by a guy, Jilly Rizzo. He was very, very close with Frank Sinatra. We go into Jilly's and he says, 'Hey, Russell, you're in town, it's nice to see you.' Russell says, 'It's nice to see you too.' He introduces me and we go in the back and sit down. Jilly comes back to us and leans down and goes, 'You know, Russ, Frank's in town.' Russ says, 'That's great, tell him I said hello.' But Jilly says, 'You don't understand, Russ, this is Frank's table.' Russ just looks him in the eyes and says, 'You know what, kid? This is my fucking table, and if he wants to sit down he can sit down with me or tell him to go fuck himself.' When Frank showed up later, he sat down with us."

Sitting with Frank Sinatra was mesmerizing, and Billy watched and listened as Sinatra and Russell chatted away like old friends. It was overwhelming and something Billy knew he'd go back and tell his family, that he'd sat down with Frank Sinatra. He knew Aunt Lottie would float to the moon on that one. Russell again introduced Billy as his boy, and Sinatra and Jilly gave him the respect that a son of Russell Bufalino deserved.

By June of 1968 Russell had stopped introducing Billy as his "boy." Instead, Billy was now his "son." And to complete the transformation, Russell decided Billy needed another lesson—this time in how to dress.

He had already discarded the combat-boots-and-leather-jacket ensemble he had worn most of his teenage years in favor of collared shirts and slacks. But Russell didn't like that look either. A clothes-horse himself, Russell favored $2,000 silk suits, silk shirts, silk underwear, and $500 custom-made Italian leather shoes. Billy had already begun wearing more jewelry, including diamond-encrusted gold rings, and had also followed Russell's lead in getting his own weekly manicures. Now it was time to complete the makeover.

"He had a favorite place in New York to buy his clothes, on Broadway, and he took me there," said Billy. "He's picking out this and picking out that. He gets me new suits, shirts, shoes, ties, socks, everything. We're there half the day, then he says, 'Okay, that's a start.'

It was thousands of dollars in clothes. I loved it. Now whenever I'd take him here and there and I'd get out of the car, people see me look the part and are nodding their heads. I still didn't know anything. I'm still new to all this. But I looked good. When we got back to Pennsylvania, Dave and Cappy and Angelo looked at me—'What the fuck?' Dave's like, 'I told you not to let my *goombadi* ruin you!' When I walked in the door at home my mom and Aunt Lottie said I looked nice. My dad took one look at me and walked away. He knew I was with Russ a lot. Everyone else could see that Russell was really bringing me along, and it was pretty fast. I can't say if Dave, Cappy, or Angelo liked it or not. Even though they were all close to Russell, they all fought for his favor. Everyone did. But I was the guy that was with him practically every day now. And I was with him that night when Bobby Kennedy was killed."

Not long after the polls had closed in California on June 4, 1968, Robert Kennedy was pronounced the winner of the Democratic presidential primary there.

He had entered the race late, in March, after President Lyndon Johnson, overwhelmed by the widening conflict in Vietnam, announced he would not seek reelection.

Kennedy's entrance into the race drew the consternation of Russell and many of his associates throughout the country. Russell particularly had never forgotten or forgiven Bobby's treatment of him during and after his testimony before the McClellan Committee in 1958. And Bobby poured salt in the wounds after his appointment by his brother, President John Kennedy, as United States attorney general in 1961. Bobby caused a lot of pain for Russell and for others. And they could never understand Bobby's aggressive pursuit given that his influential father, Joseph Kennedy, had always done business with men like Russell.

"Russell once told me that the old man Kennedy once had the biggest still in Scranton," said Billy. "And Kennedy knew all the old guys here, Volpe and Charles Bufalino. So it bothered Russell and others that

Kennedy's sons would come down so hard. But that night when Bobby got shot, Russell was happy. I know there was a lot more between them than just that hearing and I remembered that day in spring when I took him all over, to Philly and Buffalo and back to New York. I think they were trying to figure out what to do if Bobby became president. But now Bobby's dead, so it wasn't a problem anymore."

IN JANUARY 1969 THE PENNSYLVANIA Crime Commission, an investigatory unit recently formed to report on organized crime activities throughout the state, issued the first of its findings. The state attorney general, William Sennett, said in the report there were 142 known members of the organized crime syndicate in Pennsylvania and that five men led different factions. Stefano Magaddino ruled upstate New York, including Buffalo, and northwest Pennsylvania; Angelo Bruno was the leader in Philadelphia and southeastern Pennsylvania; Samuel DeCavalcante ran southern New Jersey and Bucks County, which was just north of Philadelphia; and Carlo Gambino in New York ruled northeastern Pennsylvania, with Russell Bufalino serving as his underboss.

Law enforcement in New York had always recognized Gambino as the leading Mafia figure in the country. He had the largest and richest family and was said to be the "boss of bosses" and so-called leader of "the Commission," the mob's governing body.

Russell never mentioned the report, and neither did Dave or any of the other guys. But Billy read about it in a newspaper and immediately knew it was wrong.

"I knew who Gambino was. Russell had introduced me before," said Billy. "He had a nephew who went to one of the dress factories that Russell and Angelo Sciandra had owned. The nephew wanted to get into the dress business, and Angelo told him no. So he came back again and Russell was there and he said, 'If you come back here again I'm gonna send you back in a box.' The nephew goes back and tells Carlo Gambino, and he got upset. So we're in New York and it's Russell, me,

Cappy, and young Angelo. Russell says, 'C'mon, we're going for a ride.' We go in the car and he says we're going to Carlo Gambino's house on Long Island. He and Carlo knew each other for years, and Carlo was at that Apalachin thing. They talked about the nephew in the car so I knew what it was about, but I'm driving and not saying anything on the ride out there. That wasn't my place. So we go out there and the four of us walk inside. Carlo is there with some of his guys. One of them was his underboss Neil Dellacroce. Carlo says, 'Russ, you disrespected me. You tell my nephew you'll send him back in a box? You try it and I'll send you back in a box!' Neil jumps in and says, 'Carlo, you can't talk to him that way. We'd have to kill everyone!' Neil was a classy guy. I was impressed with him. He was very sharp. When he said 'kill everyone' I knew he meant us, the guys standing there, so I'm a little nervous. He also knew that if Russell was ever taken out, there were so many people that would respond. Russell was that powerful. He and Carlo straightened it out. I remembered reading that story about the Crime Commission saying that Russell was Carlo's underboss and I knew it was bullshit. Russell wasn't anyone's underboss."

Russell and Carlo had known each other since the 1930s, and the spat was nothing more than a minor disagreement that had gotten out of hand. Both men calmed down and were wise enough not to allow any ill will to linger.

With one problem resolved, Russell had another.

The FBI had opened an investigation the previous summer concerning the transport of $25,000 worth of color television sets from Buffalo over state lines to Pittston, where they were to be sold on the black market. The TV sets had been illegally removed from a Buffalo store in April 1968. Russell was arrested and charged with conspiracy in December 1968 along with two other men associated with Stefano Magaddino. The trial began in January in Buffalo. Federal prosecutors displayed checks from several alleged coconspirators written to ABS Contracting, a garment factory owned by Russell and Angelo Sciandra. But the twelve-person jury was nonplussed and acquitted him.

When Russell returned home he learned that Billy had gotten himself into trouble over a truck hijacking. Two men had come to him looking for $20,000 to give to a source who was going to provide information on the truck being heisted. Billy gave them the money, thinking he'd earn well over $100,000 on that score. But shortly after he learned he had been deceived.

"They were to get a truckload of cigarettes and sell them and we'd partner," said Billy. "All of a sudden they came and said, 'Listen, we paid the guy but he blew off with your money.' I told Russell. He said, 'Look, that's your fault. It was a scam. Make sure you know what you're doing next time.' Nothing happened to the guys. Russell said, 'If you get yourself in trouble, get yourself out.' I was a little green around the ears. But I made sure it never happened again."

His legal problems behind him, at least for the short term, Russell decided it was time to drive to Pittsburgh and introduce Billy to John LaRocca, the powerful head of the Pittsburgh family, and his underboss Gabriel "Kelly" Mannarino.

Another Sicilian immigrant, LaRocca was only nine years old when he arrived in the United States in 1910. After his family settled in Western Pennsylvania he worked in the coal mines briefly, then rose up the ranks there and assumed the leadership of the Pittsburgh family in 1956 with the blessings of Carlo Gambino, Angelo Bruno in Philadelphia, and Russell. LaRocca appointed Mannarino his underboss. Both men had also attended the Apalachin meeting and been arrested. They were also called to testify before the McClellan Committee in 1958 but took the Fifth.

Aside from Dave Osticco, no one was closer to Russell than Kelly, who controlled much of the gambling in the Pittsburgh area. Kelly was a serious man who wore a fedora over his jet-black hair and, like Frank Sheeran, had a terrible stutter. It was Kelly who brought Russell to Cuba during the 1950s, and they both secured interests in the Sans Souci casino in Havana along with Santo Trafficante and Meyer Lansky, the indefatigable brains behind the operation. Kelly introduced Russell to Lansky, and to the Cuban dictator Fulgencio Batista.

"Kelly and Russell did a lot of business together in Cuba," said Billy. "The way Russell talked, they were making a lot of money in Cuba. He used to go there a lot. Dave went with him a few times. They'd go from Florida through the Bahamas, and then to Havana. Russell wanted me to meet Kelly and LaRocca and learn a bit about Youngstown in Ohio, which Pittsburgh controlled. I got to know LaRocca, but that first time meeting with him his eyes went right through you. When he was young he was supposedly one of twenty-two guys at a birthday party for a former boss, only they all pulled out ice picks and stabbed him in the chest and killed him."

It was during that trip to Pittsburgh that Russell decided Billy needed a gun. Russell never carried a weapon, but he felt it was time his protégé had one. And it was no ordinary gun. It was a twenty-five-caliber handgun with a pearl handle. Billy thought it was beautiful.

"We were sitting in Jenkins Sportswear, which was downtown right over the bridge in Pittsburgh, and he said, 'This is for you. If you're going to carry a gun, this will help you.' I guess that was a pretty big deal, the boss giving you a gun. I was with him all the time then, so that also meant I had to protect him. And I didn't think twice about that. He knew I knew how to use a gun from the army. But Russell thought he needed to show me. So after we got back we were at one of Russell's dress factories late at night. It was just me, him, and Angelo Bufalino, and Russell asks me for the gun, so I give it to him. He says I have to hold it like this, and point it like that, and don't get nervous and all of that. I said, 'Russ, I know how to shoot a gun.' So he goes, 'Oh yeah? You have to be responsible with this,' and he takes it and points it toward the floor and he shoots it. *Boom! Boom! Boom! Boom!* I said, 'Russ, what if someone's in the cellar?' He goes, 'Fuck them. They don't belong here.'"

CHAPTER 5

The League

It was the late winter of 1971 when the phone rang at ABS Contracting, one of the many cutting rooms Russell owned in northeast Pennsylvania. When Billy picked it up, he heard a familiar voice.

"Hello, this is Marlon Brando calling for Mr. Bufalino."

Billy didn't believe it. He put the phone to his chest and yelled out to Russell, "There's some fucking guy on the phone pretending he's Marlon Brando!"

Billy chuckled, figuring it was a prank call, but Russell looked at him with a death stare and barked, "Give me that fucking phone!

"Hello, Marlon?" said Russell. "Yes, I'm fine. How are you?"

Brando had been cast to portray Vito Corleone in the upcoming film *The Godfather,* which was set to begin principal photography in New York. The revered actor had achieved great success during the 1950s, winning the Best Actor award at the Academy Awards in 1955 for *On the Waterfront.* But his popularity had waned in recent years. Director Francis Ford Coppola thought Brando was perfect for a film that was the opposite of the stereotypical mob movie filled with psychotic gangsters and blood running in the streets. But Brando had recently come off of several forgettable roles, and Paramount Pictures executives hated him for the part.

After initially refusing Coppola's efforts to attach him to the film, Brando sought out the role and even agreed to audition to win over the leery executives. He was the only movie star among a group of actors that producer Al Ruddy signed for the pivotal roles in the film, including James Caan, Robert Duvall, Al Pacino, Diane Keaton, John Cazale, and Abe Vigoda.

Well-known for his meticulous preparation, Brando envisioned Vito Corleone as powerful but soft-spoken, cerebral but strong. A family man who saw himself as a victim of happenstance who could have been a corporate leader instead of a mob boss. But Brando needed inspiration and insight, so when he asked others tied to the production for an introduction to someone who could help him portray a mob boss, they all quietly pointed to Russell.

Russell had made his presence felt behind the scenes, playing a key role in ending months of conflict that delayed the production and threatened to derail the film altogether. He was, to the surprise of many, including Billy, intrigued by the film. It was based on the 1968 book by Mario Puzo, a bestseller that sold nearly ten million copies. Paramount had acquired the film rights. But as filming in New York neared, the production ran into one problem after another, mostly from a newly formed advocacy group, the Italian American Civil Rights League.

The nascent league was formed in April 1970 by Joe Colombo, the head of the New York family that bore his name. One of his sons had been arrested for melting U.S. silver coins, but Colombo claimed it was police harassment and formed the league with the stated goal of opposing discrimination against Italian Americans.

After gathering support, Colombo held the league's first rally that summer at New York's Columbus Circle, which drew thousands, and he hosted a benefit in November at Madison Square Garden's Felt Forum with tickets selling for as high as $250.

But the league had ulterior motives, and with it came violence. The *Staten Island Advance*, a small but well-read newspaper that was a staple of New York's least-populated borough, had been aggressively reporting on the league's activities, which included extortion and assaults. Many Italians from Brooklyn had moved to Staten Island following the opening of the Verrazzano-Narrows Bridge in 1964, which connected the two New York City boroughs.

Unhappy with its coverage, the league demonstrated in front of the paper's offices and elsewhere, tough guys with picket signs. One of the newspaper's delivery trucks was run off the road and burned while two drivers were beaten, one with a tire iron, and hospitalized.

The league was also unhappy with *The Godfather,* claiming that the book portrayed Italian Americans in a negative light. So as pre-production began on the film, set in Manhattan's Little Italy neighborhood, the league set its sights on the movie. It had strong-armed merchants there into buying and displaying league decals on their storefront windows, and the Teamsters ordered its truckers and film crew members to walk away, while league members were threatening the film's executives with phone calls telling them to "get the fuck outta town, or else."

"It was fucking chaos," said Billy. "They started production in New York and immediately there was trouble from the Teamsters, who refused to do any work. And then there were guys fucking with their trucks and knocking off equipment, like cameras and anything else that wasn't nailed down. We had guys down there every day. Andy Russo, who was a very big deal in the Colombo family, he was there. He was Carmine Persico's guy before he gave up the family and it went to Joe Colombo. Andy absolutely loved Russell, and he was really close to James Caan. I think they knew each other as kids. But there was so much going on before they even started filming."

The film's producers sought to speak to Colombo, and there would be several meetings. One was at the Park Sheraton Hotel in Manhattan, where a large number of league officials were holding an emergency meeting. Russell and Billy were there, and they listened closely as Al Ruddy set out the terms negotiated with the league.

"Ruddy said he would take out the word 'Mafia' from the screen-play, give one million to the league, stop selling some *Godfather* board game, and have a premiere of the movie in New York," said Billy. "Ruddy kept saying the movie wasn't about corrupt Italians but a corrupt society. Russell loved that. He was already pulling the strings in the background. He was the rabbi, and Colombo was consulting with him, so when Russell said it was okay, Colombo said okay. Without Russell, that movie would never have been made."

Cutting a deal with the New York Mafia shocked Paramount Pictures executives, who fired Ruddy for not just making the deal but participating in a press conference with Colombo. But the agreement calmed the league and paved the way for the production to resume after Russell passed word to the Teamsters to get back to work and for street guys to stop raiding the set. And at the urging of Coppola, Ruddy was quickly rehired.

But the real gangsters didn't go away.

Many remained lingering in the restaurants and coffee shops near the downtown set, and several even secured plum acting roles.

"Right after we brokered this peace between the producers and the league, we're at La Cantina in Little Italy and Lenny Montana comes in with this fucking camera lens he took from the set," said Billy. "He's this really big street guy from Brooklyn or Staten Island who was down there as a bodyguard for Andy Russo. Lenny comes in and says, 'Look what I got.' It must be worth fifty thousand dollars. He pulls it out from his coat and he's showing it to us and Russell sees it and yells, '*What the fuck are you doing! Bring it back! Bring it back right now, you fucking idiot, and don't ever let me see or hear about you taking anything else from there!*' Montana was a big man and I never saw him move so fast."

After Montana did what he was told and returned the camera lens, he went back to being Andy Russo's bodyguard, but not for long. The part of Vito Corleone's bodyguard, Luca Brasi, had yet to be cast, and Coppola noticed the hulking Montana, who used to be a wrestler.

"They needed someone to step in and play Luca Brasi and there was big Lenny Montana," said Billy. "Lenny was a street guy, a hustler. Andy Russo was close friends with James Caan and was there on the set every day, with Lenny beside him. So they put Lenny in the movie. He doesn't have to really speak much but when he does he fucks it up in a scene with Brando in his office. But it looks so real they keep it in the film anyway. Afterward he ran around telling everyone he was a movie star."

The crooner Al Martino tried everything he could to play the role of Johnny Fontane, the lascivious crooner and Frank Sinatra knockoff. But Coppola said no.

Martino was born Jasper Cini in Philadelphia in 1927. He had several Top 40 hits during the 1950s but was forced to leave the country over an affair he had with the wife of Anthony "Tony Ducks" Corallo, a high-ranking member of the Lucchese Family in New York. It took eight years to get him back to the United States.

"Tony Ducks threatened to kill Martino," said Billy. "So he fled to England and stayed there. After enough time had passed it was Russell who brought him back."

When he returned, Russell helped Martino secure a new record contract. He released "I Love You Because" in 1963, which was a top-five hit, and he became a popular attraction on the club circuit. But he desperately wanted the Johnny Fontane role.

"Al is close to Russell, had been for years, and after being turned down a few times he finally went to Russell," said Billy. "Al really wanted that part but Coppola said no. They wanted someone else, Vic Damone. So Russell says, 'Okay, you're not making it. The movie is dead.' Right after that Damone drops out and Al gets the role. But we had so many guys in the movie. We also had James Caan with us. He lived with us, ate and drank every night with us at Johnny D's. Russell even had him at his home with Al Martino. Russell cooked for them, and he loved it."

But Russell didn't love Marlon Brando. After he put out word that he wanted to meet a real don, Cappy and Angelo escorted Russell to the film set on Mott Street in Little Italy and to Brando's trailer. Russell walked inside for what would be the first of several meetings.

"Russell spent a lot of time with Brando," said Billy. "Russell showed him the ropes, how to speak, certain mannerisms, his quiet way, which Brando used in the film. Whenever Brando had a question, he'd call Russell. I didn't believe it the first time I heard his voice on the phone. I thought it was a joke. But it was him. Russell got the feeling that Brando thought he was above him, and you never do that to Russell. So in the end he thought he was a punk."

But Brando actually knew his place with Russell. Following a long day shooting the big wedding scene that opens the picture, Brando, who had been drinking all day, decided to drop his pants and moon the hundreds of people in the crowd, then he suddenly realized that many of the extras standing there were men connected to the Bufalino Family. Terrified, he quickly pulled up his trousers and sent word that he meant no disrespect to Mr. Bufalino.

With peace on the set, filming of *The Godfather* proceeded without incident and Russell went about his other business. On May 7, 1971, Russell, Dave, and Cappy left Medico Industries unaware they were being trailed by FBI agents. They drove along Route 315 to Aldino's restaurant for lunch with someone who had driven up from Baltimore. To the agents' shock, they learned that the lunch guest was Johnny Unitas, the legendary quarterback of the Baltimore Colts.

Unitas, known as "the Golden Arm," had won two NFL championships, in 1958 and 1959, and also played in the Colts' stunning Super Bowl III loss to the New York Jets in 1969. He was perhaps the most famous quarterback in the NFL, which is what disturbed the agents, who were trying to figure out why Johnny Unitas would drive up from Maryland to meet with Russell.

Joining them was Johnny Addie, the ring announcer at Madison Square Garden. Addie had called every major boxing match at Madison Square Garden since 1948—the introductions and the winner—

and had just announced the Muhammad Ali–Joe Frazier heavyweight world championship fight in March, which Frazier won. Addie had been a friend of Russell's for years.

The agents watched as Unitas left Aldino's around two P.M., entered the front passenger side of a two-tone brown Cadillac Coupe DeVille with Maryland plates and registration, and was driven to a local barbershop. There, a stocky man around six feet tall emerged and walked to the car and greeted Unitas. Following a brief, friendly conversation, the Cadillac took off again, this time for the Mack Novelty store, a vending machine company that Russell had a piece of. Three men came out of that store, approached the car, and all shook hands with Unitas.

It appeared that Unitas was making stops and saying hello to people he knew, which left the agents completely flummoxed. Of more concern, Russell had been widely known for years to operate one of the largest gambling operations in the country.

"It wasn't about gambling," said Billy. "Russell wanted him to do a charity event for a peewee football team, to make an appearance to help raise money, and he said yes."

It sounded innocent enough, but aside from NFL rules forbidding players and employees from associating with gamblers or gambling activities, they were also barred from associating with members of organized crime, not to mention lunching with the most powerful mob boss in the nation.

The following month the final scenes of *The Godfather* were being filmed when the Italian American Civil Rights League held its second Italian Unity Day rally in New York's Columbus Circle. The first one, the year before, at the same location had drawn fifty thousand people. Following the league's interference and success at drawing concessions from Paramount Pictures and the producers of *The Godfather*, its popularity had grown, and more than one hundred thousand were expected to attend the second rally, which was scheduled for June 28, 1971.

The league had grown since its formation, with chapters opening in cities across the United States. Russell formed one, Chapter 34, in Wilkes-Barre, and he appointed "Little" Lou Butera, a bookie and owner of the Imperial poolroom, as president. Billy was appointed secretary/treasurer and Angelo was vice president. They drove to New York to attend the rally, but on the way in Russell warned them to keep an eye out for Joey Gallo.

Born in Brooklyn and of medium height, with a sculpted jaw, receding hairline, and quick trigger finger, "Crazy" Joe Gallo had just been released from prison after serving ten years for extortion. Gallo and his brother kidnapped and ransomed senior members of Joe Profaci's family and sought to take over control of the family altogether. After Profaci died in 1962 it was Joe Colombo, not Gallo, who eventually succeeded him, and it was now the Colombo crime family.

Gallo had seethed in prison, and after his release in April he made it clear there would be no peace with Colombo. Everyone was concerned about "Crazy Joe."

"Joey Gallo hated Joe Colombo, and he hated the Italian American Civil Rights League because he was supposed to be boss of that family when he got out of prison, or at least he thought so," said Billy. "At the time the league was growing nationwide, and Russell wanted us to have our own chapter, and we did. So when it comes time for the rally, Russell, me, Louie, and Angelo are all there. It's right next to Central Park and they have a stage set up, a band playing, and red, white, and blue balloons everywhere. I'm standing next to Russell, and Louie is over here next to me. We're keeping an eye out for Gallo but there was this guy, a Black guy, and he had press credentials, and as soon as Colombo got out there, bullets were flying all over the place. So I just grabbed poor Louie Butera and pulled him in front of Russell so Lou would have gotten shot first. The Black guy was the shooter and they shot him, killed him. Colombo was shot three times and there was blood everywhere, all over his face, coming out of his mouth. They took him away in a coma. We got Russell out of there, but everyone figured it had to be Gallo behind it. So Russell wasn't happy with Joey Gallo."

THE CUTE GIRL THAT BILLY had dated when he was fifteen was now his fiancée, and Russell said it was finally time that he met her.

Ellen Ward had a sweet disposition and high aspirations. She studied to be a nurse. Ellen wasn't much more than five feet tall, and Billy had always taken it upon himself to look out for her. He had a disarming smile and such a pleasant way about him that of all of Ellen's friends, he was perhaps her parents' favorite.

"He was just a nice guy," said Ellen. "He wasn't shy, and he wasn't quiet. But he was very nice looking. We were just always comfortable together. And he spent a lot of time with my family as we grew up; he was always around. My grandmother loved him. One time he had this girlfriend and she would come by my house wondering where he was and I can remember my grandmother saying, 'I don't know what you're waiting for here.' So we dated a little bit in high school."

After graduating from St. Ann's Academy in Wilkes-Barre in 1964, Ellen dated another man, a good friend and high school classmate of Billy's who had moved to Newark with his mother. One day he had stopped on the side of a highway to help a stranded motorist fix a flat tire and was killed by a drunk driver. Billy was away on an army reserve training exercise when he heard about the accident. Upon his return to Pittston, he went to comfort Ellen.

"We were always friends first," she said.

Not long after Ellen enrolled in nursing school, they began to date again, and Billy became a regular presence in her life. In 1967, during her training at a mental hospital in Danville, Pennsylvania, Billy drove two hours each way to visit her every night.

"He'd take my girlfriend and I and go for a hamburger or soda or something," said Ellen. "He was driving a new Buick, which belonged to his father, and he was putting on one hundred miles each way. So he would disconnect the odometer so the mileage wouldn't show. I didn't know what he was doing. But then the tires were worn out and his father went down to the dealership and they were giving him a hard time about that. But then, his father wasn't the most pleasant person to deal with."

Ellen may not have been keen on Billy's father, but she loved his mother, Theresa. Ellen thought she was an angel forced to work far too hard to keep things calm in their house between father and son.

"I guess it was just his father's personality," Ellen said. "He was far different than my dad."

Billy was very different from his father as well.

While his father was grumpy and nasty, Billy did things that Ellen found endearing. At Arrow Distribution he developed a love/hate relationship with the owner, Zeke. They'd argue all the time, and on occasion Zeke would fire Billy, only to quickly drive to Billy's home to rehire him. Despite the rocky relationship, Billy loved Zeke, who ended up losing both legs to his diabetes. Following the amputations, Billy carried Zeke in his arms three days a week for his dialysis treatments. Ellen couldn't help but fall for him.

But Billy had a secret, and it had to do with Russell.

"I really didn't know anything about that for a while," said Ellen. "When Billy finally did tell me about Russell, all I knew was that he was some person from Pittston and that everyone knew him. Billy told me he would drive him sometimes to New York and that Russ liked being with him. But it wasn't until after we got engaged that I finally really met him."

Russell of course knew about the nurse Billy had been dating, and now that the young couple were going to marry, he felt it was time to meet Ellen. They all went to one of Russell's favorite restaurants, Andy Perugino's in nearby Luzerne. When they arrived, Ellen couldn't help but notice how everyone fussed over Russell.

"It was just the three of us—me, Billy, and Russell—and I didn't know if we even had a reservation," said Ellen. "When we walked in it was crowded but the headwaiter ran over to say hello to Russell and went back and moved some people who had just sat down at a table in the corner. Then they took us to that table. I didn't think much of it at the time, but I found out later it was Russell's regular table. Within seconds somebody goes under the table to put a shim under the leg so it wouldn't shake, and then someone else came by with a basket of garlic bread. I was really hungry, but just as I reached in somebody else came back who appeared to be really nervous and took that bread right off the table. He said, 'Mr. Bufalino doesn't eat garlic bread; he eats cheese bread,' so they brought that out instead."

The table secure, and with the right bread on it, Billy remained quiet as Russell and Ellen talked through most of the evening.

"We had dinner and it was very nice," said Ellen. "It was Russell and I talking and he was very sweet, very easy to talk to. After dinner we drove over to a club and sat in a booth. Billy had left us to talk to someone and Russell leaned over and said, 'Why do you want to marry this dummy?' I was taken by surprise. Then he said, 'Are you sure you want to be with him? You're a pretty smart young lady and you have a nice career starting. Are you sure? You realize that sometimes he might have to go someplace and be gone for a while. Is that gonna be all right with you?' I said I was sure."

Ellen saw it as not so much a warning as something that was going to happen, that Billy's work with Russell would take him away from her unexpectedly and sometimes for long periods and she should be prepared for it.

When Billy returned to the table, Russell got up and leaned into his ear.

"That's a nice woman," he said. "Don't fuck it up."

THE WEDDING WAS SET FOR October 30, 1971, at Blessed Sacrament Church in Hughestown with a reception for nearly three hundred guests to follow at the Mayfair Supper Club.

But the ceremony didn't go off without drama. Before the bride arrived at the church, a young woman was spotted sitting inside a car across the street. It was an old girlfriend of Billy's. He knew her as "the Indian."

Billy had met her at Arrow Appliances, where she'd come in and try to sell him vacuum cleaners. He said no to the machines, but he thought she was gorgeous and they began to see each other, even after he picked up with Ellen again. Billy broke it off once he decided to marry Ellen. Unhappy with Billy's decision after learning of his wedding plans, the woman threatened to throw acid at him and his new bride. When she was spotted outside the church, several men approached the car and found she did indeed have a bottle of acid in her lap.

"Wally was my best man and he was looking out for her," said Billy. "He thought she was the one who set his house on fire. She was fucking crazy. Gorgeous, but crazy. I used to go see her at midnight. They were calling me Captain Midnight and I'd stay with her and take her home at three in the morning and then go see all the go-go girls. Wally used to bust my balls when I got married. That crazy stuff had ended, and he said, 'I don't even know who you are anymore.'"

Ellen was told later in the day about the woman, and she recalled a phone call she had received.

"When I got my ring, this girl called me up and she tried to sell me a sweeper," said Ellen. "I didn't know that she was somebody that Billy had been seeing, the same girl. I didn't know that she was there and our best man, Wally, was really afraid she would do something," said Ellen.

Following the service, the guests flowed into the Mayfair. But there were far more than the three hundred people who'd been expected. Ellen noticed, and when she quietly inquired, Billy told her that Russell, reveling like a proud parent, had taken more than a dozen invitations and personally handed them out to some of his closest acquaintances in New York and Philadelphia, some of them a bit rough looking.

"He invited all these people," said Ellen, "and I didn't know exactly who they were."

Among those on Russell's guest list were Kelly Mannarino from Pittsburgh, Andy Russo from New York, and Benjamin "Lefty" Ruggiero, a soldier and hit man with New York's Bonanno Family. Joe Sonken, a former Chicago gangster who owned the Gold Coast Restaurant in Florida, was also there. Billy had met him before during Sonken's trips up north, and Sonken gifted them a honeymoon, a flight to Miami with first-class tickets and two weeks in a suite at the Diplomat Hotel.

Ellen didn't mind that Russell had invited some of his friends, and she didn't say a word when he had the Mayfair staff change the seating arrangements to accommodate his guests, who all sat at tables up front. After just a few short months, Russell was family to Ellen, who saw him only as a grandfatherly man who treated her with love and kindness.

"We had this connection," said Ellen. "It was also his birthday the day before, so we had an extra celebration."

Russell always claimed he had been born on October 29, 1903, and before the wedding cake was rolled in, the band stopped playing and the waitstaff brought out a birthday cake with lighted candles for Russell.

Everyone stood to sing "Happy Birthday."

Russell enjoyed the adulation and walked around the room like a proud parent. Billy's father, mother, sisters, and aunts sat at a table next to one filled with Russell's friends. William P. D'Elia's relationship with his only son had never risen above their saying more than just a few words to each other, yet he still resented the bond that had developed between Billy and Russell.

William also knew who Russell was, but it was a subject he never broached with Billy.

After the wedding, the couple drove to the Chateau, a hotel in the Poconos co-owned by Russell and Dave, and there the newlyweds spent their wedding night. The next day they found a church nearby and went to Sunday Mass before returning home to prepare for the flight to Florida, courtesy of Joe Sonken. Billy told Ellen he had to make a pit stop first at Medico Industries, and when he walked in, Russell was there with Dave and some of the other guys.

"Aren't you supposed to be on your honeymoon?" said Russell. "What are you doing here?"

"Had to take care of something," said Billy. "Anything going on?"

Russell said he was looking for someone to go to Baltimore the next day to pick up a truck filled with furniture. He then turned to the other men in the office.

"But the kid can't go 'cause he's married now," he said sarcastically.

Billy took the hint. "I'll go."

Russell gave him the keys to a car and told him to have someone drive down with him. The honeymoon was postponed.

Billy enlisted Wally, and when they returned with the truck, Billy took a love seat and chair for the new home he and Ellen had just purchased in Hughestown.

"When he told me we weren't going on our honeymoon, I was so innocent and unaware about whether this was okay or not that I thought, 'Well, this will give me a chance to get a washer and dryer,'" said Ellen.

THE ITALIAN AMERICAN CIVIL RIGHTS League, Chapter 34, Wilkes-Barre, held its first annual dinner dance three weeks after Billy's wedding, on November 20, 1971, at the Mayfair. Lou Butera, Angelo, and Billy, all Chapter 34 officers, wore black tuxedos with frilly shirts and black bow ties. The event drew over three hundred people, with entertainment provided by a forgettable lineup of singers and comedians.

Tables were sold in packages, and the closer you were to the stage, the higher the cost. A center front table was $500. Russell, of course, sat up front. The event raised over $100,000 and was a great success. Under Russell's orders, the money went directly to local people and organizations in need. Billy was in charge of Chapter 34's finances and wrote checks out to the parents of a blind baby born with cancer to pay for ongoing hospital treatments and tires for their car, which had been worn out by all the trips back and forth to the hospital.

"We weren't like the United Way, where you had to fill out an application and wait for them to decide who can get what," said Billy. "That's not how ours worked. If we knew somebody in need, they got it, no applications, no questions asked."

Chapter 34 also held benefits for special-needs children, including an annual Christmas party. But because of the large sums of money that were collected, there was constant friction with other charities, especially with the United Way, which tried to flex its muscle, claiming the money should be donated to them and they would decide who would get it. The United Way even went so far as to try to stop the chapter from buying a van for an organization that needed it to transport children. Russell stepped in and said no, it was the league's money and the league would decide who got what. The United Way backed off.

But just a few days after the inaugural dinner a tall, fearsome, familiar figure from New York arrived in Pittston representing the league's national office, which also wanted a share of the money.

"Lenny Montana came to see us with Gerry Lang, whose real name was Gennaro Langella. He was also with the Colombos," said Billy. "They were with the mother league, and they walk in and we're all friendly and everything and then they tell us, 'Here's the deal. You probably grossed one hundred, maybe one hundred fifty thousand from the dinner dance. Any money you get, we split it up fifty-fifty. That's the way it is with other local chapters, and that's the way it is with you.' We were all friends, but when it came to money, all bets are off. So I tell Russell what they told us and he says, 'Tell them to go fuck themselves. I'm going to handle it.' I tell Lenny, 'Go back to

New York and tell them that Russell is handling it.' So we kept all the money, and the mother league never said anything about it. Russell knew what the mother league was doing with the money. He helped start the league. So he said no, he wanted to give it all back to the community, and there was no one big enough to say no to Russell. So that's what we did, every year. There was no bullshit. No applications, no committees. People came to us and Russell left it up to me to make sure every penny went to charity. And it did. But the mother league? No. They had other ideas. Joe Colombo was in a coma and out of the picture, so they were going in a different direction."

JUST A MONTH LATER BILLY and Ellen were planning to celebrate their first Thanksgiving together as a married couple. She was too tired to cook or entertain, so they would eat at her parents'. Billy was in New York with Russell and not due back until six P.M. It was seven when he arrived at his in-laws', and before he could even sit down, the phone rang. It was Russell.

"The fucking dinner was on the stove and as soon as I walk in the door I take the phone and go, 'Yeah, Russ, what's up,'" said Billy. "He says, 'I left my shaver in the bathroom. Go pick it up and bring it back to me.' Okay, what am I going to say? My wife and everyone says I'm out of my fucking mind. But I go over to his house, pick up the shaver, and drive back to New York. I walk into the suite and he's playing cards with four or five guys. I said, 'Here's the shaver,' and he goes, 'See, I told you the kid would do it.' It was a test. He wanted to see just how loyal I was, and if I'd leave my family on a holiday for him. He told them he thought I would, and he was right."

WHEN *THE GODFATHER* PREMIERED A few months later, on March 14, 1972, it was a massive hit.

Al Martino was now a movie star, as was Alex Rocco, who portrayed Moe Greene, the casino owner shot in the eye. Rocco was a former associate of Boston's infamous Winter Hill Gang who fled for

California after beating a murder charge. He also spent time in prison for wrecking a diner and beating its owner with several other men. Al Lettieri, the dark, dangerous drug trafficker Virgil Sollozzo, was the brother-in-law of Patsy Eboli, whose brother Thomas was boss of the Genovese Family and was another close associate of Russell's. And of course Lenny Montana, whose turn as Luca Brasi became a cultural time stamp.

"The movie came out and at the premiere Lenny was holding up Raquel Welch high on his hand," said Billy. "Lenny was a good guy, but he was a street guy, muscle. One day he's stealing cameras from the set, and now he's a movie star. We all went to see it—me, Cappy, Angelo. But Russell didn't go to the premiere. Al Ruddy offered him a private showing, but he said no. He didn't want to see it. And he never did see *The Godfather*. Ever."

CHAPTER 6

Gold Coast

No one knew much about the young couple that had moved into the home in Hughestown, another quiet, pretty borough in a region filled with tree-lined streets and single-family homes.

The neighbors seemed nice enough, or at least they pretended to be even after word quickly spread about Billy and the man he worked for. It was a taboo subject only spoken about in private, and usually in whispers.

Most everyone in the Pittston area had a "mob guy" on their block or knew of someone who did. Billy was friendly enough, waving hello and telling people who asked what he did for a living that he was a manager at Arrow Distribution.

Ellen, who worked as an intensive care unit nurse and faithfully attended Mass on Sunday, said the same thing. She had no reason to say anything else because Billy never told her what he was doing with Russell aside from driving him around.

"All I knew was that he was selling appliances and sometimes he went with Russell and drove him to different places," said Ellen. "I never really thought about it then. Some might think it's stupid. Bill never talked about it, so it wasn't on my mind."

Their families lived nearby. Pittston was the next town over, and they visited often, as did Russell. And Papa, as Ellen called him, was delighted when she announced she was pregnant and expecting her first child in the fall.

"He was just ecstatic," said Ellen. "But Carrie—we called her Aunt Carrie—she and Russell could never have children. I'm sure it bothered Aunt Carrie. But they were thrilled for us. And Russell, he was more of a father figure to Bill than his own father was, so he felt as if he was going to be a grandparent."

Billy was excited by the news. He didn't want to wait to start having children, and Ellen made it clear that she planned to be a stay-at-home mom. So as the late winter cold became sharp enough to bite through the skin, Billy sat in his office at Arrow Distribution, having just helped load dishwashers onto a truck destined for a hotel chain owned by an associate from another family. He was trying to warm his hands when the phone rang. It was Russell.

"Get down here," he said.

"To where?"

"Florida, ya dummy. I have to send Angelo back up north and I need you here with me. He'll pick you up from the airport tomorrow."

So Billy did what he was told and booked a flight for the next morning. When he arrived in Miami, Angelo was there to pick him up, accompanied by an old man everyone called the Professor. His real name was Tuminello. He was a short man in his midnineties who had spent his career as a musician playing the trombone. He was also a member of the Masons and had earned the distinction of reaching the highest Mason degree, master Mason.

Billy got into the car and was introduced to the Professor, who spoke with a heavy Italian accent, and Angelo told him they were going to meet Russell at Joe Sonken's place.

Sonken was from Chicago but had fled the city in the 1940s for South Florida following the Al Capone years. In Miami, he had become a popular restaurateur and was the owner of the infamous Gold Coast Restaurant. After opening in 1948, the Gold Coast was known not just for its steaks, fresh fish, and pasta, but for the celebrities who dined there, among them Cary Grant, Frank Sinatra, and Sammy Davis Jr. It was also known as a notorious hangout for its gangster clientele. Carlo Gambino, Meyer Lansky, Santo Trafficante, and, of course, Russell all ate there often.

As they approached the restaurant, Billy could see from a distance the big brown sign with red and gold letters: *Joe Sonken's Gold Coast Restaurant.*

Once inside, Angelo and the Professor were directed to a table off to the side while Billy was taken to Russell, who was seated with seven or eight other men. They were Teamsters union officials in town for two weeks of executive meetings at the Diplomat Hotel, and Russell introduced each one. The last one was a small man who was sitting next to Russell.

"This is my son, Billy," said Russell. "Billy, this is Jimmy Hoffa."

Hand outstretched, Hoffa stood up, but Billy towered over him. Hoffa was only five feet five inches tall, if even that, Billy thought. But when they shook hands, Billy felt as if he were shaking with a man twice Hoffa's size. His grip was that strong.

"Nice to meet you, kid," said Hoffa. "Russell tells me a lot of good things about you."

"It's an honor to meet you, Mr. Hoffa."

Russell nodded toward where Angelo and the Professor were sitting and Billy left to join them. When he sat down a waiter rushed over, and Billy ordered an eggs purgatory.

"A what?" said the waiter.

Billy explained that it was a poached egg with marinara sauce. The waiter left with the order, but before Billy could say a word to Angelo, a small, round middle-aged man with an open-collared shirt came bouncing out of the kitchen breathing fire.

"Who ordered a purgatory in my place?!" he yelled.

It was Joe Sonken.

"You fucking guinea gangsters from Pennsylvania, we don't serve that shit here!" he yelled.

Sonken's outburst caught Russell's attention, and he yelled over, "Hey, Joe, that's my guy. You can't talk to him like that."

Sonken laughed and went back into the kitchen. His meal order secure, Billy turned to Angelo.

"So what's going on?"

Jimmy Hoffa had just been released from prison. He had served four years of a thirteen-year federal sentence at the Lewisburg prison in Pennsylvania following his conviction for jury tampering, mail and wire fraud, and several other charges. His freedom in December 1971 was secured with a pardon from President Richard Nixon. But unbeknownst to Hoffa the pardon came with several strings attached, the most onerous being that he couldn't run for the Teamsters presidency again until 1980.

The deal had been negotiated by Frank Fitzsimmons, whom Hoffa had handpicked to serve as the acting Teamsters president until his return. But Hoffa was furious. Unwilling to accept the terms of his pardon, he sought Russell's counsel and help to restore himself to the leadership of "his union."

The two men had known each other since the mid-1940s, when Russell's younger cousin William Bufalino arrived in Detroit. William had left Pittston for the U.S. Army Air Forces in April 1942, and the same year, he received his law degree. By 1945 he was a lieutenant stationed at the Army Air Forces base in Romulus, Michigan, located just southwest of Detroit. It was there that he met and married Marie Antoinette Meli. She was the daughter of Frank Meli, a Sicilian immigrant and member of the Detroit "Partnership," a group of leading gangsters who oversaw organized crime in Detroit and the surrounding region.

The wedding was a major social event with over 1,500 guests at the Book-Cadillac Hotel in Detroit. Russell and Carrie were there, and they were introduced to Hoffa.

With his law degree in hand, William remained in Detroit and assumed control of the Belvin Distribution Co., a jukebox sales and service firm whose real owners were William's new family, the Melis. William made a $30,000 investment in the company, half the funds sent from a Pittston bank controlled by Russell and the other half from Russell himself.

Russell now had a piece of the Detroit jukebox business.

Not long after, William became president of the powerful American Federation of Labor associated Jukebox Union. But in 1947 he resigned at Russell's urging to assume the presidency of the newly formed Teamsters Union Local 985, also known as a "Jukebox Local," which was controlled by Jimmy Hoffa. William's placement there cemented Russell's friendship with Hoffa and gave Russell enormous influence within the Teamsters and, eventually, its rich Central States Pension Fund.

William would later rise to become the Teamsters' national lawyer and Hoffa's personal attorney after he assumed the Teamsters presidency in 1957. With that insider's view, William would share everything with his cousin in Pittston. Most of the time he didn't have to, since Hoffa and Russell were the best of friends and Hoffa told him most everything anyway.

As the Teamsters grew into a national powerhouse, Russell used his enormous influence in cities where he and many of his friends had business interests. If he required a strike somewhere to influence a negotiation or to prove a point, the Teamsters there would picket. If someone sought a loan, they'd be directed to the Central States Pension Fund. With Hoffa and his cousin William in Detroit, Russell funneled loans for projects across the United States, for which he'd receive a fee.

Hoffa insisted that each Teamster loan, and the interest owed, be repaid. But under Fitzsimmons the Teamsters were decentralized and it was the locals that were responsible for the loans, including collection. The lack of central authority led to loan delinquencies, and many loans lent to "friends" went unpaid. Under Fitzsimmons, 36 percent of loans from the Central States fund were delinquent or had defaulted.

Hoffa knew who was taking the money, and it infuriated him.

"The one thing about Jimmy, he was always for the union, and he always made sure those loans were paid back, with interest," said Billy.

Fitzsimmons had also steered the Teamsters' political allegiance in 1972 to the Republican Party and put the full power of the organization behind President Nixon in his quest for reelection.

That also didn't sit well with Hoffa. While grateful for his release, he had no intention of abiding by the terms of his deal with the government and had put in place a strategy that would allow him to regain the presidency of the Teamsters.

But he first had to meet with Russell.

For years Russell had maintained two homes in South Florida. One was a small bungalow in Hollywood, while the other was a large place on several acres in Hallandale Beach. During the winter months he'd stay there for weeks at a time.

When Hoffa requested the meeting, Russell knew why, and he wanted to impress upon his friend that he should move slowly and quietly. Many people were watching, he said.

The two men had been close for nearly thirty years, and they enjoyed a prosperous and respectful relationship. It was Russell who introduced Hoffa to Frank Sheeran. Russell had spotted Frank in Philadelphia and heard he had been doing various jobs for extra money and inquired about him.

Frank had seen combat in Italy during World War II and spent over a year on the front lines. After the war he worked as a truck driver and had been a member of the Teamsters Local 107 in Philadelphia since 1947. With his widening interests, including those in Cuba and with the Teamsters, Russell needed someone by his side, and Frank became his part-time driver and bodyguard.

Soon after, Russell asked him to apply the deadly skills he had learned in Italy, and Frank was one of a select few who could coldly dispatch Russell's enemies on command. Once inside Russell's inner circle, Frank sought a bigger role with the Teamsters, and Russell introduced him to Hoffa. Frank eventually moved to Detroit to work for Hoffa and his Local 299 before taking his current position in Wilmington, Delaware.

For his part, Hoffa loved everything about Frank, from the tree trunks he called wrists to his hands, which were so big a handshake felt like a vise grip. Russell had employed Frank as muscle, and Hoffa did the same.

Before ending their meeting, Russell and Hoffa had other matters to discuss, including a Central States loan for $4.5 million granted to the Pocono Downs racetrack near Wilkes-Barre. Russell had obtained the loan as well as another for an investment in a coal company, also in Pennsylvania.

To show his appreciation, Russell gave Hoffa the contract for the "sports service" at the Pocono Downs racetrack. The sports service handled all the parking at the track. The contract was drafted in the name of Hoffa's daughter, Barbara.

But before they parted, Russell again cautioned his friend to go slow and not ruffle any feathers. There were men—friends—who had expressed their disapproval upon hearing that Jimmy was ignoring the terms of his pardon and trying to regain the Teamsters leadership.

Billy knew that Russell was concerned for Hoffa. Things had changed since he had been away, and Russell hoped Hoffa would heed his advice. But his friend was stubborn.

On his way out of the restaurant Hoffa stopped to shake hands with Billy.

"Look out for my good friend over there," Hoffa said, looking over at Russell.

"I will, Mr. Hoffa," said Billy.

"Call me Jimmy."

"Okay, Jimmy."

BILLY REMAINED IN FLORIDA WITH Russell for a few days before they returned home together. They then drove to New York with Angelo. After dinner at Johnny D's, Russell was in the mood for the Copa, only he decided he wanted to sit at the bar upstairs, and upon arriving a booth was cleared for him, Billy, Johnny, and Angelo. With the exception of Johnny, the men were wearing their Italian American Civil Rights League pins on their lapels. Each pin had diamonds and a small ruby to recognize the status of the chapter's officers.

The smoke-filled bar was loud and crowded with familiar faces. Among them was Joey Gallo, who was there with an entourage. Russell had little use for Gallo, and neither did many others following the shooting of Joe Colombo, who remained paralyzed. An open contract had been put out on Gallo's life, but the brash gangster not only remained alive, he traveled freely and visited the same clubs frequented by his rivals. The Copa was one of them.

Billy saw Gallo there and pointed him out to Russell, who said to ignore him and then left the table.

"Russell gets up to go to the bathroom," said Billy. "We were all wearing our league pins and Russell comes back and sits down, and Joey Gallo comes up to the booth. The balls on this guy. Everyone knows there's a contract on him, but he's there celebrating something. I think it was his birthday, and he'd been drinking with his people. Russell must have passed him coming back from the bathroom and Joey comes over and points at Russell's pin and says, 'Take that fucking pin off.' Russell goes, 'Why don't you go fuck yourself.' So I get up to say something but Joe's bodyguard, Pete the Greek, steps between Joey and Russell and goes, 'Joey, take it easy. Do you know who he is?' Joey waves his hand and says, 'Yeah, I know. He's a boss, I'm a boss. We're all bosses.' Pete leads Joey away, but Russell is pissed. 'Fucking cocksucker. Disrespectful.' Whatever Russell was thinking, he was saying. Russell never got mad, but you don't talk to him like that. Joey was wild. I had bumped into him before. He knows Russell is angry so he immediately leaves the Copa and takes his group with him. Some people who saw what happened come to the booth to talk to Russell. No one could believe that Joey would disrespect him like that. It was a half hour or so later we hear Gallo got shot at Umberto's downtown. A lot of people thought Gallo was behind the shooting of Joe Colombo and figured this was finally payback from Colombo's people. Russell? He never said anything about Gallo being killed. Nothing. And I didn't ask him."

MORE THAN SIX HUNDRED PEOPLE, many dressed in tuxedos, gowns, or other formal attire, filled the Mayfair Supper Club on October 28, 1972, for the second annual dinner dance sponsored by the Italian American Civil Rights League, Chapter 34, Wilkes-Barre.

The huge crowd, double the size at the debut event the year before, had come to see Al Martino.

The crooner was a certified movie star, having wooed audiences with his brief but critically acclaimed role as Johnny Fontane in *The Godfather*. When Billy called him on behalf of Russell to perform at the dinner dance, Martino was more than happy to oblige the man he called his own godfather.

The dinner dance was always held around Russell's birthday, or the day he claimed was his birthday, October 29, and at the beginning of each dinner everyone—the politicians, the judges, the businessmen, and the wise guys who had driven or flown in from other parts of the country—all stood up for a toast to wish him a happy birthday.

No one said it, but as everyone lifted their glasses and sang, they all knew that the man they were honoring had had a difficult year. A vicious storm had swept through the region in June, and more than seven inches of rain had fallen. When it was over, Hurricane Agnes had left much of the Wyoming Valley underwater as homes up and down the banks of the Susquehanna River were flooded, including Russell's.

The torrential rains fell all along the East Coast, and in Luzerne County alone more than twenty-five thousand homes and businesses were lost or damaged. Russell's home on East Dorrance Street was just blocks from the river, and by the time the rain stopped, the flood-waters had reached the ceiling.

Russell and Carrie moved in with her cousins the Sciandras while their house was repaired. Billy convinced his father to do the plumbing. They still barely spoke to each other, but just enough for Billy to ask his dad for the favor.

With Carrie secure, Russell spent more time in New York City. He had to. He was now in charge of three crime families: his own, the Magaddino Family in Buffalo, and the Genovese Family in New York. Tommy Eboli, the Genovese boss, had been shot in July in Brooklyn after a visit with his girlfriend.

The hierarchy of mob leaders who made all the big decisions, the Commission, had approved the murder after Eboli had refused to repay a $4 million loan he secured from Carlo Gambino to front a drug operation. Enraged at the slight, Gambino responded. Eboli was shot five times in the head, his death instant.

Russell's association with the Genovese Family ran deep. He had been close to Vito Genovese, the family patriarch. When Genovese was imprisoned in 1959 it was Eboli, his capo, who became acting boss. After Genovese died in 1969, Russell stepped in to run the family until Eboli assumed the title of boss.

But Eboli's murder left a troubling leadership vacuum at a time when cooler heads were required given the Jimmy Hoffa situation. Hoffa had ignored Russell's advice to "go slow" and instead moved with speed that summer to regain his position as Teamsters president. Certain Genovese Family members were among a broader group of men who pushed back hard.

Among them were Anthony "Tony Pro" Provenzano, a capo in the Genovese crime family and head of a Teamsters local in New Jersey, and Anthony "Fat Tony" Salerno, another high-ranking member of the Genovese Family based in New York. In 1961, Hoffa had appointed Provenzano an international vice president of the Teamsters, making him the union's second-most-powerful member. Provenzano's New Jersey local was among the strongest in the nation, and he and Hoffa had worked closely together. But Provenzano was later convicted of extortion and was imprisoned with Hoffa in Lewisburg. There, a feud developed between the two men over Provenzano's Teamsters pension, which he lost with his felony conviction. Hoffa didn't forget the incident. Neither did Provenzano.

Not wanting the friction to escalate, Russell agreed to assume temporary control of the Genovese Family. He had done so once before, and now he was stepping in again.

"Russell was very close with many of the guys there, like Fat Tony, so it wasn't a big deal. No one questioned it. Who could anyway?" said Billy. "But it also allowed Russell to keep a lid with them on things with Jimmy."

The dinner dance in Wilkes-Barre that October was a huge success for the league and for Billy, who, along with Angelo, served as a chapter "captain."

And Russell was more than pleased with the event. Luzerne County judges Bernard Podcasy and Arthur Dalessandro were among the featured speakers, and Billy made all the presentations. But Billy's thoughts weren't on the dinner. Ellen was expecting their first child in a few days, and like every other first-time parent, his apprehension was palpable.

When Carolyn D'Elia was born on November 3, Billy walked on air, and Russell couldn't have asked for a better birthday present. They went out for a few celebratory drinks and when they returned to the hospital, they were so loud the head nurse kicked them out. When Carrie saw her namesake, she cradled the baby in her arms.

The moment was bittersweet for Carrie, but Russell floated in the same clouds as Billy.

"He just loved her," said Ellen. "And he was very protective of me. When I was pregnant with her I wasn't feeling good one night and Billy had gone out and I couldn't find him. I called some people that we knew but they didn't know where he was, so then I called Russell. I would never bother him with something like this, but I said I wasn't feeling good and I couldn't find him. No one could. I said I didn't think he's out anywhere and then Papa said, 'Oh yes he is. Don't worry about it. I'll find him.' And he did. He found him right away at some new restaurant a friend of his had opened and Bill came right home."

No one was more surprised than Billy, who was shocked when he was told he had an urgent call.

"I had no idea how he found me," said Billy. "No one, I mean no one, knew about this place. No one. But he called me there and said, 'What the fuck you doing? Your wife is about to have a baby and is sick. Get the fuck home.'"

After the birth of his daughter, Billy left Ellen and returned to Manhattan with Russell, who had his new responsibilities with the Genovese Family. That meant even more visitors coming to see him at Johnny D's and Vesuvio.

"Russell had his hands full," said Billy. "He was meeting with all these Genovese people and dealing with all their problems. And he was still meeting with the entertainers playing the Copa that week. That never changed. No matter how busy he was, he found time to meet them."

Russell had been going to the Copa for years. Some even whispered that Russell had a piece of the club. Whether he did or not, he loved the place and forged relationships with many of the entertainers who performed there. Over time, it became a tradition for the headliners and their managers to lunch with Russell at Johnny D's ahead of their performances. Tony Bennett, Jerry Vale, and Peggy

Lee were among the singers who broke bread with Russell. Even Liberace, the famed flamboyant pianist, paid his respects.

"We had him there once for lunch. I'll tell you, he was class," said Billy. "After I started with Russell we had over one hundred people come through who were entertainers. When Liberace shows up, there were like fourteen people in the back. Danny Gorey was there. He was a big, tough guy, a bit of a con man but also a muscle guy Russell would use. If you wanted to bust up a joint you'd send him. But Danny was a chain-smoker, so he sat away from Russell. He hated cigarette smoke. If you lit up a cigarette near him he'd go, *'Put that fucking cigarette out!'* That's funny because Russell used to smoke Chesterfields, with no filters. But he quit. Danny knew his place. Guvy Guarnieri, Russell's top guy from Binghamton, was also there too but he wasn't smoking. He was just asking Liberace some dumb questions. He goes, 'What's it like to be a fag? Do you like being a fag?' So Russell turns around and goes, 'Stop being stupid and stop busting his balls.' It was kind of embarrassing. But Liberace smiled and let it go and he and Russell continued to talk. Russell could talk with anyone, so they were both very relaxed. Sometimes someone would come and they'd be all uptight and nervous meeting Russell. Not Liberace. A little later he gets up and says to Russell, 'Thank you very much. I appreciate you having this interview.' He goes to the front and signs some autographs and then leaves. When we ask for the check, we're told that he paid it on the way out. We couldn't believe it. Liberace paid the check? I thought he was a very classy guy. It was the first time in my life I ever heard of an entertainer paying a check."

CHAPTER 7

Deportation

The call from the law office of Jack Wasserman in Washington, DC, was not unexpected but was still a blow nevertheless: Russell had to leave the country.

The government had been trying to deport Russell since the Apalachin fiasco in 1957, and for sixteen years Russell had kept its agents at bay.

Immigration authorities had secretly issued a deportation order in 1961 and arranged a passport and one-way ticket to Italy. The plan was to pick Russell up without warning and send him on his way. But the Italian authorities at the consulate in Philadelphia got wind of the plan and tipped off Wasserman, and he successfully filed motions to keep Russell in the United States.

Wasserman had filed more appeals with the Board of Immigration Appeals, the most recent ones in 1967 and again in 1971, but they were denied each time. He filed a final appeal with the U.S. Court of Appeals for the Third Circuit in Philadelphia in November 1972, but in January 1973 Wasserman informed Russell that the court had upheld the deportation and Russell had to leave immediately.

The decision was based on Russell's "failure to establish good moral character," his lying under oath regarding his birthplace and other false testimony, and his two fraudulent entries into the United States in 1956 during his return from Cuba. But the court's ire was focused on Wasserman, an immigration specialist who the court said was "in charge of tactics which have held petitioner in this country despite the fact that he deliberately and falsely asserted United States citizenship."

Believing he was finally bound for Italy, Russell spent the two weeks leading up to his departure settling his business affairs, laying down instructions with Dave, Cappy, Angelo, consigliere Eddie Sciandra, and Billy. Nothing would change, said Russell, other than Billy was going to join him in Italy with his family while he continued to fight the government from there. Carrie would eventually come too.

Billy didn't mind, only he had to sell the idea to Ellen. He was surprised when she said she didn't mind either. Italy, she said, sounded very nice.

As his deportation approached, hundreds of people visited to bid him farewell. He and Carrie had been staying with Josephine Sciandra, the widow of former boss John Sciandra, while repairs continued on their flooded house. The heads of crime families throughout the nation and their underlings were there. Others, such as local businesspeople, politicians, law enforcement, and even a few Catholic priests, waited in line outside to pay their respects. The mood was so dire, it was more akin to a wake.

Russell was so certain he was bound for Italy that upon his arrival at the immigration office on N. Broad Street in Philadelphia on March 27, 1973, he had already booked a seven P.M. flight to Rome for that evening with Pan American.

"Me, Angelo, and Jim Moran, a lawyer from Philadelphia—we brought him down there to Philly," said Billy. "They told Russell to report at eight in the morning to Immigration. We showed up with me carrying a black suitcase filled with forty pounds of toilet tissue.

They said toilet paper in Italy was rough. They put Russell in a cell but within an hour there's already an issue with his paperwork and they tell him they may have to keep him overnight. So I decided to make some phone calls. I'm calling this senator and that senator. I reach one guy in Washington and he says, 'Here's what you do. When they take him to the steps, run around behind him and push him down. He gets injured, he doesn't go.' It was stupid. So as the day goes on, all we know is that he was going. They were just waiting for the call."

Russell had tried to exert his great influence for a last-minute reprieve following the appeals court decision in November, and there were whispers that $1 million had been transferred to friends in Italy to persuade the authorities there to refuse his entry.

"There wasn't any money," said Billy. "We thought something might happen because of who Russell was and who he knew. We hoped something would. But he thought he was gone. He told me to get out there in two weeks. 'Tell your family you're moving out to Italy.' But at a quarter after four an Immigration guy comes out—his name was Bertness—and he says, 'Well, boys, he's going home with you. We got to let him go. We just got word from the Italian consulate. We say he wasn't born here, they say he wasn't born there. So he's a man without a country. They said, "You keep him."'"

Billy and Russell emerged from the federal building via a side entrance and into chaos. Reporters and television crews surrounded Russell and yelled out questions while nearly twenty friends and family members tried to cover him. One federal employee quipped that Marlon Brando must have been coming out of the building. Russell's cousin Larry Bufalino jumped into his arms, held him tight, and with tears in his eyes yelled, "Thank God! Thank God!"

Angelo put a thick arm around Russell, and he and Billy escorted him to a waiting gray Cadillac Fleetwood. Before entering the car, Russell turned toward the reporters. "I'm not resigned to being deported," he said. "I hope there's a way I can stay . . . I think it's a goddamn shame, what they're doing to an individual in this country. The whole thing is a stupid nothing."

Billy, Angelo, and Jim Moran accompanied Russell inside the car and they drove to Dante & Luigi's, one of Russell's favorite Philadelphia restaurants, for a victory dinner. When they finally returned home later that night, they first went to see Carrie.

"We pull in and everyone is happy and I hug Carrie," said Billy. "We were both so happy I broke her ribs."

But the good humor was tempered a few days later when the Internal Revenue Service placed a $21,000 lien on Russell's home. The agency said it was for federal back taxes. A few weeks after that, on Thursday, April 19, the U.S. Immigration office in Philadelphia announced publicly what they'd told Billy and Russell the day he was released—the Italian foreign ministry refused to issue a travel document for Russell to enter the country.

Now that the decision had finally been announced, Russell, Billy, and several other friends went to the Club C&C in Scranton to celebrate. Billy thought it was a good time to generate some favorable publicity and convinced Russell to talk to a reporter about his experience. The notoriously secretive Russell at first said no, but Billy explained that he knew the reporter, who had agreed to tell the "real story" about Russell Bufalino.

"We were having dinner and Russell was talking to the reporter in a back room," said Billy. "He was from the *Scranton Times*. We knew him. He said he had no money and was losing his job so he came to us to help him. He said if he could get an interview with Russell, it would save his job. He used to hang around here at the restaurant, the dress factories. I gave him two or three dresses, I think it was for a daughter. So I said, 'Okay, you want to talk to Russell? Only if you tell the real story. You got to tell the real story.' So Russell is in the back talking to him when the FBI comes in. They open the door and yell out they have a warrant for Russell's arrest. Russell came out and said he wanted to see the warrant, and they said he'll see it when he sees it, 'Come with us.' So Russell's getting mad and yelling that this was an illegal arrest, that it was harassment again. And he was right. He just beat the feds on the deportation, so now they come do *this*? Two agents come over to handcuff him and Russell says, 'I never gave you guys any trouble. Knock it off.' Then he says, 'You guys are in your fifties, I'm in my seventies. Let's put the gun and the badges down and let the best man win.'

"They cuff him and take him out and we walk over to the federal building, which was just a block away. That was Good Friday, and they arrested him then thinking there were no judges until after Easter. But we get to see a magistrate and we're there all night until Russell finally gets out on a fifty-thousand-dollar bond. I think it was around two or three in the morning when we got out of there. Thing was, we didn't know what it was for. All they said was that the warrant charged him with violating the Hobbs Act. We're like, 'What the fuck is that?' We found out later it was about the vending machines. They arrested a bunch of guys that weekend, in Scranton and up in New York State, and they said Russell was using violence to drive out competition. A week later that reporter's story came out, the one who promised to tell the real story. The headline was 'Bufalino Real "Family" Man, According to FBI.' The first thing the article says is that Russell was the head of the Bufalino Family. I was like, 'Fucking cocksucker!'"

Russell was the focus of more attention a week later when national newspaper columnist Victor Riesel reported that federal law enforcement officials believed that Russell was one of the newest members of the Mafia's national commission.

Riesel had written about national labor issues and the mob for years, going back to the early 1950s. His tough-talking, no-nonsense column routinely excoriated members of organized crime for their misdeeds. Among his regular targets then was William Bufalino. In a February 1954 column, Riesel had reported that William was part of a conspiracy involving the Teamsters in Detroit to extort millions from workers, businessmen, and the federal government through threats and violence. Riesel's work was so prickly, someone intentionally blinded him by throwing sulfuric acid into his eyes in April 1956.

His response was to put on a pair of dark sunglasses and continue writing.

While Riesel's most recent column about Russell and his place on the Commission drew the interest of the FBI and the media, Billy simply dismissed it as gossip.

"Russell was never on the Commission," said Billy. "He was always above it."

Just two months later, on May 6, 1973, Russell was indicted by a federal grand jury in Buffalo along with twenty-three other men and charged with robbery, perjury, extortion, and gambling. Prosecutors said Russell ran a $36,000-a-night dice game in Rochester.

He had been in control of the Magaddino Family for several years, which extended his reach to Buffalo. But he already had a firm grip on Binghamton and the Southern Tier, and his top guy there, or capo, was Anthony "Guvy" Guarnieri.

At sixty-one, Guvy oversaw all the gambling in the region and was involved in union busting. He also shared with Russell an interest in the Tri-Cities Dress Co. in Binghamton. Guvy was another one of Russell's guys who attended the Apalachin meeting, and he was also alleged to be involved in a plot with Russell to bomb two rival vending machine companies in the Binghamton area.

"We used to take Russell up there to Endicott all the time to see Guvy," said Billy. "So we'd go up there, Russell would cook. They'd play cards. Sometimes we'd stay, sometimes just leave him there. But that was like a hangout for everyone up there in Endicott. One of his other guys up there was Mr. Luigi. He was supposedly a contract killer from Buffalo. They moved him here to Pittston. One time Kooch was busting his balls and I said, 'Kooch, stop fucking around with him, he'll shoot you.' There was no doubt in my mind that he was once a shooter. When he died he had fifty-seven thousand dollars in the bank. Nobody claimed it.

"But Russell liked going up there. One time we went to pick him up and the tire blows out. He's yelling, 'You cocksucker. You pig. We never had tires like this. Now let's change the tire.' I said, 'I can't change the tire. There's no tire iron.' He goes, 'No tire iron? What the fuck is wrong with you!' I didn't tell him why, but the week before, when I was with this guy Johnny Catal, he used the tire iron to beat the fuck out of a guy at a golf course on a back road. He got arrested. I forget which magistrate was on this, but I said, 'C'mon, you have to do me a favor and get this guy out.' He said, 'If you saw what happened to this guy, you'd put him in jail. He was all wrapped up like a mummy with a little opening for his mouth and eyes.'"

Despite the arrests and the constant media attention, the summer had been a good one. And the latest headlines revealed that federal prosecutors had finally caught on and described the gradual leaching of power away from Stefano Magaddino to Russell, whom they publicly acknowledged was the boss of Buffalo.

Russell was now firmly in control of a vast region that included New York State, much of Pennsylvania, and parts of New Jersey and New York City. And he also had immense influence within the Teamsters, the most powerful union in the country.

The Bufalino Family had never been more dominant. Yet it had not grown. While there were plenty of associates, for years the number of soldiers, or "made" men, remained around sixty and was thinly spread out across four states. And they were not getting any younger. Russell was just a few months away from turning seventy, while Dave and Cappy were in their sixties and Angelo was in his forties. Guvy in Binghamton had turned sixty, as had consigliere Eddie Sciandra, and many of the others were just as old.

Despite his advanced age, Russell wasn't thinking about immediate succession. But he was thinking about the future, and new blood. So that fall, as he and Billy were exiting the Lincoln Tunnel and heading back to Pennsylvania following a business meeting in New York, he looked over to the man he had long called his son. It was time to pop the question.

"He was just sitting back in his seat and had his eyes closed, like he always did, and after a while he sits up and just blurts out, 'So, are you going to be with me?'" said Billy. "He caught me off guard. He said I'd always be his son and he'd always love my family, but he needed to know if I was going to be with him. I just looked at him and said, 'Sure, Russ, you always know I'd be with you.' That was it. He stopped talking and put his head back. So when we pull up to his house later he tells me to walk inside with him. Carrie is up and Russell says, 'Give the kid the title. I'm giving him my Cadillac.' She wasn't happy about that. She said she thought they were going to trade it in but Russell said, 'No, I'm giving it to him.' It was a '73 Cadillac Fleetwood Brougham, gray and black. It was a gift for saying yes. But the thing was, I didn't know what I said yes to. Being with him? He was like a father to me, so of course I would always be there with him. He couldn't have been talking about being made. My mother was Irish, so I didn't even think that was possible. So I just figured he needed to hear me say it, that I would always be with him in this life, that I made the choice and that was it. I didn't think much of it after that. We had the dinner coming up, so I was probably focused on that."

The Italian American Civil Rights League, Chapter 34, Wilkes-Barre, scheduled its third annual dinner dance for Saturday, October 27, 1973.

Billy, as secretary-treasurer, was again in charge of the talent, only Russell let it be known that this dinner was an especially significant event—they would also be celebrating his seventieth birthday. Billy knew he had to go the extra mile and bring in some real talent. So he called Dick Linke.

He had met Richard "Dick" Linke during one of the trips to California that Russell had sent him on while he was dealing with his legal problems in Buffalo. A reporter for the Associated Press in the 1940s, Linke switched to public relations and later worked at Capitol Records. It was there, in 1953, that he found an amiable young actor and comic, Andy Griffith. Linke was so high on Griffith's talent that he left Capitol to become his personal manager. As Griffith's popularity rose, Linke helped develop and served as a producer on his hit television program, *The Andy Griffith Show,* which ran from 1960 to 1968. Griffith's success drew more talent to Linke's firm, and he soon was managing a stable of actors and singers such as Frankie Avalon, Ken Berry, Jerry Van Dyke, and Bobby Vinton.

"Russell had been sending me out to California and I was spending a lot of time in Beverly Hills and became very close to Dick," said Billy. "He was married to a Vegas showgirl. Her name was Bettina. She was fucking gorgeous. You'd give up your wife and three kids for a fucking weekend with her. They had a beautiful home at a country club and got divorced and married again a few times. I'd have married her a fourth time, she was *that* gorgeous. But with us, Dick knew the drill. If his people wanted to play the big venues, like the casinos in Vegas, they had to do the little things. So he would provide us talent for our civil rights dinner dances and he'd tell them all it was for charity and they weren't getting paid, but we'd treat them well. So we started with Russell's birthday, and I knew he'd be happy when I told him the headliner that year would be Frankie Avalon."

The handsome Avalon first appeared on television on *The Jackie Gleason Show* in 1952. He later starred with John Wayne in the feature film *The Alamo,* had a smaller role in 1961's *Voyage to the Bottom of the Sea,* and had his breakout role in the teen hit *Beach Party* in 1963, in which he starred with Annette Funicello.

His résumé soon filled with numerous film and TV appearances, including on the popular *The Patty Duke Show.* But Avalon was a singer at heart, having scored several top ten hits in the 1950s and early 1960s, and a number one hit with "Why" in 1959.

Avalon would be joined at the dinner by the DeJohn Sisters, Jackie

Forrest, Frankie Lyndon and the Belmonts, and comedian Dick Capri, who would serve as master of ceremonies. Northampton County Court of Common Pleas judge Richard Grifo was the keynote speaker, and the "assisting officer" helping Billy, chapter president "Little" Lou Butera, and vice president Angelo Bufalino sell tickets was Russell's cousin Larry.

Tickets for the event were $50 each and $500 for a table. Leading local businessmen purchased blocks of seats and tables. Among them was Louis DeNaples, the owner of an auto parts business and growing garbage landfill who had done cleanup work for the local counties following Hurricane Agnes. He knew Russell and wanted to be at the event, which was sold out weeks in advance. And of course, Russell had his own guest list, men from all over the nation. Leading organized crime figures from New York, Philadelphia, Buffalo, Miami, Chicago, Kansas City, and Los Angeles came to pay homage, and Russell put them all up at his Howard Johnson's.

During the dinner, Russell brought Billy to each of their tables. Billy knew many of the men, while others were introduced to Russell's "son" for the first time.

Unbeknownst to Billy, the heavyweights hadn't come just to celebrate Russell's birthday. Instead, Russell had something else planned. Many of the men remained in Pittston at the Howard Johnson's, and when Russell summoned Billy to meet him at the hotel the following Tuesday afternoon, Louis DelVecchio guided Billy to a large conference room, where he was greeted by some of the most important Mafia figures in the United States. He had just seen them all on Saturday at the dinner and they'd stayed a couple of extra days at Russell's request.

"I walk in and the first person I see is Kelly Mannarino from Pittsburgh," said Billy. "There must have been thirty, forty guys there, but they were all made men. I saw Dave and Cappy and Angelo in the back with Russell. Kelly stuttered something to me and Russell calls me over and I go up to him and everyone gets quiet. Russell puts his hand on my shoulder and says, 'You all know Billy as my son. Well, you're all here because he's one of us now.' That was it. There was no sword or gun on a table or saints burning in your hand, no blood oath, and not a lot of words. None of that. I mean, I was half Irish, so I couldn't be made, right? It didn't matter. Russell just said it. I was his boy, his son. And when Russell said something, that was it. It was over in ten seconds. And then everyone in the room came up to congratulate me. I wasn't sure what Russ had in mind that night we were driving back from the city, when he asked if I was going to be with him. I never really thought that could happen. But Russell said it, and that was it."

And Billy was the last made member of the Bufalino Family.

CHAPTER 8

Good for Everybody

Billy and Ellen's second child, Miriam, was born on September 1, 1974.

Just like they had with Carolyn, Russell and Carrie fussed over the newest addition to the D'Elia family.

Russell and Carrie had spoiled Carolyn with far too many Christmas and birthday gifts. Russell just couldn't help but indulge her. He was so smitten with Billy and Ellen's firstborn, he had even offered to babysit. Ellen wasn't quite sure what to make of the offer. But when she and Billy had to attend a wake and couldn't find anyone, they took Russell up on his offer.

"We needed a babysitter so Russell said, 'Oh, I'll watch Carolyn,'" said Ellen. "He had bought her a rocking horse and we put it in the living room with the TV. We weren't gone very long and when we came back we looked inside through the window and we couldn't believe what we saw. Papa was on the rocking horse with Carolyn's bonnet on his head. He's rocking back and forth on the horse and Carolyn is jumping on the couch and she was swinging this gold pocket watch Papa had. It had a long gold chain on it and diamonds, and Carolyn is twirling the watch over her head and yelling and kinda like urging Papa on. It was some sight. And he must have given her cookies because they were all over the place—on the sofa, on the floor. It was a mess. But they were having so much fun."

Billy had also been having fun.

Being a member of the Bufalino Family was a transformative event that changed his life forever. He'd thought he had it good just being Russ's "son," but now his elevated stature provided immediate and immense financial and personal benefits. Associates came to him with potential scores and business opportunities, and everywhere he went the notoriety of being a soldier, newly baptized and fully embraced by the Bufalinos as well as crime families in other cities, added an additional level of respect. And under no circumstances could he be harmed.

So it was as a made man that Billy traveled to Cherry Hill, New Jersey, on October 18, 1974, to attend "Frank Sheeran Appreciation Night" at the Latin Casino to honor the head of the Wilmington, Delaware, Teamsters Local 326.

The Latin Casino was a pit stop in South Jersey that was part of the same circuit featuring performers at other mob-friendly clubs like the Copacabana. Al Martino, Liberace, and Peggy Lee had all played there, as did Jerry Vale, who was the headliner on this night with the beautiful Golddiggers. The club also had the same type of clientele: celebrities and wise guys from New Jersey, Philadelphia, and sometimes New York.

More than twelve hundred people, many arriving in limousines and luxury cars, filled the club to pay homage to Frank, who had become an important figure within the Teamsters. So important was he that mingling in the room with notable crime figures and union leaders were Philadelphia's top city officials, including the district attorney, who wasn't troubled in the least attending a dinner for an accused murderer who was being fêted by other murderers, accused or convicted.

And why *wouldn't* they come? After all, Jimmy Hoffa was the guest of honor. Since the meeting in Miami with Russell in early 1972,

Hoffa had visited all of his old friends in New York, Philadelphia, Chicago, and Detroit, and within Teamsters headquarters in Washington. With support from key factions in hand, Hoffa was emboldened and threw down the gauntlet.

But the Teamsters had become a truly different union from the one Hoffa had presided over, at least politically. Frank Fitzsimmons had developed a very close relationship with President Richard Nixon, who sought the support of the powerful union, much to the dismay of the FBI, which had intimate knowledge of the union's deep underworld associations.

Hoffa filed a civil lawsuit on March 13, 1974, against President Nixon and his attorney general, William Saxbe, alleging they had conspired to impose a ban on his union activities until 1980. Hoffa wanted the restrictions lifted, which would allow him to challenge Fitzsimmons for the Teamsters leadership in 1976.

He also broadly hinted that he would expose Teamsters corruption under Fitzsimmons. Most important, said Hoffa, was fixing the pension funds. Too many loans to "friends" had gone delinquent or defaulted, and he was going to remedy it.

But the more he said, the more people got nervous, and some wanted him dead.

Russell said no.

But as he traveled down to Philadelphia and then into southern New Jersey with Billy and Angelo, Russell prepared them both, saying it was time to talk to his old friend and business partner.

"We knew Jimmy was going to be there," said Billy. "We would have gone anyway. We were all close with Frank, especially Russell. But Russell said he needed to speak to Jimmy. He was saying in the car going down there he was stubborn and wished he'd just shut his mouth and leave things be. They had been friends for a very, very long time but Jimmy was becoming a problem. You could see it. The Teamsters had changed, the way they did things, and Jimmy's filing lawsuits and saying things in public—things were coming to a head. Russell thought he could talk to him."

But the talk would wait until after Frank's celebration. Many of the Teamsters were wearing "Jimmy in '76" buttons, which only added to the underlying tension. Hoffa and Frank wore them too as everyone sat to eat their New York strip steak, baked potato, and vegetable.

Near the end of the meal and before the dessert, Hoffa was introduced. He walked up to the podium and recalled his long relationship with Frank and how he'd call him at three A.M. most mornings, for what, he didn't know.

"I think he just wanted to let me know he was on the job, out in the street, at that hour. I seldom knew what Frank was talking about much after ten," said Hoffa, to laughter and howls. He continued on but did not discuss the darker side of their relationship. When Hoffa was done, he gave Frank Sheeran a traditional Teamsters gold watch. Then Frank spoke.

"At the dinner Frank made a speech," said Billy. "He had the stutter but he made it through it, and when he's done he looks at us and Russell and says, 'Seee, Russellll. I diddnn't fuckinnnng stutterrrrrr.' Everyone was hysterical. Afterward, Jimmy Hoffa comes over to us and Russell said, 'Jimmy, remember my boy Billy?' Jimmy said of course he did and we shook hands. Russell had sent me to Chicago a couple of times. That's where I met Joey Glimco. He was one of Hoffa's main union guys, the one with the loans. We were looking to do something and I had to see him. So between meeting Jimmy at Joe Sonken's a couple of times, when he came to Pennsylvania and the business with Glimco, he knew who I was. Then Hoffa goes into his pocket and pulls out a gold Teamsters watch and gives it to me. I don't know why but it was a nice watch. We hung around a while after that and then drove into Philadelphia. Russell was going to talk to Jimmy there."

Russell, Billy, and Angelo met up with Angelo Bruno, the boss in Philadelphia, and Frank and Hoffa at a familiar bar in South Philly, and they all sat down at a table in the rear. After ordering a round of drinks, it was time to talk to Jimmy.

"Russell tries to talk to him," said Billy. "He says, 'Jimmy, you have to stop this. There are some people who don't want you to do nothin'. You have to watch your back.' Jimmy isn't having any of it so Russell says, 'We'll give you a local, you'll make three hundred thousand a year, you have your pension. Go relax and play with your grandkids.' Jimmy was stubborn. He just said, 'Russell, you're my friend, and with all respect, I wouldn't do anything to you or Frank, but I built that fucking union from nothing. I have to do what I have to do and I'm getting my union back.' That was it. Russell didn't say anything else to him. That wasn't Russell's way. You have to understand that Russell never talked in circles. He spoke plainly and right to the point, so there was no confusion. But Jimmy wasn't hearing Russell, and he didn't want to. So a little later Frank was taking Jimmy out for hot dogs. Jimmy loved hot dogs, especially Lum's hot dogs. There was something special about them. So Russell pulled Frank aside. 'Just talk to your friend and see if he will listen to you.' Frank said, 'Russ, he'll never hurt you. You know that. He loves you like a brother. But you know he'll do what he has to do.' They walked out, and that was it. There was nothing Frank was going to say to change Jimmy's mind. Jimmy was a tough guy. I respected him because Russell respected him, but Russell knew he had a problem coming down to Philly that day, and it got bigger after that meeting. I think everyone knew after that Jimmy had to go. Russell knew it too, but he loved the guy, and even as things got worse, I think he was still protecting him and hoping he'd change his mind."

But Hoffa continued to run an active campaign for the Teamsters presidency and he continued to appeal the condition of his parole that barred him from holding any union office until 1980. He even promised to take his case to the U.S. Supreme Court if he had to. Fitzsimmons, once Hoffa's close friend and compliant associate, called him a "bum" in a March 1975 speech.

But the real concern for Russell and others continued to be the pension funds, particularly the Central States fund. It had over $1 billion in investments in Las Vegas casinos, Florida real estate, and hundreds of other projects—loans given to people that no bank would consider. Yet despite his unease, Russell knew that Hoffa would never hurt him. So as the chorus grew for Hoffa's permanent removal from the living, Russell wouldn't listen, until he had to.

In early June 1975, the *Sacramento Bee* and *Time* magazine each reported that a U.S. Senate committee that had been investigating the CIA's ties to the Mafia discovered the agency had enlisted organized crime figures to kill foreign leaders, including Fidel Castro, and to help with reconnaissance for the failed invasion of Cuba at the Bay of Pigs in April 1961.

And both publications identified Russell as a participant in those failed CIA plots.

The *Time* story, "CIA Mafia Spies in Cuba," said Russell and two other men, James "Jimmy Doyle" Plumeri and Salvatore Granello, were recruited by the CIA to help in its preparation for the invasion of Cuba.

The *Time* story said that during the 1950s Russell had varied interests in Cuba, including its casinos, and just hours before Castro took control, he fled, but in his haste he had to leave behind $750,000 buried in a secret location.

Plumeri and Granello were also both big players in Havana and shared business interests with Russell, including the casinos. The CIA somehow got wind of the story about Russell's hiding his money and used that as the carrot for his cooperation: help us, and we'll help you get to your money. Russell still had contacts in Cuba and used them to provide surveillance information about the island prior to the April 1961 invasion by U.S.-supported Cuban exiles. And before and during the attack, he was on a boat off the coast of Havana with

Plumeri, Granello, and two CIA agents waiting for permission to land on the island. But the twelve hundred or so exiles were slaughtered on the beach where they landed, and those who survived were taken prisoner.

Russell returned to the United States empty-handed.

The *Sacramento Bee* provided even more details and explored Russell's deep relationship with Cuba and the CIA in a shocking story that began:

> A Pennsylvania Mafia boss and two members of a New York City Mafia family were among the sources of information that the Central Intelligence Agency used to prepare for the ill-fated Bay of Pigs invasion of Cuba in 1961, a former employee of the agency has told *The Bee*.

The story was based on an interview with an unidentified former CIA agent, who said Russell had meetings with CIA agents in New York and Florida.

Surprisingly, Russell publicly refuted the stories, telling the *Scranton Times*, "It's a lie. The entire story. I don't want any credit for anything I didn't do and in this case I'm not involved. Someone is suffering illusions of grandeur."

But it wasn't just the CIA that knew about his ties to Cuba.

The Senate Select Committee to Study Governmental Operations with Respect to Intelligence Activities, headed by Senator Frank Church of Idaho, was born from the 1973 Watergate Committee investigation, which uncovered that the national intelligence agencies were carrying out questionable domestic security operations at the behest of President Nixon, who was subsequently forced to resign. In addition, the *New York Times* had reported in 1974 that the CIA had been spying on anti–Vietnam War activists for more than a decade.

To better understand exactly what the CIA was doing, the committee began its probe in January 1975. And among its charges was to investigate the CIA's involvement in deposing foreign leaders, including Fidel Castro. It was through that effort that it learned about the CIA's recruitment of Sam Giancana, the former mob boss in Chicago, and Johnny Rosselli, a leading gangster from Los Angeles, as well as of Russell, Plumeri, and Granello, for assistance in the Bay of Pigs invasion.

"I knew about Cuba," said Billy. "Russell would talk about it from time to time. Dave went there with him back in the fifties and he'd reminisce, saying something like, '*Goombadi*, you remember this in Cuba?' Then he'd tell another story about Russell in a restaurant. They went into a Havana restaurant and Russell did his thing and yelled at the waiters. Someone there told him, 'Russ, you can't do that here. You can't yell at the waiters. You do that, the whole place will get up and walk out!' But Russell said he had a lot of business in Cuba. He had a piece of a couple of casinos, the Sans Souci and another one. I think it was the Nacional. Kelly Mannarino got him into it. He introduced Russell to Meyer Lansky. Russell introduced me to Lansky one time in Florida. We went to get breakfast someplace and he was there. You could tell they knew each other. They all had a piece of the casinos together. Kelly also introduced Russell to Fulgencio Batista, the dictator there. Russell said that he and Batista had gotten pretty close, so close Batista trusted Russell with his children. He'd send his daughters during the summer up to Camp Tegawitha, this kids' camp in the Poconos, under Russell's protection.

"Russell said they had a good thing in Cuba. There was a lot of money there, but they screwed it up. Everyone got greedy, especially the Cubans. The original deal with Batista was for him to get five percent a year of the casino take. Then it went up to ten percent, then each year after that he wanted a little more. It didn't stop. They were making so much money at first they didn't care, until Batista kept wanting more. So Russell said there was this kid, Fidel Castro. He came looking for help but Russell said they told him they were with Batista. But now they're getting pissed at Batista because he's asking for too much of a cut, so they start dealing with the kid, Castro. Russell always called him 'the rebel in the woods.' He said they threw him a couple of bucks figuring if he won, they could do business with him. What the fuck, right?"

But Russell's support of Castro went beyond money. He also sent Castro arms. Russell and Kelly Mannarino devised a plan at the height of the revolution in late 1958 to fly stolen U.S. Army guns and ammunition from an airport near Pittsburgh and deliver them to Cuba. The U.S. government got wind of the plan and intercepted the 121 stolen rifles at the Allegheny Valley Airport. There were other shipments of arms, but unbeknownst to Russell, it didn't matter. The gangsters had no future in Cuba.

"Russell and Kelly had the casinos and figured they'd cut a better deal with Castro than they had with Batista," said Billy. "But when Castro wins, he takes over the casinos and gives Russell and everyone else twelve hours to get out of Cuba. No baggage, no money, no nothing. Russell had a lot of cash there and didn't know what to do with it. So he buried it. It was more than they said, close to a million. Russell told us the money was still there. We'd joke around about who was going there to get it."

When the stories were published, Plumeri and Granello were already dead, having both been mysteriously killed after the newspaper columnist Jack Anderson, who first hinted of a CIA/mob plot in 1967, reported in 1970 their connection to the CIA. Plumeri was found on a street in Queens with a plastic bag over his head. He had been strangled. Granello's body was found in a car trunk in Manhattan, shot four times in the head.

But Russell's name had never appeared in any report in connection to the CIA or Cuba—until now. And to make matters worse, Giancana was subpoenaed by the committee and scheduled to testify later in June. Rosselli was also subpoenaed. Russell wondered if he'd be called to testify, as well as Jimmy Hoffa: it was Hoffa who had served as the middleman, introducing the CIA to Russell in 1959.

"Russell got into that believing he was going to get his money back and get his businesses up and running again in Cuba," said Billy. "They all did. But President Kennedy fucked up. They screwed everybody, Russell, Santo Trafficante, all those guys who thought they'd get back on that island. They felt deceived."

Two weeks after Russell's ties to the plots were exposed, and on the eve of his testimony before the Church Committee, Sam Giancana was found dead in his Chicago home. He had been shot several times in the head and neck, apparently by someone he knew. He had been frying sausages and onions for himself and his guest. When his body was found the next morning, he had $1,400 in cash in his pocket, mostly in $100 bills.

"I knew people in Chicago and they said it was his family, his own people," said Billy. "There was too much going on with the committee, so they took care of it. It was good for everybody. Who asked them to do it? Russell didn't say a word to me about Giancana. Nothing. And I wasn't going to ask him. He had a lot on his mind."

Aside from the CIA and the committee, Russell and Guvy had to travel to Buffalo, where their conspiracy trial was finally set to begin on July 15. It was the case from 1973, in which they were charged with extorting $100,000 from a store owner in Geneva, New York. Russell had just been acquitted in April in the separate vending machine extortion case in Binghamton and now had to face another jury.

Federal prosecutors had an informant, Joseph Zito, a Bufalino soldier in Binghamton who worked for Guvy. Facing a twelve-year sentence for extortion, Zito said he had information on Russell and Guvy and was looking to cut a deal. The FBI obliged, and Zito testified that he'd been sent to rough up several owners of local vending machine companies.

But the testimony didn't sway the jury, which acquitted Russell and Guvy on July 24, 1975. Russell returned to Kingston to prepare to travel to Detroit. He and Carrie were attending the wedding of his cousin William Bufalino's daughter, his goddaughter.

The wedding was set for August 1, 1975, at William Bufalino's home in Grosse Pointe, Michigan, just outside of Detroit, and joining Russell and Carrie were Frank and his wife, Irene. But instead of flying there, they decided to drive.

"Frank didn't want to fly," said Billy. "Something about not wanting to get onto a plane because a union representing an air transportation company or something was striking and he didn't want to cross the picket line. When they left Russell's house a couple of days before the wedding, I loaded Russell and Carrie's luggage into the trunk of Frank's car—I think it was a new Lincoln Continental—and said goodbye to them. Frank drove; Russell was in the front and the women in the back. I didn't speak to him again until they came back a few days later. By then it was all over the news that Jimmy had disappeared. But when they got home no one said anything about Jimmy. Not Russell, not Frank, not the wives. There was nothing unusual except for all the FBI guys watching us from across the street. They were all over Russell. But as soon as they got back, you could tell Frank was upset."

Hoffa's sudden disappearance captured the nation's attention. Two days before the wedding, he had gone to the Machus Red Fox Restaurant in a Detroit suburb to meet with Anthony Provenzano and iron out their long-standing issues. Anthony Giacalone, a Detroit underworld figure, was to accompany Provenzano.

Hoffa was seen at the restaurant but was alone. He left there and was never heard from again.

The FBI immediately focused on the hierarchy of organized crime, theorizing it feared Hoffa would regain the presidency of the union and push out disloyal union leaders, many of whom were members of or had ties to the mob.

And among those whom investigators believed had the most to lose was Provenzano. At the time he was under investigation for steering $6 million in New Jersey Teamsters money to a condominium project in Fort Lauderdale, Florida. The FBI also knew of the great rift that had developed between Provenzano and Hoffa.

The Provenzano probe was one of many involving organized crime and Teamsters funds, and the FBI admitted that its investigations weaved through the relationships between many individuals and connected firms, and that through the use of corporate structures, tens of millions of dollars had been stolen from the pension funds.

Amid the intense pressure from the FBI, Russell summoned Billy a couple of days after returning home from Detroit. They were going to drive to New York for a meeting, only Russell wouldn't say with whom until they got into the car.

"It takes two hours or so to drive to New York, so Russell waits a little while, and as we're driving in he tells me what's going on," said Billy. "He says we're going to the Vesuvio for a sit-down with Fat Tony Salerno, Tony Provenzano, and with Frank Sheeran. They wanted to meet with Frank to make sure that he doesn't come after them for Hoffa. They knew Frank was very close to Hoffa and was very angry, and that he knew that they were behind it and was going to kill them. So Russell said we were going to the Vesuvio to meet with the two Tonys, and that Frank would meet us there and he'd tell them himself that they would not have to worry and they wouldn't have any trouble from him. There would be no payback, no revenge.

"This was the first time I was hearing about Hoffa, that the two Tonys were responsible for Jimmy. So we get to New York and go into the Vesuvio and Frank walks in right after us. He was never a happy guy, but now that I knew what was going on I could tell he *really* wasn't happy. He's pretty quiet. More quiet than usual. Just before the two Tonys come in I'm standing next to Russell when he grabs Frank's arm, pulls him closer, and says to him, 'Don't be smart. Don't make any smart remarks or say anything stupid. Don't say nothin'.

You hear me?' Russell wanted this to go smoothly. Frank said yeah, he understood.

"The two Tonys come in a little while later and Fat Tony has the cigar in his mouth. I never saw him without one. He and Tony Pro are looking around. I don't know what they were worried about. We knew the FBI was watching us outside. They were all over the place. The Tonys came in with another guy; it could have been Sal Briguglio, but I can't say I'm sure. He was one of Tony Pro's guys who was supposed to be the shooter. I only met him once or twice before. We all shake hands and everyone exchanges pleasantries and then Russell and Frank sit at the table with the two Tonys and I sit near them at the bar. I was just a few feet away. Frank said his piece and promised he wouldn't give them any trouble. You could see the two Tonys were relieved when they got up. We all shook hands again and they left and that was it. But I don't think Frank's promise meant forever. I can tell you one thing. I knew there was no way the two Tonys would have done that with Jimmy without Russell signing off on it. I'm sure all that committee stuff and Cuba was on his mind. He loved the man, but it was just too much. I don't think Frank figured that out, that Russell had to be involved. And Jimmy got cooked. Russell didn't tell me that, but you just know. They had places there, undertakers, just a few minutes away where they could cremate him quickly. After that, the only time I ever heard Russell say something about Jimmy was a couple of weeks later at my house. We were having a barbecue and my dad was there and he yells out, 'Hey, Buff, where's Jimmy Hoffa?' He was joking but it was a pretty stupid thing to say. Russell looks at him and says, 'Bill, when you find out, you let me know.' And that was it. Russell never mentioned Jimmy again."

CHAPTER 9

The Box

From the moment Russell and Frank returned to Pennsylvania from Detroit with their wives, FBI agents were glued to Russell, watching his every move. They were stationed across from his home in Kingston, trailed his car, and were across from Vesuvio in New York City.

The bureau had assembled a task force for its Hoffa investigation and assigned over two hundred special agents from field offices throughout the country.

And it seemed like all of them were tracking Russell.

"They were pretty much everywhere," said Billy. "Russell ignored them. He didn't say anything and didn't want them to think that they bothered him, which they didn't. Russell really never let anyone bother him."

Whether it bothered him or not, Russell was a chief suspect in Hoffa's disappearance.

A federal grand jury was empaneled in Detroit, and from September 2 to December 11, 1975, a total of ninety-five people were subpoenaed. Of those, twenty-two invoked their Fifth Amendment right against self-incrimination and refused to testify. They included Anthony Provenzano; Detroit gangster Anthony Giacalone; Hoffa's foster son, Charles "Chuckie" O'Brien; Salvatore "Sally Bugs"

Briguglio, the stone-cold killer and union official who worked under Provenzano in New Jersey; New Jersey Teamsters Thomas and Stephen Andretta, who were brothers; and Frank Sheeran, as well as, of course, Russell.

Representing all of them was Russell's cousin, William Bufalino.

William had ended his long relationship with Hoffa after his release from prison in 1971, choosing instead to remain a Teamsters attorney. William often said that Russell was his closest friend, that his relationship with his cousin was tighter than that of brothers.

"Yeah, they were close, very close," said Billy. "I liked Bill. He'd come out to see us all and then go sit with Russell. He didn't do anything without Russell's approval. Nothing."

After the conclusion of the grand jury testimony, the FBI held a two-day conference in January 1976 at its Washington headquarters to review the evidence it had gleaned over the six months since Hoffa's disappearance. The results, memorialized in the HOFFEX Memo, theorized that Hoffa had been murdered and that Anthony Provenzano was likely behind it. But it also suggested that any move on Hoffa would have to have been approved at "very high levels within the Organized Crime structure."

The only "high-level" person subpoenaed who fit that description was Russell.

The investigation continued to focus on just a few suspects, including Russell, Frank, Provenzano, Salerno, Briguglio, O'Brien, Giacalone, and the Andretta brothers, but the evidence was too thin to make any arrests.

So the FBI tried a different strategy.

In February 1976 two men, one large and one small, walked into a Manhattan jewelry store and convinced the owner, Herbie Jacobs, to give the larger of the two $25,000 worth of diamonds after they invoked the name of Russell Bufalino.

Jacobs had done business with Russell for years, with Russell supplying him with stolen and smuggled diamonds to fence. It was big business, and it was even believed that Russell had a secret ownership stake in Jacobs's business.

Jacobs had no reason to doubt that the man invoking Russell's name, Jack Caringi, was anything but legit. So he accepted the $25,000 check. But it bounced, and Jacobs called Russell, telling him that one of his "friends" had used his name to buy diamonds and had given him a bad check.

"We were in Florida and the phone rang and Herbie said he had a problem," said Billy. "This guy came in with Russell's cousin Larry. Herbie said he gave him twenty-five thousand credit and took his check because he knew you. Russell says, 'Why did you do that?' and he hangs up. I tell Russell, 'Don't get involved. This looks like a setup. Some guy no one knows gets twenty-five thousand credit?' I'm like, 'No, fuck, don't do it.' Russell says, 'They would do that to me?' He couldn't believe they'd do that to him, which is why they did it."

They finally tracked down Caringi, whose real name was Jack Napoli, a six-foot-five-inch-tall petty crook from Brooklyn. Several weeks later, on April 12, Napoli walked into Vesuvio to apologize to Russell.

"Napoli walks in. He's a big guy. As big as me," said Billy. "He goes in the back and sits down and tells Russell the diamonds are gone. Russell was very upset that he used his name, but he goes, 'Listen, you're a young guy. Why don't you get a fucking job? Go see the jeweler and he'll work with you. You get a payment plan and pay the guy off. Straighten your life out.' Napoli looks at him like he's grateful and goes, 'You're right, Mr. Bufalino. I will. Thank you, thank you very much.' He leaves. But twenty minutes later he walks back in and says, 'Mr. Bufalino, I decided I ain't paying nobody.' Russell got up and kicked him in the balls. He's irate and cursing at him. He says, 'You ever use my name to rob innocent people again, I'll kill you with my bare hands!' Napoli ran out of there. But I said to Russell, 'Why would he leave here so nice and then come back twenty minutes later and talk like that to you?' Something wasn't right."

Another alleged Hoffa conspirator, Anthony Provenzano, was indicted in June for a fifteen-year-old murder. Federal prosecutors alleged that in 1961 he hired four men to lure a union official to his summer home, where they beat him and then garroted him with a rope. The indictment came from the work of the Organized Crime Strike Force, which was probing Hoffa's disappearance.

Provenzano's arrest was a harbinger of things to come.

So was the drum found floating on the surface of Dumfoundling Bay in August 1976 near North Miami Beach.

When police opened it, they found a decomposing body with no legs. It was Johnny Rosselli.

The flamboyant, seventy-one-year-old Rosselli had been visiting his sister's home near Miami when he disappeared ten days earlier. The autopsy revealed he had been tortured, possibly shot first in the stomach by the killer or killers, who then took a knife to carve the bullet out. His legs were hacked off, and, still breathing, he had been wrapped in chains and placed inside the drum. He was apparently still alive and asphyxiated as the drum sank to the ocean floor. The gases emitted by his decomposing body eventually lifted the drum to the surface.

Almost immediately, Rosselli's murder was attributed by many to his involvement with the CIA's attempts to kill Fidel Castro in the early 1960s, and specifically his testimony a year earlier before the Church Committee. Rosselli had testified five days after Sam Giancana was killed on the night before he was scheduled to testify.

One senator who served on the committee, Howard Baker of Tennessee, said he didn't believe Rosselli had revealed all that he knew, in part because he was "visibly shaken by Giancana's murder."

Rosselli's death so soon after that of Giancana was too much of a coincidence and detectives were looking for a direct connection. CIA director William Colby acknowledged that the agency had used the underworld figures in attempts to kill Castro but was adamant that the CIA had nothing to do with their murders.

Billy knew better than to ask Russell about Rosselli.

And given all that swirled around Hoffa, it was little surprise when FBI agents arrived at Russell's home before nine A.M. on October 27, 1976. They took him into custody, but it didn't have anything to do with Rosselli or Giancana. Instead, it centered on Billy's original suspicions about Jack Napoli.

Russell was charged with extortion and conspiracy for threatening Napoli's life while trying to retrieve the $25,000. Arrested with Russell were Herbie Jacobs and two other men from New York. Russell was released on a $50,000 bond. The case was presented to a grand jury in September in New York and was being prosecuted by the Organized Crime Strike Force in New York.

"We didn't know it at the time, but Napoli was wired," said Billy. "The whole thing really was a setup. The whole thing. From the very beginning. Russell's cousin, Larry, was an informant. About two years before that there was a cop we were doing business with in the Diamond District. He said, 'Billy, I gotta tell you but I'm not telling Russell because he's going to be pissed. But you need to tell him that his cousin Larry is an informant.' I go to Russell and say, 'This cop so-and-so wants to give you a message. Larry's a snitch.' Russell said, 'I don't fucking believe it. He's a fucking Bufalino! No Bufalino would do that!' I said, 'He's a snitch, Russ. I'm the messenger. Don't kill the messenger.' But Russell just wouldn't believe it. It was Larry that took Napoli to see Jacobs about the jewelry. When Jacobs first called Russell about it, he said, 'What the fuck? What did you give him the diamonds for? I'm not getting involved.'

"When Napoli left the Vesuvio the first time and everything was straightened out, he went back to the FBI guys and they said, 'Go back.' They didn't have anything on tape they could charge Russell with. So when Napoli comes back in the second time and tells Russell to his face he's not paying for the diamonds, he did it on purpose to get a reaction out of him. That's what the FBI wanted. You think he really would have done that otherwise, insult Russell? But this was all about Hoffa. No one had been arrested, so they found other ways to go after them."

Russell's arrest produced headlines across the country, but it didn't stop him from celebrating his seventy-third birthday.

Three days later, on October 30, Russell was fêted at the annual Italian American Civil Rights League, Chapter 34, dinner. A birthday cake was rolled out for him, and speakers, including the Lackawanna County district attorney, praised Russell for his humanitarianism. Seated in the audience were two Luzerne County judges, Bernard Podcasy and Arthur Dalessandro.

No one mentioned the recent indictment. But it did weigh on Russell's mind and as Christmas approached, he looked forward to his annual retreat to Florida. But first there would be welcome news. Billy and Ellen were expecting their third child.

Carolyn was now four and Miriam two, and Papa and Aunt Carrie were a big part of their lives. They visited the D'Elia home often, usually to see the children, but sometimes Russell had some business to discuss with Billy. Those visits were fun compared with the ones at Russell's home. Carrie kept a tight leash on the horseplay. The children were limited to playing in the kitchen and the adjacent room next to it, and a gate prevented them from exploring the rest of the house. Russell would yell, "C'mon, Carrie, they're kids. Let them play!" But Carrie feared what they could do to the walls and furniture. Other times Russell would bellow, "Carrie, give them the chocolate, they're fucking kids!"

Ellen tried her best not to feel insulted.

Her life with Billy was what she had expected given the early warning from Russell. Ellen had her hands full with the two small girls, and Billy was gone most nights well into the evening, and sometimes early morning. But he always returned home whenever he was in town and was a good father, and he was becoming a good provider. Aside from his regular paycheck at Arrow, he'd come home with hundreds and even thousands of dollars in his pockets, the result of business that he would never discuss with Ellen. He kept her in the dark about that part of his life. The less she knew, the better.

For her part, Ellen read the papers and had an inkling of some of the things he was involved in with Russell. One thing Billy did share was that there were never drugs. Whatever the government may have said or what had been reported in the papers over the years, Russell was not involved in the drug business, period, and he expected his people to follow his lead. Same with prostitution. He told Billy he never wanted to take advantage of people, and Ellen took that as a sign of good faith.

She had remained an observant Catholic and attended Mass each Sunday, sometimes with Billy, often without him. She also volunteered her time with different charities, including the diocese's Catholic Charities, and helped Billy out with the Italian American Civil Rights League dinners. But there were nights, even days, where Billy was away, and it wasn't like she had gone into this with her eyes closed. Russell had warned her, and she'd made her choice. So she often relied on her close-knit family if she was ever in need of help and continued on as if her husband were nothing more than an appliance salesman. As it was, that was all she knew.

But Ellen learned a bit more during Russell's extortion trial, which began in August 1977. Billy took Russell to New York and stayed with him there, and would escort him into the courtroom and remain there for each session.

As the trial progressed, Jack Napoli wasn't the best of witnesses. But after eight days of testimony it took the jury just an hour to find Russell guilty. He knew he was facing some significant time in prison when he posted his $50,000 bond and left the courthouse.

Jack Napoli entered the witness protection program.

Four days later, on August 15, 1977, Ellen gave birth to a son. She and Billy named him Russell, and they tried to enjoy the time with their newborn and his namesake, who was scheduled to be sentenced on September 23. But the sentencing was delayed until October 21, and when Billy took Russell into New York to learn his fate, the news was not good. He received four years in prison and a $20,000 fine.

Russell proclaimed his innocence and said, "If you had to deal with an animal like that, Judge, you would have done the same thing."

Prosecutors pleaded for him to be jailed immediately. But the judge, citing the countless letters he'd received attesting to Russell's "good character," allowed him to remain free on bail while he appealed his conviction. A week later, courtrooms, prison, and appeals were replaced by Frankie Avalon and Andy Griffith, who were coming to Wilkes-Barre to help him celebrate his seventy-fourth birthday.

The annual dinner dance coincidentally fell on the same day as Russell's birthday, October 29. And given Russell's pending prison sentence, and the likelihood he wouldn't be there for next year's dinner, Billy thought it best to bring in a couple of headliners. So he called Dick Linke in California, and he sent Frankie Avalon, Andy Griffith, and a funny new talent, ventriloquist Jay Johnson.

The dinner was familiar terrain for Avalon, who had performed at events like these across the country. But Griffith and Johnson had not, so Linke told them to shut up, keep their eyes open, and not ask any questions—and not to expect to get paid. It was a charity event for some "friends" who would treat them well.

Over eight hundred people were there, the largest dinner attendance yet. The room was filled with friends from across the country, politicians, law enforcement officials, and local businessmen, including Louis DeNaples, who again purchased an entire table and sat up front with his brother Dominick, their wives, and their families.

Gruff but smart, DeNaples came from a large but very poor family. He later grew an auto parts business into one of the largest in the region, and then, in 1970, he and his brother started the DeNaples Hauling and Refuse Co. One of their first garbage-hauling contracts was with their hometown, the borough of Dunmore. From there they opened a private landfill in Dunmore and by 1973 it was called Keystone.

"Russell knew DeNaples well. We all did," said Billy. "Cappy was from Dunmore, and he introduced Louie to Russell and Dave and then to me. Louie and Russell were both big into cars. After the '72 flood, Carrie had a Pontiac Tempest that got flooded, and Louie got the car and gave it back to Russell refurbished. We'd go down there to his yard and his father, Patrick, would be there. Just a sweetheart. Russell and I would hang out and talk to him and to Louie. He was also building up his garbage business and we'd help him when he needed it, opening it up to people we knew, getting people to pay, things like that. That's when he became a superstar and I'm sure having Russell on his side helped him a lot. But DeNaples was about to go on trial. Something about him and a couple of other guys taking some money from the government for cleanup work they did after the hurricane."

Russell was presented with his customary birthday cake along with a rousing "Happy Birthday" salute. And at the end of the evening virtually everyone stood in line to shake hands with him. Avalon, Griffith, and Johnson stood in line too, and when they finally reached Russell, he invited them out for pizza.

"We got into a limousine and went to Bernie's Pizza in Exeter," said Billy. "It was owned by a couple of local brothers, Bernie and Dick Foglia. They were members of our local chapter. I sat next to Andy. We hung out and talked for a while. Very down-to-earth. Then Russell came over and said he had to leave but he told them the limo driver was to take them anywhere they wanted to go to. I heard there was some misunderstanding and they almost went all the way to New York City, but the driver turned around and got them back to the hotel. They didn't want any misunderstanding with Russell."

As Thanksgiving approached, Russell and Carrie left early for their home in South Florida. He usually wintered there after the holidays, as did dozens of other organized crime figures from families in New York, New Jersey, Chicago, Detroit, Pittsburgh, and most other cold-weather cities who always migrated south this time of year.

Russell had always enjoyed Florida. He'd bought his Hollywood home there in the early 1950s and it served as the launching point for his visits to Havana. The Miami area was a mob hub over the winter months, a place to meet, eat, and do business, and they always did it at Joe Sonken's Gold Coast.

"Russell ate breakfast, lunch, and dinner there," said Billy. "I became really good friends with Joe Sonken. I'd call him and say, 'Hey, Joe, I got a guy that needs a hundred thousand dollars.' He'd scream and yell, 'You fucking gangsters, leave me alone!' But the next day he'd be there with a bag of money ready for you."

Russell thought his escape to Florida would lead to several months of quiet time, but it didn't. He was subpoenaed there just before Christmas by the state attorney general about the Johnny Rosselli murder, but he refused to answer any questions.

Three months later he was again the subject of headlines and queries from reporters. On March 27, 1978, Salvatore "Sally Bugs" Briguglio was standing in front of the Andrea Doria Social Club in New York's Little Italy when he was accosted by two men, who knocked him to the ground. One of the men pulled out a gun and shot him four times in the head and chest before they jumped into a car with New Jersey license plates and sped off.

Russell didn't speak of Briguglio's murder. But Billy could only wonder if Frank Sheeran had broken the promise he'd made that day at Vesuvio with the two Tonys.

Briguglio had worked for the union once headed by Anthony Provenzano, who was finally tried for the 1961 murder of the union rival and was found guilty and given a life sentence in June 1978.

Less than three weeks later, on July 10, 1978, the U.S. Second Court of Appeals in New York denied Russell's appeal for a new trial, and he was ordered to report to prison. His attorneys filed a motion with the U.S. Supreme Court to allow him to remain free on bail while they prepared another appeal, but Justice Thurgood Marshall denied the petition and Russell was ordered to report to the Metropolitan Correctional Center in New York by August 10, 1978. He would remain there until his transfer to the federal prison in Danbury, Connecticut.

His fate now a certainty, Russell told the men closest to him to come to his home. He had to settle his affairs, and he was going to name the acting boss.

One by one they arrived. Dave, Cappy, Angelo, and Billy, as well as Sam Gelso and Sam Cometta, both old friends of Russell's. They all went downstairs and sat and listened intently as Russell explained with precision his plans moving forward.

"We had a meeting downstairs in Russell's house," said Billy. "Sam Gelso and Russell went back a long time. His son Charlie was an attorney that Russell had started to use. Really smart guy. Russell and Sam were like this. He made a lot of money, Sam. And Sam Cometta was there. He was in his eighties or something. Another guy Russell went back with. They got close when Russell first came to Pittston. One time, Russell was cooking crabs at Club 82, a place he had in Pittston. One of the crabs gets out and starts crawling toward Sam, and *boom!*—he shoots it. Russell goes, 'What are you doing, you senile old fuck? We could have ate that!'

"So we all sit down and Russell tells everyone that even though he was going away, he was still in charge. But he said, 'Don't do anything until you see Billy. I don't care if it's for this or that, you go see Billy. Everything runs through him because he's going to come see me. And lay low. Don't reach out to people until we can check them out first. Some people will tell you they're with us or Russell said this. Don't pay attention to any of that shit.'"

Billy was probably the most surprised to learn that Russell's orders would go through him, which made Billy the most important member of the Bufalino Family outside of Russell. And to make his ascension official, Russell said that Billy, and only Billy, would have the key to his kingdom. The other men looked at each other. They knew what that meant.

Russell kept three safes downstairs, all filled with his most important possessions. But one safe in particular was far more important than the others. It was where he kept his most precious valuables, papers as well as cash.

Everyone called it "the box."

"That didn't sit well with some of the guys," said Billy. "When Russell said that I was getting the key, Dave looked over and said, 'My *goombadi* ruined you! You're all right. You got the box!'"

The other men said nothing. Noticeable in their silence were Cappy and Angelo. They had both been with Russell for a very long time, far longer than Billy, and despite Russell's clear affection for "his son," each of them believed they should have been entrusted with Russell's most valuable possessions.

And Cappy felt even more slighted that Billy, and not he, would be Russell's emissary to the outside world. So did consigliere Eddie Sciandra, who didn't even make the trip from his home on Long Island. Russell had called him the night before and said Billy would be in touch. Eddie knew what that meant.

Russell decreed that it be Billy, and so it was. It was Billy who had direct, daily access to Russell, and now he had the key to the box.

At that moment, aside from Russell, Billy D'Elia was the most powerful member of the Bufalino Family. Before long, men on the street began calling him "Big Billy."

Once the meeting was over, they shared several toasts and each gave Russell a kiss on the cheek and a hug.

Billy gave Russell a longer and warmer embrace.

"I won't let you down," he said.

"I know you won't," said Russell.

Billy returned the next day with Angelo to take Russell to New York and to the Metropolitan Correctional Center, where Russell was due to report. When they arrived at his home to pick him up, Russell was saying goodbye to Carrie. She didn't cry. Carrie had been used to his being away for so many years, what was four more, she figured. Carrie was a Sciandra. Her father and brothers weren't part of this life, but her cousins were, and like Russell, she knew what was expected.

"He looked at me and said, 'Take care of the old lady,'" said Billy. "Then me and Angelo took Russell to New York and we go to the apartment. He had to report to MCC the next day, so that night we went to Johnny's and had a big dinner and he said goodbye to people from New York and some people who came up from Philadelphia. Then we go to Vesuvio and people would come to see him there. They were big send-offs. But it also gave him the chance to tell certain people that I was the guy to go through. The next day we took him to MCC. He said to me, 'Just remember one thing: this is the life we chose, and the government will get their grain of salt.' Then he walked in. He wasn't mad or scared. Absolutely not. And he never complained, ever."

Russell's first two weeks at the city detention center, a drab concrete structure, were hot and uncomfortable, and there were bugs everywhere, giant roaches crawling on the floors and walls from cell to cell, especially at night when the lights went out. But surprisingly, he was released during his third week there. His fiftieth wedding anniversary was approaching, and much to the chagrin of the prosecutors, he received a special three-day pass. A grand party had originally been scheduled for September 1, but given his current circumstance, it was canceled.

"They invited four hundred people to Gus Genetti's but instead they sent out four hundred letters saying the party was canceled," said Billy. "They let him go home for a couple of days and Carrie cooked. She made veal cutlets, pasta, *zuppa di* clams. So that was their anniversary party. Ellen was there and we had the kids over. Russell just loved it."

Billy drove Russell back to MCC, but from there he was transferred to the Dade County prison in Miami. The Florida state attorney general sought Russell's testimony in a loan-sharking case against

Frank Gagliardi, a Miami gangster otherwise known as "Frank the Wop," but he refused. So he was given a six-month sentence for contempt of court.

The Dade County prison was worse than MCC in New York, uncomfortably hot with even bigger bugs and food not worthy of a dog. Billy wanted to get Russell out of there, but Russell refused and wouldn't allow Billy to visit after he got wind of a plan that would place Russell inside a hospital, which would ensure better treatment.

"You think guys are going to respect me if I pull something like that?" Russell said.

He was later sent to Danbury, which was just two and a half hours away by car from Kingston. After Russell reported there, Billy followed his command and visited him every Wednesday and Sunday. And every day at home he or a member of his family received Russell's calls. He'd speak to Ellen and the children, who were told their papa was away in college and building bridges there.

"He would call my house every day, five to ten times a day," said Billy. "And Russell made sure to talk to the kids and to Ellen. There were so many calls the government asked Charlie Gelso how many people lived in that house. Charlie was his attorney now. They didn't believe Russell was talking to my family. They were all collect calls, and he didn't need permission. He could make as many as he wanted. When I got on the phone I knew the government was listening, so we'd just talk in code. He'd say, 'You remember that thing?' and I'd go, 'Yeah,' and he'd say something that I would understand and I'd go take care of it. Sometimes he was looking for people. He could never find his cousin Angelo. All these years later and he's still saying, 'What the fuck, I can never find him when I need him.' He always said he gave Angelo nosebleeds."

Unbeknownst to the government, Billy and Russell had developed a system for Russell's most important calls, and it involved Ellen's sister Ann. She lived directly across the street, and Russell would call there knowing the FBI wasn't listening.

"Her sister would open her front door and yell out, 'Billy, phone call!' and I'd go run across the street and talk to him," said Billy. "We'd also talk twice a week when I went up to the prison on Wednesday and Sunday. Carrie would come usually once a week, and sometimes I took Ellen and Angelo. He'd talk to them for a little bit and then he'd come to me. There were no barriers or anything. We sat right next to each other so we could talk. We were taking good care of him there. We'd tip the guards, and they'd get him good food, make sure he was comfortable. That first year when he got there they even let him have a Christmas party for the inmates and these kids that were next door at this orphanage. He somehow arranged it through the Holy Name Society. Every inmate had to sponsor a problem kid. I think there were three hundred there. So Russell calls and says these kids are cold, they need coats, they need hats. So I get the clothes. I order pizzas from New York. Someone else sent chicken. Then he said, 'You know, these kids have never seen a show. Bring some entertainment.' I say, 'What would you like?' He says, 'Bring a singer, a comedian, a magician.' So we end up getting an eighteen-piece band. Compliments of Gene DeLuca Music. So they bring us into the prison and we put the big show on. But these kids, they were rough. Which one had a knife? Which little kid punched an inmate in the face? Only Russell could make something like that happen. He talked to the warden. It was a lady warden, and she let it happen. Russell wanted the party and he got it. He used to say, 'The impossible we could fix right away. Miracles take a day or two.' Russell knew how to make things happen. He enjoyed himself."

As Russell's acting boss, Billy was also enjoying himself.

He was Russell's conduit to the outside world, and Billy dutifully took care of his business. Law enforcement, specifically the FBI, had begun tracking his movements after he was spotted visiting different cities and locations. But it didn't raise alarm bells since they still thought of Billy as Russell's driver.

"The government didn't know," said Billy. "They don't have a clue. They think it's Eddie Sciandra in New York, or even Dave or Cappy or Guvy in Binghamton. But it was me. Now, I knew everyone across the country. I talked with them, negotiated with them. Some I called friends. And I could go into any city and get anything I wanted. Anything. Russell didn't think any of our other guys were cut out for that, and he was probably right. Cappy and Angelo were dependents. And Dave? He was important to Russell, but for this, he just didn't have the personality for it. We had a deal once where I told him I'd collect the money and give him half the cash. But he said he wanted me to turn over the cash to him and then he'd decide how much to give me. I said, 'Don't even think about it.' He was pissed, but he came back later and said, 'Okay, give me half.' That's not how Russell did things, and I did things Russell's way, so everyone knew what to expect from me. But outside of our thing, nobody knew me. And I was fine with that."

While the government was oblivious to the new pecking order of the Bufalino Family, there was a festering problem within it, and it didn't take long for Billy to be tested.

Eddie Sciandra and John Francis, who had ties to the Westies, a violent Irish gang in New York, called Billy and said they had a problem and needed to meet at Russell's house. They said they had already spoken with Carrie, something about paying the lawyers, but they wouldn't say exactly what the issue was until they met.

"I already knew what was up," said Billy. "It wasn't too hard to figure out. They show up and I said, 'You want me to tell you why you're here? Okay, Carrie called you and says I'm taking money or other things out of the box, and you guys think I'm stealing.' They go, 'Are you crazy! We would never think that.' But they did, and they wanted to prove it. They wanted to show Russell I wasn't any good. So we go downstairs and I open the box and there are twenty envelopes. Each one has an amount written on the outside and cash and jewelry, or just jewelry, on the inside. So one says, 'I bought a ring for fourteen hundred,' the other says, 'I sold a piece for ten thousand.'

Every envelope had the money in it. So we go through it and every-body is satisfied I'm not stealing. They said, 'That wasn't it, we just wanted to talk to you.' Oh yeah, about what? Eddie and John, they got a little jealous. That's what it was. Eddie was Russell's consigliere, and John and Russell had a lot of other business, some of it rough. So now that I'm the guy talking to Russell every day and doing Russell's business, and I'm telling guys what to do and I'm the guy with the key to the box, they just didn't like it. So they wanted to check on me and to squeal to Russell, but there was nothing to check.

"The next time I went to see Russell in Danbury, I told him what was going on. He said, 'Fuck 'em.'"

CHAPTER 10

In, Out, and in Again

Russell had spent nearly two years in prison when he got word that Angelo Bruno had been murdered.

The longtime head of the Philadelphia family was sitting in his car when someone walked up from behind and aimed a shotgun at the back of his head.

Russell's dear friend died instantly.

Someone showed Russell the newspaper with the grisly photo of Bruno sitting dead in the front passenger seat, his head, or what was left of it, tilted backward, his eyes closed, and his mouth open and filled with blood, with more blood soaking his neck and jacket. His driver, John Stanfa, was injured but survived.

Russell didn't hide his anger.

He had known Bruno since the 1940s and over the years they had formed a deep relationship, often meeting for drinks or a meal at Skinny Razor's place, the "Friendly Lounge," or other favorite Philadelphia restaurants and bars. Like Russell, Bruno had an interest in a Havana casino and shared a close relationship with Carlo Gambino in New York.

Russell and Bruno talked almost every day until Russell learned that the FBI had tapped Bruno's phone. They were so alike, Russell was known as "the Quiet Don" and Bruno "the Gentle Don." His death deeply saddened Russell.

"Angelo was a gentleman," said Billy. "He wasn't as flamboyant as Russell and not as smart. I don't think anybody was as smart as Russell. But he and Russell went way back. When Russell was in Philly for a court thing, a couple of Angelo's guys were at the same hearing but didn't have a lawyer. So Russell told Charlie Gelso to take care of Angelo's guys. That was their relationship. But they weren't equals. We were at a wedding in Philadelphia, the daughter of Phil Testa, who was Angelo's underboss. They called him 'Chicken Man' because he used to be in the poultry business. They had the reception at the Bellevue-Stratford. So Russell and I go, and we were sitting on this side of the room, and Angelo was on that side of the room. One of his guys comes over and says, 'Russell, Angelo's over there. Why don't you go up and say hello to him.' Now, this is supposed to be Angelo's town. But Russell said, 'Look, I'm here. If he wants to say hello he can come to me.' A half hour later Angelo comes snooping around and says hello to Russell. Now, keep in mind they were good friends, but Russell didn't have to say hello to anybody. Everybody said hello to him."

Bruno's murder had also angered the New York families, because it had caught them by surprise. Killing a boss required the sanction of New York, and since this hadn't been sanctioned, they all wanted it dealt with immediately. After Russell was consulted in prison, the decision was made.

"In a family, you can't kill a boss, not without permission. That's a no-no," said Billy. "Russell wasn't part of the Commission. I always thought he was above it. They'd always consult with him on the big decisions and they did on this, and Russell signed off with the other bosses. They found the guy who did it, one of Bruno's top guys, and killed him. They killed some other guys who were part of it too. And then all hell broke loose in Philadelphia. Chicken Man Testa took over but then he was killed a year later. Someone put a bomb under his porch and they blew him up at his home. It was always crazy down there in Philly. They didn't behave like that anywhere else."

Bruno's death would set the stage for years of turbulence in Philadelphia, but at the time it was more of a distraction for Billy, who had another pressing, more personal issue to deal with. His mother, Theresa, had been diagnosed with breast cancer. It spread quickly, and after spending several weeks in the hospital, she passed away on April 8, 1980.

Her funeral was the first time anyone could recall seeing Billy cry.

"We always got along," said Billy. "I really loved her. She knew what I was doing for a living, or at least she had a good idea. But she never, ever asked me."

After burying his mother, Billy stopped talking to his father. They barely said two words to each other anyway. William P. had retired from the Pittston Fire Department and still spent his time at the bar and tending to his tomato plants. Billy had never eaten any of those tomatoes and didn't want to. Bad memories could never be forgotten. And now, with his mother gone, along with Aunt Lottie, who had been told by William P. to leave the house, he figured he'd erase his father completely.

There was more sadness in July when Kelly Mannarino died. He had cancer and was hospitalized for two weeks before succumbing. Kelly and Russell had worked together since the 1940s and he was perhaps Russell's closest friend. They shared Cuba, Castro, and the casinos together and were both at Apalachin, and Kelly controlled most of the LaRocca Family's gambling operations in Western Pennsylvania. Yet after forty years as a leading organized crime figure, he had never been convicted of a federal crime. A regular visitor to Joe Sonken's Gold Coast, he once bought $30,000 worth of candy and dropped it off there. Everyone was eating candy for months.

Billy delivered the news of Kelly's death during his visit to the prison that weekend, and Russell mourned the loss of another close friend.

He had been getting by during his two years in Danbury. The medium-security facility featured a dormitory-like setting where most of the inmates slept on beds lined in rows, and Billy made sure he ate well. He continued to visit twice a week and other days talked to Russell daily on the phone. Despite the circumstance of his imprisonment, Russell was pleased. Business was good during his absence, and Billy had proved him right. He had become an important figure within and outside the family, and his steady stewardship had even caught the attention of another law enforcement agency.

The Pennsylvania Crime Commission released its ten-year report *A Decade of Organized Crime* in September 1980, and included in its nearly three hundred pages was a mention of one new member of the Bufalino crime family.

> While most of the members listed in the 1980 report are the same as those identified in the 1970 report or in subsequent state and federal disclosures, there is one addition to the list that has piqued the curiosity of Mafia watchers in this region. He is William D'Elia of Hughestown.

The Crime Commission first noticed Billy at the funeral for William Medico in 1972 but knew little about him, saying only that he served as a bodyguard for Russell and was on the board of directors of the local chapter of the Italian American Civil Rights League. The crime commission didn't realize just how important he was, yet his travels and regular meetings with other organized crime figures prompted them to open a D'Elia file.

They also had received bits of news from several informants. One was Charles Allen, a Philadelphia crime figure accused of two murders, who claimed that Billy was at Medico Industries when Frank Sheeran and Charles "Chuckie" O'Brien, Jimmy Hoffa's foster son, received a delivery of dynamite.

"I was there, but it didn't have anything to do with Medico," said

Billy. "Frank used to have Allen drive for him. He was once in prison with Hoffa. He was his gofer. Now he's driving Frank around and I'd meet with him and Frank at Aldino's. But one day we're at Medico's and Frank shows up with Chuckie and they go around to the back parking lot, and some other car pulled up and they transferred the dynamite. I don't know where it came from. We had five or six construction firms that were licensed to carry it. But that was it."

When Ellen read the report and saw Billy's name in it, she didn't know what to think. Reading for the first time anywhere that Billy was directly connected to the Mafia was more than unnerving.

"When that report came out it was an upsetting time for me," said Ellen. "I thought that it would be good if I could have a nervous breakdown. But I had little kids and I couldn't."

And she didn't really discuss it with her husband. He was gone most of the time anyway. And she didn't bring it up with Russell during his daily calls from prison.

The Crime Commission said that despite Russell's imprisonment, he remained one of the most powerful Mafia figures in the country and his family was the most powerful in the state, ahead of the Bruno Family in Philadelphia and the LaRocca Family in Pittsburgh. The commission believed that Russell was still in charge and that consigliere Eddie Sciandra was his acting boss. Billy had no idea where they were getting their information from, but he welcomed it. Let the government focus on Eddie. If that's what they thought, he reasoned, let them keep thinking it. He'd continue to meet with Russell and do his bidding.

During his stay in Danbury, Russell had plenty of time to stew over Jack Napoli. He could not accept that he had been set up by being disrespected. He believed the fit of anger with which he'd responded had been justified. Yet the government had used it to put him in prison.

But Russell did more than just think about Napoli, which is what prosecutors alleged in a federal indictment on January 1, 1981, the details of which claimed he'd enlisted the head of the Los Angeles family to kill Napoli.

Jimmy "the Weasel" Fratianno was the acting boss of the Los Angeles family when Russell met with him at the Rainbow Room in New York in 1976 following a performance by Frank Sinatra at the Westchester Premier Theater.

Fratianno later became a government witness following his 1977 arrest for the murder of a Cleveland union official, Danny Greene, who was killed by a car bomb. Promised just five years in prison—he only served twenty-three months—Fratianno was placed in the witness protection program, and among the many scraps of information he gave to the government was one about a meeting he had with Russell at the Rainbow Room.

Fratianno had just arrived with an underling, Mike Rizzitello, after watching Sinatra perform. Russell and Billy were there, along with a host of leading organized crime figures from across the country. Fratianno said Russell pulled him aside and relayed how he was facing trial for an extortion plot and wanted someone who was going to testify "clipped." Russell said the witness was Jack Napoli, that he was under government protection, and that he was hiding in Northern California near San Francisco. Fratianno and Rizzitello met with Russell two days later at Vesuvio and Russell passed along a business card. Written on the back were Napoli's name and aliases, and the words "Walnut Creek" and "pork store." But the question on their minds was, how did Russell know the location of someone in witness protection? The program was supposed to be, in theory, impenetrable.

"In the prison system in the United States, there's a system where you can get word. A network to get information. In this case it was from a U.S. marshal. So that's how we found out he was in Walnut Creek," said Billy. "Russell just knew people, and he found out where he was."

After driving up to Walnut Creek, which was northeast of San

Francisco, Rizzitello was stopped by police on August 9, 1976. They searched him and discovered the card Russell had given to him.

Russell was released from Danbury on May 8, 1981, after serving 33 months of a 48-month sentence, with 458 days of good-behavior credit. He exited the prison looking sharp, with a gray suit, light blue shirt, gray tie, and black leather shoes. After the bulletproof glass door closed behind him, he shook hands with a prison guard and slid into a waiting gray limousine. Inside were Billy, Angelo, and attorneys Charles Gelso and Michael Casale. But they weren't returning to Pennsylvania. Instead, they drove to Manhattan, where Russell faced new charges. The indictment had been handed down in January charging Russell with conspiring to kill Jack Napoli.

He was taken into custody by federal marshals, was arraigned, and posted a $50,000 bond.

"As soon as he walks out of prison they hit him with new charges," said Billy. "We had to go back to court on Monday, so when we're done at the federal building, Russ and me stay at his apartment for the weekend. After we go back to the courthouse on Monday, they give us six hours to get him home. But Russell says, 'Fuck 'em.' He wants to go to Madison Square Garden. Gerry Cooney is fighting Ken Norton. It was a big fight, and Russell wants to see it. I remind him that we have to get him back home, but he wants to go to dinner and then we go to the Garden. Danny Gorey meets us at the restaurant. He's always got a cigarette in his mouth and is blowing smoke everywhere, so you can imagine that Russell isn't happy. Our tickets are at ringside, and to get there at the Garden you have to go up these steps. We're running late and Russell is running up these steps. Danny Gorey can't make it. He smokes too much and he's coughing, and Russell passes him saying, 'Don't be a cocksucker. Have another one.' As soon as we get to our seats Cooney knocks out Norton and the fight is over in less than a minute, and that's when Danny finally reaches us. He looks like he's going to have a heart attack. He missed the fight. Russell tells him to keep walking, we're leaving."

Carrie welcomed Russell home with the aroma of a fresh tomato sauce she had prepared. He went into his living room, which he called "the den," to sit in his favorite leather lounge chair and watch the news. Not that he was looking to see anything specific. Russell was just trying to find something that would get his mind off his last few years and the uncertain years ahead.

Another indictment, this one conspiracy to commit murder, hung over him, and at seventy-seven he reasoned he didn't have many years left, and he surely didn't want to spend the last of them behind bars again. But the government had been persistent in trying to right its Jimmy Hoffa investigation, which had produced a number of suspects but no arrests.

The reception for Russell's return home was low-key, just Carrie and Billy's family. Carrie had visited Russell nearly every weekend during his thirty-three months away, and when he arrived home her only goal was keeping her husband from mingling with men who had prison records, which unfortunately included many of his friends and associates. She knew that even a phone call with a convicted felon could violate Russell's probation and return him to prison.

So it was with more than a hint of concern that Carrie reviewed the guest list for the Italian American Civil Rights League, Chapter 34, dinner dance at Gus Genetti's in Wilkes-Barre on September 5. Just weeks after his release, Russell was the guest of honor.

Nearly nine hundred people, the largest number yet, would come to honor Russell and to hear Tony Bennett, whom Billy had booked as the star attraction. Also watching were FBI agents from their organized crime office directly across the street from Genetti's, and they noted the wise guys, many of whom had arrived the day before to attend a private party hosted by Russell.

Each year the organized crime figures would assemble the night before the League dinner and feast on the same main course—freshly served goat personally prepared by Russell. And to throw off law enforcement, the private dinner was never held at the same place twice.

But crime commission agents, tipped off about the entre, learned that the goat had always come from an Italian market in Scranton. So on the day of the private dinner, they'd just follow the goat.

The following night the same men would all be at Genetti's, mixing in with the politicians, judges, and civic leaders. But Carrie insisted that the dinner dance would be Russell's last public appearance. The September issue of *Philadelphia Magazine* reported that Frank "Frankie Flowers" D'Alfonso, believed to be Angelo Bruno's replacement as boss of the Philadelphia family, was a front man for Russell, who the magazine said was really the new boss there as part of an agreement with the New York families. Russell had added Philadelphia to his vast territory, while New York got everything east of the Delaware River, which included South Jersey and the rich casinos in Atlantic City.

But Russell told Billy the story wasn't true, and even worse, it brought unwanted attention. Russell had another trial ahead of him, and all he wanted to do was relax.

To make him comfortable, Ellen bought him blue jeans. Russell had never worn jeans, but he'd have them on whenever he and Carrie drove over to the D'Elia home for dinner. He'd play with their kids for a while and then sit and watch a new cable news channel, CNN. Russell was a student of history with varied tastes and interests that went beyond his day-to-day business and life.

But the children always wanted his attention, and he'd give it to them. He also still loved to cook, and Ellen would assist him, though she favored Carrie's *capretto*—baby goat meat—stew and always remembered what Eddie Sciandra had once told her about Russell's cooking: "Don't let him fool you, Ellen. He puts too much salt in everything."

Aside from cooking, Russell kept himself busy in other ways, especially at the D'Elia home, where he became Ellen's Mr. Fix-It.

"He loved to do stuff," she said. "He'd come over and fix a door or my garage door, or a faucet. He knew how to use tools and was always handy."

Meanwhile, Billy remained on the street and continued to oversee Bufalino Family business. Much of it was good, with some bad sprinkled in.

One of those occasions that didn't play out well occurred when two men from Miami looking to set up a gold deal sought him out, and Billy agreed to meet them at the Woodlands. He and Russell had been going to the cavernous dinner club for years. It featured several bars and restaurants, a health club, hotel rooms, and a large banquet facility for weddings and special events. It was a sort of home away from home.

Billy already knew the men. One was Hal Chandler, who ran the Diplomat Hotel, and the other was a guy he knew as Mike Z, a vice president at the Fontainebleau Hotel. They said they were going to buy gold from someone in Chicago and asked Billy to be their middleman.

"It was snowing and they're from Miami and they're in Miami suits and freezing their balls off," said Billy. "So they sit down in the cigarette smoke with me and this guy from Chicago, Wayne, and he says they're mining three hundred thousand worth of gold. 'But before they give us their money, we want to deliver the gold to you first because you're a neutral party.' Everyone is fine with that, so they set up a day to transfer the money for the gold. But it was all a scam. The gold wasn't real but Wayne still wanted the money. So I tell the story to Russell thinking maybe he could help with a call to Chicago, and we meet with the Miami guys at the Woodlands. Russell says, 'Listen, I just got out of jail and I'm going to jail in another year and a half. I don't really want to get involved.' So the Hal guy says, 'Well, Russell, we figured that was going to happen. They told us in Miami if you think that cockeyed old fucker up in Pennsylvania is going to help you, you're crazy.' Russell's fucking veins bulged out of his neck. He looks at me and goes, 'You! You're going to Chicago!' So I go there and I tell this fucking Wayne to shut his mouth, he's not getting nothin'. So I quashed the whole deal. And it was all because the Miami guys insulted Russell."

Russell didn't take any more meetings after that, and as his trial approached the government tried again to deport him, to no avail. Instead, they hatched another plan and called attorney Charles Gelso with an offer and asked if he could accompany Russell the next time he visited Philadelphia.

"We went to Immigration every week down in Philadelphia," said Billy. "Russell had to report there. It was crazy, but what can you do. So there was a guy there and he said, 'Mr. Bufalino, once I got to know you, I really liked you a lot. I don't want them to put you in jail for the rest of your life. If you would just sign an order for deportation, you'll leave the country and I can guarantee you'll never have to go on trial.' Russell looked at him and said, 'Listen. I was born in America and I'll fucking die in America.' That was the end of that deal. He believed in what he believed."

But Russell's belief in himself would be his undoing once the trial was underway in New York.

Billy again stayed with him at the New York apartment and drove him back and forth to the courthouse, where he stayed and watched the proceedings. But from the very beginning, the trial didn't go well.

The government's chief witness was Jimmy Fratianno, who relayed the story of the 1976 meeting at the Rainbow Room in New York where Russell asked him to kill Napoli. Prosecutors also presented evidence that Russell had recruited an inmate serving time with him at Danbury to kill Napoli. Stephen Fox was a member of the Pagans, a ruthless East Coast motorcycle gang involved in drug trafficking, selling stolen property, and murder-for-hire. Fox had several prior convictions, and at Danbury he had befriended Russell. Prosecutors said Fox eventually agreed that upon his release he'd fly to California and kill Napoli. Instead, he violated his parole and fled to Florida. Upon his capture there, Fox, hoping to barter for minimal prison time, said he had some interesting information about a major organized crime figure that he could share.

Meanwhile Mike Rizzitello, Russell's codefendant, claimed the card he'd carried with Napoli's name and location meant nothing to him because he couldn't read or write. Rizzitello was originally from New York and had hung around with Joey Gallo, for whom he was allegedly the top hit man. Rizzitello eventually moved to Los Angeles, where he served nine years in prison for robbing several restaurants in 1962. After his release, he met Fratianno, who was the acting boss of the Milano Family there, and he became a capo under his watch.

But he couldn't stay out of trouble. Rizzitello was convicted of insurance fraud in 1976 and a mail-billing scheme in 1977. Sentenced to three years in prison, Rizzitello was behind bars in 1978 when he was indicted for running a $100 million–a–year pornography business and also stood accused of shaking down pornographic film dealers.

Fratianno told prosecutors about Rizzitello's role in the porno shakedown as well as his being the point man in Russell's attempt to kill Napoli. For his part, Rizzitello repeated his story that he couldn't read or write.

"During the recesses at the trial we're all sitting in the hallway and Rizzitello's sitting there off to the side by himself reading a paper," said Billy. "I said, 'Russ, look at this.' Russ goes, 'Hey, stupid, what are you looking at, the pictures? You can't read, you fucking dummy!'"

With the trial going badly, Charles Gelso declined nightly dinners with Russell and Billy to focus on the testimony. Despite Fratianno's damning accusations, Gelso felt good about Russell's chances for acquittal. But then Russell made a bold, fateful decision, one that Gelso couldn't talk him out of.

"Russell said he wanted to testify," said Billy. "You never get up there on the stand. Charlie flipped and told him it was suicide, that Russell being up there would only give the prosecutors the opportunity to not just question him but bring up things about him. Like his association with Vito Genovese and Carlo Gambino and Apalachin. All that stuff. But Russell was stubborn. He didn't want to hear it. He thought he could just go up there and tell the jury that anyone would have said what he said. But once the jury heard about the other parts of his life, that was it."

The jury took less than two hours to reach a guilty verdict. Mike Rizzitello, who didn't testify, was acquitted.

While prosecutors were thrilled with the outcome, they were outraged when Judge Kevin Duffy agreed to release Russell on $50,000 bail while he awaited sentencing. He was nearly seventy-eight, and Duffy didn't believe he posed a danger or a flight risk.

With the sentencing set for November 17 and Russell facing a considerable prison term, prosecutors saw an opportunity. Nathaniel Akerman, the assistant U.S. attorney who led the team that gained the conviction, wrote to Charles Gelso on October 29 offering Russell a deal—become a government informant and tell all he knew about Jimmy Hoffa and other matters related to organized crime, and in return he would receive a minimum sentence or even a suspended sentence and avoid jail time altogether, along with other perks. Acker-man waited for Gelso to reply.

The following day, October 30, a federal jury in Philadelphia con-victed Frank Sheeran of labor racketeering. Prosecutors alleged he had taken bribes from a New Jersey Teamsters official for what they described as a "corporate shell game" in which Sheeran and others used nonunion labor for several labor-leasing firms and pocketed the difference in salaries. The charges against Frank and Russell were born from the same investigation begun in 1975 with the disappear-ance of Jimmy Hoffa. Unable to charge them in the Hoffa case, pros-ecutors cast wider nets.

Following Frank's conviction, prosecutors there offered the same deal to him as Akerman had to Russell—become a government informant, tell all you know about Hoffa and other business, and you'll be rewarded. Sheeran, facing seventy-seven years in prison, said no.

Meanwhile hundreds of people wrote letters in support of Russell to Judge Duffy, each one attesting to Russell's many kindnesses to them and to the community. Among those participating in the campaign was a newly ordained Catholic priest, Father Joseph Sica, who also wrote to Pennsylvania governor Richard Thornburgh and his wife, Ginny.

Short and balding, with a wide girth, Sica was from Dunmore, the same town as Cappy, and there was some sort of connection between Sica and Louis DeNaples, the businessman and Dunmore resident, but no one knew what that was.

It seemed like Sica had just popped out of thin air, and he quickly endeared himself to Russell, who was so taken with him, he introduced Sica to Carrie, and together they wanted to support a deep desire he had to help children.

"Russell went to go visit his lawyer Mike Casale, who was in the hospital, and there was a young priest with Casale and Mike introduced Russell to him," said Billy. "He just got out of priest school. So I'm watching this priest and he was all over Russell. He says he wants to raise money for children and Russell says sure and he tells me to help him."

The idea was for a fundraiser that would be held at a theater in Williamsport, which was about seventy miles west of Wilkes-Barre. Russell provided the same entertainment he had for the orphans' benefit he hosted at the Danbury prison, including the Gene DeLuca orchestra. The event raised thousands.

When it ended, Billy and Russell were invited for coffee and cake at the home of one of the organizers, and they were presented with plaques for their help with the event.

"Sica is there and he just hugs Russell and kisses him on the cheek," said Billy. "He says, 'I wish you were my father.' I knew right there we were going to get fucked. When we were putting together that show Father Sica was at my house almost every day for supper. Ellen was helping him with the preparations. We had the show and it went well. After, Russell says to me, 'What are you doing with this kid?' I said, 'Russ, he's all right.' He goes, 'I didn't ask if he was all right. What are you doing with him?' I said, 'We're going to be okay.' Russ looks at me. 'Last time I'll ask you. What are you doing?' I said we split whatever we got. He goes, 'How much did you get?' I told him twenty-eight thousand. He says, 'Are you crazy? You guys are gonna take money from a priest? Let him keep it all.' So he got it all. A couple of days later he shows up at my house in a fucking brand-new red Trans Am."

The car didn't sit well with Billy, and Ellen was irate. She devoted a lot of time to the church and to its charitable endeavors, including Catholic Charities. She was outraged. But Sica's actions also drew the scrutiny of the diocese.

"I get a visit from Monsignor Kenneth Horan, who was the head of Catholic Charities," said Ellen. "He was a good friend and he was close to the bishop and he knew Russell. It was late at night and I was home scrubbing floors, and in walks Monsignor Horan and he was with another priest. I'm thinking, 'What the hell is going on here?' It's ten o'clock at night. He never visits like this. So we said hello and hugged each other and he said, 'Listen, Ellen, I have to ask you something. I got called in to the bishop. He said there was a discrepancy in the money the parish was supposed to receive for the fundraiser. The bishop said Father Sica told him that Russell Bufalino took the money.' I was shocked. I told him that Russell would never take money from anybody like that, from a church organization or from anybody. So we're talking and then Billy came home."

"I walk in and the monsignor is there with Ellen," said Billy. "And he goes to me, 'If I ask you a question, will you tell me the truth?' I said sure. He said, 'I'll give you my word it will never get out of this room. How much did Russell take off of Father Sica from the fundraiser?' I told him he didn't take a dime, and we didn't because Russell told me not to. So Monsignor said he knew Russell wouldn't take money, and that he would go back and tell the bishop that. Sica took it all and blamed Russell. I told him to get Sica out of here before I smashed him. Monsignor said, 'You're supposed to forgive.' I said, 'That's your job, that ain't my job.'"

A week later, Father Sica pulled up to the D'Elia house in his red sports car, walked up to the front door, and rang the bell. When Ellen opened it and saw who it was, she couldn't hold in her anger.

"I wouldn't let him in," said Ellen. "I told him, 'Don't ever come near my house again. It was a terrible thing you did.' He took the money, I'm sure. And Russell had gotten him his suit when he was ordained and bought him his shoes. Russell and Aunt Carrie thought he was wonderful. I never told Russell and I asked Billy not to tell them, and he didn't. They were treating Sica like he was their own kid. I never told Russell what he did with the money. Maybe I should have."

Sica continued on as if nothing had happened and apparently was never disciplined by the diocese. So like Ellen did, he gathered letters in support of Russell and even wrote a letter to Governor Thornburgh, requesting he intervene.

As the sentencing date approached, Ellen was desperate and wrote to Judge Duffy asking if she could visit with him. She was surprised when he agreed. As Ellen made her preparations with several friends to drive to New York, she was approached by Father Sica, who asked if he could accompany her.

"Father Sica wanted to come. He thought it would help if a priest was with us," said Ellen. "So I put what he did with the fundraiser aside. When we get there I asked the judge if there was anything we could do to help Russell. I told him that Papa was upset and that if someone threatened you like that you'd get angry too. And if it was anyone other than Russell no one would think twice about it. Judge Duffy was very nice to me. He realized that we cared about Russell and he understood what we were saying. But he said there was nothing that could be done. He said if Russell hadn't taken the stand he probably wouldn't have gotten convicted. Russell had this crazy idea that it was okay for him to get up there and tell the truth. It was not a good idea for him to get up there at all. I think he just prejudiced the jury."

Unbeknownst to Ellen, having Father Sica with her may not have been the best of ideas either. Duffy, in all certainty, had been made aware of a caustic encounter the priest had previously had with the FBI.

"Russell was home on bail, and the FBI was watching Russell's house, and Sica would go outside and yell at the FBI agents, calling them motherfuckers and whatever," said Billy. "I'm sure that didn't make a good impression."

On November 8, 1981, after being found guilty of labor racketeering and mail fraud, and after declining the offer to cooperate with the government, Frank Sheeran was sentenced to eighteen years in prison. Soon after, Charles Gelso wrote back to Nathaniel Akerman and said he'd discussed the offer with Russell, but his reply was also a firm no.

"Although Mr. Bufalino is well aware of the enormous benefits, financial and otherwise, he could receive as a Government witness, he cannot and will not avail himself of those benefits by giving false testimony," wrote Gelso. "Mr. Bufalino has no information on the matter suggested by your correspondence and will not falsely implicate others to obtain favorable treatment from the Government."

Billy drove Russell downtown to the federal courthouse on the morning of November 17, 1981, and Russell was prepared for what was in store for him. The government, he said again, would get its grain of salt, even with an old man nearing eighty. And it did. Billy watched as Duffy sentenced Russell to ten years in prison.

Duffy ordered that he'd remain free on bond pending his appeal and Russell said nothing to the reporters waiting for him outside. Billy took him back to the apartment, where they packed a few things, and then there was a quiet ride home to Pennsylvania, where he would see Carrie and strategize about his appeal.

Russell knew that a ten-year prison sentence for a seventy-seven-year-old man was a virtual death sentence, so he tasked Billy with securing legal help for Gelso, who was preparing Russell's appeal. But they didn't want just another lawyer. Charlie Gelso was good, so good that Russell didn't want anyone else representing him. But Russell needed someone with great influence, a mover and shaker, a power broker who, like Russell, could make the impossible happen. There was but one name, and Billy made an appointment for he and Russell to have a visit with the devil himself.

CHAPTER 11

The Fixer

Roy Cohn had, for years, been among the most powerful behind-the-scenes dealmakers in New York.

No one was more ruthless or conniving, or even hated, and he enjoyed a national profile that allowed him to threaten, cajole, or terrorize most anyone.

He represented some of the most well-known people in New York, including real estate mogul Donald Trump, New York Yankees owner George Steinbrenner, and Steve Rubell and Ian Schrager, the owners of the swanky and popular celebrity disco Studio 54. He had also counted organized crime figures as clients, men Russell called friends, such as Carmine Galante and Anthony Salerno.

The famed—many believed infamous—attorney gained renown in his twenties during his untiring hunt for communists. As the chief counsel for Senator Joseph McCarthy and his House Un-American Activities Committee, Cohn destroyed the lives of hundreds of people, many of them artists and entertainers, with just the slightest accusation of sharing communist sympathies. Cohn reveled in his ruthlessness, and he even sent Julius and Ethel Rosenberg to their grisly deaths in the electric chair in 1953 after successfully prosecuting them as spies for the Soviet Union.

Now, years later, Cohn was at the height of his power and influence. He was the preeminent fixer in New York, using threats, intimidation, and the courts to bulldoze people for his clients. He also guarded his privacy zealously, refuting for years rumors that he was gay and threatening anyone who thought of saying so publicly. There was no one more powerful, and for the right price he held out hope for most anyone, even those who had already been convicted.

"We needed help, and it was Tommy Gambino's idea, Carlo's nephew, for Charlie Gelso to draft Russell's appeals and then have Cohn sign them," said Billy. "Having Cohn's signature was supposed to mean something. We didn't know him, but we knew two dentists in Wilkes-Barre who did know Cohn. They were very, very close to him and we asked them to set up a meeting for us."

The dentists were both gay and had attended the bacchanalian orgies Cohn hosted at his estate in the Poconos. At Billy's request and on behalf of Russell, they reached out to Cohn and a meeting was scheduled at the Woodlands.

"Cohn had a house in the Poconos—I think it was in Cresco—and he was whitewater rafting, so he comes up to visit and told us to bring our paperwork," said Billy. "We meet, we talk, we all get along. He knows who Russell is and he plays the role as if he can help him. So he agreed with our plan to have Charlie Gelso write up the paperwork for the appeal and Cohn would sign it. He knew everybody and had the clout. The plan is for me to go meet him at his office the next week in New York with ten thousand in cash. So I go to his office, which may also have been his home, and went upstairs. He's a thin, little guy with an ugly face and a gravelly voice and he goes like this: 'Promise me one thing. If you ever get in trouble again, don't come to me in the twenty-fifth hour.' I said I wouldn't. So I give him the envelope with the ten thousand cash in it. Then I go back to see him the next week. I have another envelope with ten grand in it. But instead of an office they take me upstairs out on the roof. I couldn't believe what I saw. It was hot and sunny, and he was sitting in a beach chair with one of those sun visors under his chin. He has nothing on but a fucking Jockey bathing suit, one of those little things. There are two little cocker spaniels there and two guys that looked like linebackers in white shirts with no sleeves and very short black shorts standing on each side of Cohn feeding him and the dogs scrambled eggs. I gave him the envelope, he lectured me again about going to him in the twenty-fifth hour, and I left thinking this was beyond the call of duty. It was fucking crazy."

For the next six weeks Billy traveled to New York to give Cohn his $10,000 cash envelope, with the exception of one visit to Cohn's estate in the Poconos. The title to the expansive home said it was owned by a friend of Cohn's, but everyone knew it was Cohn who owned it. Billy drove there with Ellen, who had no idea who she was going to be meeting with or why.

"We drive up and there are all these luxury cars parked to the side," said Billy. "BMWs, Mercedes, Cadillacs, Rolls-Royces—there must have been forty of them. We park and walk up and there are all these people there, nearly all men, and I don't know any of them. But it's a big party. This guy stops us. His name is Russell Eldridge. I learn later he's Roy's assistant and handled all his business, like collecting all the money from the gay movie houses. Roy was big into porn and some other things. He says to Ellen, 'Honey, why are you here?' She says she's with me. Then he looks at me and says to her, 'Why are you with him?' I tell him who I am and I'm there to see Roy and he says this may not be the place for us. He said the night before some guy was having sex with dogs. So this is great. I didn't want to be there with this nut. Ellen just looks at me. She has no idea what's going on. He says to her, 'Let me give you a little advice. When you go home, any money he has laying around, pack it up and hide it. Hide anything you can because you don't want to have nothing if he goes away.' Then he turns to me and says that Roy gets about forty calls a day and answers only five and that I should call him first. I said, 'Fine, but tonight we have a dinner appointment with Roy.' So he goes inside and we're out there awhile feeling really uncomfort-able and he finally comes back and says, 'Okay, Roy is waiting for you.' We go inside and we sit down with Roy and he introduces us to another guy, says he's a senior official with the U.S. Department of the Interior. The four of us sit down and have a nice dinner and Ellen enjoys herself, but near the end Roy tells me again to promise him we wouldn't wait until the last minute to reach out to him. I said sure. I saw him one more time after that. Charlie Gelso wrote up the entire brief and I brought it to Roy, who signed it. But even Roy couldn't help. This was still all about Hoffa. At that point it was pretty desperate, so we really tried a Hail Mary."

The famed boxing trainer Angelo Dundee had been a regular at Joe Sonken's Gold Coast Restaurant going back to the 1960s. He was friends with Russell, and they talked boxing together and did busi-ness together, with Russell backing several of his fighters. Dundee had been the longtime trainer for Muhammad Ali, and the former champion had just retired in December 1981 after losing a decision to Trevor Berbick in the Bahamas. At Billy's request, and on behalf of Russell, Dundee agreed to go to Washington, DC, to plead for Russell, and he brought Ali with him.

"We had Angelo with us," said Billy. "So Dundee takes Muham-mad Ali with him to meet with Ted Kennedy, who was crazy about him, especially all the old Cassius Clay stuff. They tell him that they have a good friend who is facing a lot of time in prison who got set up by the FBI but he's almost eighty years old and they need help to keep him out of prison. So Kennedy says sure, he doesn't want to see an old man go to prison. He'll see what he can do and asks for his name. They say it's Russell Bufalino. Dundee said Kennedy got so angry he kicked him and Ali out of his office, but not before yelling, 'Absolutely not! As long as there's a Kennedy alive no one will ever lift a finger to help Bufalino!' That had to do with the old shit with the brothers, John and Bobby."

Unbeknownst to Billy, there was another secretive effort to keep

Russell out of prison, and it had to do with the newly elected president, Ronald Reagan, and his choice to serve as labor secretary, Raymond Donovan.

The FBI had begun an investigation into Donovan amid allegations he had long-standing mob ties through the Schiavone Construction Company in Secaucus, New Jersey, of which Donovan was a part owner and executive. Among the men whom Donovan allegedly knew were Anthony Provenzano, Salvatore Briguglio, and another man, Fred Furino, a New Jersey Teamsters official.

Furino and Briguglio had been childhood friends in Hoboken and later worked as truck drivers and served as organizers for Provenzano's Teamsters Local 560 in Union City, New Jersey. Furino had also been called before the grand jury investigating the disappearance of Jimmy Hoffa, but he'd declined to answer questions about his relationships with Provenzano and Briguglio or their whereabouts the day Hoffa disappeared.

William Bufalino had been scheduled to represent Furino, but U.S. district judge Ralph Freeman in Detroit ruled that it would be a conflict of interest, given that William Bufalino also represented many of the other suspects in Hoffa's disappearance—among them Briguglio and Provenzano.

On January 22, 1981, the FBI interviewed Furino regarding his knowledge of alleged bribes given by Donovan in the 1970s to Briguglio for "labor peace" on behalf of Schiavone Construction. Furino, who the FBI believed was the late Briguglio's "bag man," denied any knowledge of the bribes as well as making alleged cash pickups for Briguglio from Donovan or even knowing Donovan.

But in April 1982, more than a year after his interviews with the FBI, Furino took six polygraph tests, with all of them indicating he'd lied about not knowing Donovan. Furino was subpoenaed to testify before a grand jury investigating Donovan but disappeared. He was found dead on June 11, 1982, in the trunk of his car in Manhattan, a single bullet hole in his forehead.

Time magazine reported ten days later about Furino's failed polygraph tests, his pending grand jury appearance, and an FBI memo stating that Donovan had socialized on a regular basis with Furino and Briguglio.

But after Furino's murder a Binghamton, New York, man, Michael Klepfer, was indicted on conspiracy charges for attempting to bribe the owner of a West Hazleton, Pennsylvania, bakery company to end a strike. Also charged was his father, Ellis Klepfer, the owner of a trucking company for which Michael was an executive. Ellis Klepfer was also a longtime member of the Bufalino Family, a Binghamton associate working under Guvy Guarnieri.

Hoping to avoid a long jail term, Michael Klepfer said not only that he knew Furino, but that Furino had told him Donovan laundered $20 million for the Teamsters into Reagan's 1980 presidential campaign in return for pardons for Russell and Provenzano. Klepfer also said that Furino had been murdered over fears that he would testify about the plot before the grand jury.

But for reasons that went unexplained, Klepfer later retracted his statements after refusing to take a polygraph test, and he was charged with lying to the FBI.

Klepfer pleaded guilty to one count of lying in a plea-bargain arrangement in which the conspiracy charges for attempting to bribe the bakery executive were dropped. Facing a five-year sentence, Klepfer received a mere six months in prison. And in a very unusual meeting, the federal judge in the case conferred privately for more than an hour in his chambers with Raymond Donovan, who had traveled to Syracuse to meet with him.

Despite the guilty plea, Michael Klepfer insisted that what he'd told FBI investigators was an accurate depiction of what Furino had told him. The judge said he believed him.

Furino's murder and Klepfer's claims produced some headlines, which eventually went away. And any hope of Russell's receiving a presidential pardon were dashed. With a ten-year prison sentence ahead of him, Russell accepted his fate and made his preparations to report to the federal prison in Leavenworth, Kansas.

The week before their departure, Billy drove Russell into New York for a party at the Midwood Lounge in Brooklyn. Russell owned a piece of the bar/restaurant near Brooklyn College with Charlie Fratello, perhaps one of the toughest men in New York, whom Russell relied on for so-called wet work. It was there where he would privately say goodbye to his closest friends in New York. Soldiers, capos, and other leading figures from each of New York's Five Families came to pay their respects, among them Andy Russo from the Colombo Family and Anthony "Tony Lee" Guerrieri, a member of the Gambino Family and close associate of a rising capo, John Gotti.

Billy remained by Russell's side the entire evening while another friend, Artie Rinaldi, picked up the tab.

"Artie was the best gambler I ever saw," said Billy. "You couldn't talk to him until late in the morning. He'd look through all the newspapers and go through all the horses, baseball, basketball, and football. He was a sharp dresser, a real classy guy who was so good, no one would take his action. So I'd bet for him for a while. When Russell was away in Danbury, he gave money to Carrie every week."

The following day Russell laid out his instructions, which were similar to the ones he had given prior to his incarceration at Danbury. There would be multiple calls per day to Billy, along with regular visits. But since Leavenworth was halfway across the country, the visits would be limited to twice a month.

His affairs in order, Russell said goodbye to Carrie, who as usual remained stoic. For Ellen and the children, seeing Papa off was heartbreaking.

Russell and Billy flew to Kansas City and drove to Leavenworth, which was one of the oldest federal prisons in the country and just across the state line, about twenty miles north of the city. As they approached the prison entrance, Russell had a change of mind and decided he wanted to go for coffee.

"Keep going," he said, motioning them along with his fingers. Since leaving the airport they had been trailed by FBI agents inside an unmarked car, and it followed them to a place called Country Kitchen. Russell had another hour to report, and he ordered dry rye toast and orange juice. They returned to the prison just ahead of the twelve forty-five P.M. reporting time. As they were about to climb the steps, Billy went to grab Russell's arm, but he brushed him away.

"I'm walking in here on my own two feet," he growled. "I'm not giving these bastards any satisfaction."

CHAPTER 12

Moving On

"Lawmen say it is just too soon to tell whether Bufalino will try and run mob dealings from Leavenworth, Kansas, as he did from jail in Connecticut in the 1970s. But the Crime Commission suspects that Bufalino can lose some of his power if his stay in jail approaches the ten years of his sentence. . . . Should that happen . . . some of Bufalino's crime captains could scramble to succeed him, and there's little doubt there's a lot at stake."

The local television news report pointed to Eddie Sciandra, Dave Osticco, and Guvy Guarnieri as potential replacements for Russell during his imprisonment, and perhaps permanently. It was all guesswork. Some reporters claimed they had sources within law enforcement, but no one within the FBI or the state or local police had an inkling as to what was really happening inside the family.

As for his so-called top lieutenants, Russell never considered them replacements. Besides, they had their own problems.

The FBI had begun a special investigation in 1979 of the Bufalino Family, which it dubbed RABFAM (Russell A. Bufalino Family). Led by the agency's Philadelphia office, it had learned much about Russell during the Hoffa investigation and now sought to understand the full breadth of his power and influence in everything from the Teamsters to political corruption.

Among the many criminal activities noted by the agents during their investigation were instances of bank fraud, loan-sharking, and interstate transportation of stolen property such as jewelry and furs. The family also remained heavily involved in the garment industry. But there were cracks, and it was from those small openings that law enforcement could see the depth of Russell's power and influence and that of his family.

Just a year earlier Congressman Daniel Flood had pleaded guilty to a single charge of conspiracy to violate the federal campaign laws for taking cash payoffs. Flood had been tried for taking hundreds of thousands of dollars under the table from lobbyists and contractors, but he was acquitted after a lone juror refused to find him guilty. Suspecting that juror had been compromised, prosecutors prepared for another trial and were going to include additional charges that focused on Flood's long-standing relationship with Medico Industries: he had in fact steered tens of millions in defense contracts to Medico for years in return for cash and, more recently, access to the company's private jet.

The FBI had wired Medico's offices and captured Russell discussing Philip and William Medico as capos in his crime family. William had died in 1972, but the FBI had known about the Medicos and Russell going back to the 1950s, with informants providing detailed reports on their close friendship and business relationships. William, who was Medico's general manager, and Russell were said to be particularly close. In 1969, the Associated Press reported that Medico had received $12 million in army, navy, and air force contracts, including one contract for the production of rocket warheads for use in Vietnam. After learning about the tapes, and that one of his top advisers had agreed to testify against him, Flood accepted a plea deal.

"Russell never liked Flood," said Billy. "He thought he was just too much of a showboat. He had that mustache and spoke like he was onstage somewhere. He had his uses over the years. But he came to one of our league dinners and asked Russell if he could say a few words. Russell said no and turned him away. How many guys could tell a congressman to fuck off?"

Among those targeted in the RABFAM investigation were Russell, Dave, Cappy, Frank Sheeran, and Billy, and the probe was so wide-ranging it required the help of other field offices throughout the country, including those in Kansas City, Las Vegas, and Miami, as well as the use of several informants.

It was one of those informants who tipped off investigators about Dave Osticco, saying he'd fixed the jury in a trial involving Louis DeNaples.

DeNaples and two other men had been charged with defrauding the U.S. government of $525,000 by falsifying documents for reimbursements for cleanup work they said they did after Hurricane Agnes. Following his November 1977 trial, a single juror held out for acquittal, causing a hung jury. Not wanting to face another trial, DeNaples pleaded no contest to a single fraud charge. He paid a fine and was spared prison, yet was now a convicted felon.

The informant said that Dave had bribed the juror who held out, and the informant shared that with an FBI agent in Scranton, who passed along the tip to a young assistant U.S. attorney there, Eric Holder.

Holder wanted to speak to the informant, Frank Parlopiano, who claimed that a man named Charles Cortese had confided to him that his wife, Rose Ann, was a member of the DeNaples jury and that he persuaded her to acquit DeNaples. For the price of $1,000 and new tires for her car, she was the lone holdout for a conviction, leading to the hung jury.

"Cappy asked Dave if he could help Louie with the trial," said Billy. "It was Cappy who introduced Louie to us years earlier; they were both from Dunmore, so we already knew him well. Dave said he'd take care of it and he approached the husband, but he'd had to have gone through Russell first. He liked Louie."

Dave, now seventy, was indicted on October 20, 1982. Billy, Angelo, and Charles Gelso accompanied Dave to his arraignment, where he posted a $50,000 bond and promised to show up for all court appearances.

Meanwhile consigliere Eddie Sciandra, sixty-nine, whom the government and media strongly suspected was Russell's acting boss and logical successor, began serving an eighteen-month sentence in New York following his conviction in March 1982 for income tax evasion.

And Guvy in Binghamton was in no position to assume a new role either given the various investigations surrounding him.

The prosecutorial onslaught against the Bufalino Family was taking its toll, and one by one aging gangsters were being imprisoned or dying off. Meanwhile, with Russell locked up, the mood surrounding the Italian American Civil Rights League, Chapter 34, had soured, as was evident at the annual dinner dance. Fearing that the recent arrests and investigations would deter local businessmen, politicians, and county officials from attending, the group was renamed the Italian American Humanitarian League. It didn't help. The November 1982 dinner attracted only half the number of people who had attended the year before. Nearly all the politicians, judges, and law enforcement officials who'd readily attended past dinners skipped this one, with many believing that Russell would likely die in prison—and the Bufalino Family with him.

But a few weeks later, on November 23, Russell returned to Scranton.

He was transported from Leavenworth to testify before the Pennsylvania Crime Commission. He was placed on a prison bus with other inmates for a long ride to Texas. Upset over his treatment, Russell got Billy to call Roy Cohn to intervene, and Cohn called Jim Kanavy, a special agent with the Pennsylvania Crime Commission in Scranton, to plead for permission for Russell to fly back. Cohn said Russell would pay for it. Instead, the marshals put Russell on a plane, and it was Kanavy who picked him up at the airport, along with an-other agent and two Pennsylvania State Police troopers. After enter-ing the state police car, Russell was in a foul mood. Billy had gotten him a $1,000 suit to wear along with alligator shoes, but the marshals insisted he wear his prison boots. During the drive to the courthouse Russell sat between Kanavy and the other agent, Steve Keller, and intentionally leaned into them. Realizing he was upset, Kanavy poked Russell and asked why he wore such ugly shoes.

"You should find out what happened there," said Kanavy.

"I learned something a long time ago, kid," said Russell. "When you got a problem, you have to take care of it at the source."

Russell lightened up after that, and he and Kanavy spoke the rest of the way. Kanavy, who had investigated the Bufalino Family since 1973, found Russell to be disarming and cordial, and very smart, so smart he thought he could have been the head of a major U.S. cor-poration. Of course, Kanavy thought, he was amoral and would kill you in a heartbeat.

After arriving at the courthouse Russell was flanked by attorneys Charles Gelso and Mike Casale and compelled to testify under a grant of immunity from prosecution. Billy and Angelo sat in the rear.

During the contentious four-hour hearing, Russell admitted knowing Frank Sheeran, Jimmy Hoffa, Vito Genovese, and Carlo Gambino; denied having anything to do with Hoffa's disappearance; denied holding any interest in Medico Industries; and said he couldn't really remember anything else. Questions about his involvement in everything from smuggling Sicilians into the United States through Venezuela to trafficking in pornographic films went unanswered. Like the boxers he loved, he dipped and dodged, feinted and frowned. Near the end, the hearing became so heated that Charles Gelso was removed by the state police.

When it was over, Russell was escorted out in handcuffs and put on a plane back to prison.

Prior to Russell's imprisonment, Billy had for years visited Kansas City to meet with the Civella Family. Nick Civella had led the family since the early 1950s, had been at Apalachin at Russell's invitation, and along with Russell had a hand in the Teamsters' Central States Pension Fund. He was sent to Leavenworth in 1980 following his conviction for trying to bribe a prison official on behalf of a nephew, who was seeking a transfer to a minimum-security facility in Texas.

Civella was a familiar and welcome face for Russell, and the two old friends spent as much time as they could together talking about current business. But Civella was sick with cancer and had applied for an early medical release. His son Tony was doing some of the heavy lifting during his father's incarceration, and Billy would get off the plane and visit with him before heading to Leavenworth.

Like the dutiful son that he was, Billy flew to the Midwest twice a month to meet with Russell, and the chitchat about life back home would quickly morph into talk of business. Russell remained in charge, and with every visit he'd dole out one command or assignment after another: go to New York for this, fly to Los Angeles to meet with that one, and stop in Kansas City on the way back to take care of something else.

Once a month Carrie would accompany Billy. On those trips they'd fly first-class and take a limo from the airport, and Billy put her in the finest hotel room he could find.

"She wouldn't go with anyone else, only me. And it had to be first-class all the way," said Billy.

But as the months passed and with Russell entering his eighties, the dynamic of the Bufalino Family was changing.

Underboss Dave Osticco was convicted of obstruction of justice for tampering with the jury in the Louis DeNaples trial and was sentenced to eight years in prison. In February 1983, capo Philip Medico died of natural causes, and in July 1984 Stefano LaTorre, the oldest member of the family, also died of natural causes. He was the last of the original "Men of Montedoro" who'd founded the family.

Meanwhile hit man Charlie Fratello was charged with first-degree murder for killing a man in Pompano Beach, Florida, and sentenced to life in prison.

As made soldiers of the Bufalino Family either died off or were locked away, the family business began to change. While gambling remained a mainstay, the family was no longer influential in Teamsters circles, and its hold on garment manufacturing was a thing of the past. The family needed fresh ideas, and Billy sought out one after another.

In the meantime, Russell's passion for boxing brought a heavyweight title fight to Scranton. He had managed fighters before and had an interest with Angelo Bruno in the contract of the former heavyweight champ Sonny Liston. Russell had the closed-circuit television rights to Liston's fight with Cassius Clay—soon to change his name to Muhammad Ali—in Lewiston, Maine, in 1965, in which Liston was knocked out in the first round, with many observers suggesting he took a dive.

Even in prison Russell was kept abreast of new talent. He gave Billy instructions to get a piece of the contract of James "Buddy" McGirt, a teenage aspirant from Long Island who would go on to win the light welterweight title.

Years earlier, Russell had had a hand in organizing a local boxing group, the Friends of Boxing Club. For its president, Russell tapped Louis DelVecchio, the longtime manager of Russell's Howard Johnson's motel in Pittston, where Russell organized many of his underworld meetings and put up many of his guests.

Among the fighters DelVecchio knew well was the current heavyweight champion, Larry Holmes, who grew up just eighty miles to the south in Easton. Holmes fought his first professional fight in Scranton in 1973, and since then he had visited the region often. When he did, he stayed at the Howard Johnson's.

DelVecchio invited Holmes to fight in Scranton. And despite objections from Don King, who promoted his fights, Holmes agreed.

With Russell's approval, DelVecchio promoted the bout, which was set for Sunday, March 27, 1983, at the old Watres Armory in Scranton.

The bout had boxing journalists and officials scratching their heads. The Watres Armory, an old brick fortress that looked like a prison from the outside, could only seat up to seven thousand spectators. And the fight, billed as "Larry Holmes' Homecoming," had a minuscule purse compared with what Holmes could earn in a typical larger venue in Las Vegas or Atlantic City. When asked, "Why Scranton?" he said he owed the city since it was where he fought his first professional fight.

Challenging Holmes for his fourteenth title defense was Lucien Rodriguez of France, a fighter with mediocre skills with virtually no chance of winning.

NBC carried the fight, with Marv Albert announcing at ringside, and it lasted the full twelve rounds. But Rodriguez was overwhelmed by Holmes, who won by unanimous decision.

"Lou DelVecchio knew Holmes," said Billy. "Don King knew about it and who was involved and stepped aside. Everyone else was wondering, 'What the fuck is going on. Scranton?' I gave Holmes a brand-new Admiral refrigerator, an A La Mode, which just hit the market, and it had an ice-cream maker. And he did a commercial for me in front of the A La Mode. When Don King found out Holmes got one, he called to say he wanted one."

It was the first and last championship fight ever held in Scranton.

Billy flew out to Leavenworth soon after and filled Russell in on the fight. He also sought his counsel on another idea. Billy wanted to get into the chicken business, and he sought a meeting with Paul Castellano, then the head of the Gambino Family.

Russell had known Castellano for years, going back to the 1950s, and Castellano was among those Russell invited to Apalachin. A protégé of Carlo Gambino, Castellano became the boss of that family following Gambino's death in 1976. But unlike Russell, Castellano flaunted his wealth. He even built an expansive home on Staten Island that was dubbed "the White House" for obvious reasons. But one of Castellano's main businesses was poultry. Two of his sons had a distribution company that provided chicken to many of the major supermarkets in the New York area, and Castellano also owned several neighborhood meat markets, including one on Avenue S in the blue-collar Marine Park section of Brooklyn.

"I wanted to sell chicken and I told Russell I wanted to meet with Castellano, but he said, 'Don't go. You're going to waste your time,'" said Billy. "Castellano was partners with Frank Perdue and got all the chicken that he needed from him."

Frank Perdue owned Perdue Farms, one of the largest suppliers of chicken in the nation. With his balding head, sharp nose, and folksy voice, Perdue became a national celebrity with an advertising campaign proclaiming, "It takes a tough man to make a tender chicken."

Russell told Billy that Perdue had been doing business with Castellano for years and that Castellano had been helpful to Perdue with union issues at his company.

"You'll never get a deal," said Russell.

Billy didn't try, even after Castellano and his bodyguard Thomas Bilotti were shot and killed outside of Sparks Steak House in New York in December 1985. Billy knew John Gotti, the capo behind the murder, who became the recognized leader of the Gambino Family. When Billy spoke to Russell on the phone about Castellano's murder, Russell didn't offer an opinion. He wasn't a fan of Big Paul.

"He never said anything about it one way or the other," said Billy. "But I'd become good friends with John."

With the chicken business a nonstarter, Billy found other opportunities.

He had been sought out by a local marketing consultant, Thomas Joseph, for help in obtaining printing contracts. Joseph guaranteed Billy $1,000 per week and a percentage of every contract he secured. Though he spent a lot of time in New York, Billy had his old Philadelphia contacts, and through them he was introduced to people in Atlantic City who got him appointments with several casinos. Printing contracts with Bally's and others soon followed, including one with the Republican National Committee. He and Joseph traveled to Washington, DC, for a ceremony at the White House, where Billy took a photo with President Reagan's chief of staff Donald Regan and the CIA director William Casey.

Billy was also doing work with Louis DeNaples. Since DeNaples acquired the Keystone landfill in the 1970s, he and Billy had become closer business associates, with DeNaples relying on Billy for various services, including protection from crime families in New York and New Jersey eager to get a piece of DeNaples's landfill. Among those was Carmine Franco, an associate of the Genovese Family and major garbage figure who had begun to consolidate the trash-hauling business from the New York metropolitan area down to Philadelphia and had tried to move in on DeNaples.

DeNaples asked Billy to intercede on his behalf, and once Franco and others learned that DeNaples was with Billy, they stayed away. Billy also collected on a debt owed by Franco to DeNaples.

Billy kept Russell abreast of everything he was involved in, and he always gave Carrie a piece of whatever he earned. She was surviving Russell's incarceration, attending Mass and visiting with her small circle of friends and family, as well as with Billy and Ellen. Their children were getting older, with Carolyn now a teenager. But they would join their parents for the visits, and Carrie welcomed them.

Nearing forty, Billy was emerging as an important figure. He had a knack for negotiating, and more and more he was being called in to help settle one thing or another, similar to what Russell had done for years. But his celebrity was expanding, and it caught the attention of a very large man from New York who spoke with a distinct voice.

At six feet one inch and over three hundred pounds, Robert Whitehead was an imposing figure with boundless energy and expensive tastes in everything from clothing to food. He spoke with a faux-British accent, was fluent in French, knew a little Italian, and also claimed to have attended Yale, though Yale had no record of his attending. An opera buff, Whitehead made large contributions to the Metropolitan Opera House at Lincoln Center and owned two private jet planes, a Falcon 50 and a Learjet. He also said he was from California, and had a wife and three children living on Staten Island.

Whitehead operated an investment business in midtown Manhattan but advertised himself as a loan broker who could close large business loans for those unable to secure traditional bank loans.

Whitehead knew a con man, Malcolm Lauer, whose talents lay in fleecing anyone for anything. Lauer had previously met Billy and their friendship had blossomed, and it was through Lauer that Billy was introduced to Whitehead, who was seeking someone of Billy's reputation.

Whitehead's firm, Banker's Trust, provided businesses with bridge loans of up to $6 million. He claimed to have a network of investors who would provide the funding for the short-term loans, but he required a deposit, usually 10 percent of the loan amount, or a letter of credit, to secure the loan. Most of the borrowers, typically businesses in distress and in desperate need of cash, could not obtain letters of credit. So they had to come up with a deposit.

"Mal wanted me to meet him and came with me," said Billy. "I asked Whitehead what did he need and he said he was looking for someone to give him credibility, and that if I came to his office I would probably help him get loans. For that, he would pay me $2,000 a week. He advertised in all the financial papers and magazines. But I found out pretty quickly he was just another con man. People would come see him and he'd say, 'My dear fellow, I will give you two million in three weeks.' But if you read the contract you had to give him $200,000 down on a $2 million loan. He'd take their money and when they'd call looking for the loan, he'd say it was held up for some fucking reason or another. Then, when they realized there was no loan, the only way they could try to get their money back was through arbitration, because it said it in the contract they had signed. These people don't read anything so they were fucked, and Whitehead just wanted me to protect him whenever he fucked up somebody."

In addition to the weekly salary, Whitehead offered Billy several carrots, including a suite at the Helmsley Palace and a limousine with a driver.

"He'd tell people I was his partner," said Billy. "But I said don't tell people I'm your fucking partner because I'm not your partner."

Partner or not, Billy enjoyed the hotel and, like Russell had for years, now stayed in New York from Sunday through Wednesday. In addition to the work he did for Whitehead, he continued with the jewelry business Russell had introduced him to so many years earlier in the Diamond District, and he met often with members of other New York families, including the new head of the Gambino Family, John Gotti.

"I asked John to do a big favor for me with a union in New Jersey, and he took care of it," said Billy. "So I sent him some money, five thousand, to say thanks. He sent the money back with a message: 'John says you're his friend. You don't take money from friends.' Classy guy."

Billy became a fixture at the Helmsley and had his own table at Harry's Bar, where he'd hold many of his meetings. One evening he arrived at Harry's to find that his table had been given to the actors Jack Klugman and Vic Tayback. The two men were friends, and Tayback had replaced Klugman in the Broadway play *Twelve Angry Men* when Klugman had to withdraw after having a polyp removed from his throat. Klugman had roles in many movies and starred along with Tony Randall in the popular television series *The Odd Couple*. Tayback was known nationally for his role as Mel on the CBS program *Alice*.

"I get there and they tell me there were some people at my table, a couple of actors and their friends, and I told them to get them the fuck out of there," said Billy. "So they say, 'Of course, Mr. D'Elia,' and someone goes up to them and tells them to get up, you're sitting at

Mr. D's table. They protested and they weren't happy about that. But they got up. I had a ball at the Helmsley."

And business with Whitehead, it turned out, was good, even better than Billy had envisioned. But he could not believe the number of gullible, and wealthy, individuals who would do business with him.

"One guy from Texas answered one of Whitehead's ads in one of those financial magazines and wanted to borrow twenty million dollars," said Billy. "That was the most ever. So Whitehead sent a jet for him and brought him to New York and delivered the contract stipulating the loan had to be backed by cash or letter of credit. Of course he gave him the cash, two million. Fucking insane."

With the suite at the Helmsley in New York, making routine trips to Philadelphia, and being called throughout the country to settle various disputes, Billy was rarely at home, which didn't sit well with Ellen. Making matters worse was Ellen's deep disdain for Whitehead.

She was home raising three children, and her marriage to Billy had reached a breaking point. During the little time he spent there, they always argued. When Whitehead called for Billy and Ellen picked up, there was nothing she wouldn't say to him to express her deep dislike for both of them.

"He would call and tell her that I was his 'best friend in his whole life,'" said Billy. "She'd just tell him, 'No, listen to me. Don't call here because I'm going to shoot him. I don't know how I'm going to do it. We're getting a divorce. Then I'm going to shoot him.' Whitehead would go, 'Dear lady, don't talk about my best friend like that!' and she'd hang up on him."

Whitehead was so infatuated with Billy he asked him to be the best man at his wedding, despite already being married with three children. Whitehead had a girlfriend and he wanted to buy her an engagement ring. So Billy took him to Forty-Seventh Street in the Diamond District.

"I take him down and he's looking at a ring that costs a hundred and twelve thousand dollars and goes, 'Oh, my girlfriend will love it!' I tell the salesman, 'Listen to me. He wants that ring. Do not put that ring in his hand until you have the fucking money in front of you. Got it? Because he's going to fuck you out of it, and then you're going to be looking at me. And when he gives you the money, make sure you count it three times.'"

The end for Billy and Robert Whitehead came over a weekend in Atlantic City. That Friday, Whitehead fleeced two lawyers from California after they gave him a check for $260,000 as a deposit for a loan. They thought that since they had given it to him after the banks had closed at three P.M. they had plenty of time to stop payment by Monday if they smelled something fishy. After they left, Whitehead called a bank where he and Mal Lauer had an outstanding loan for $60,000 and told the banker there he needed to cash a check. When the banker told him that the bank was closed, Whitehead said the check was for $260,000 and part of it would pay off the $60,000 loan.

"He says, 'My dear fellow, I was going to give you the sixty thousand dollars out of that for the loan we have with you,'" said Billy. "So now the greedy bank guy wants the money and is trying to figure out how to do it because the bank was closed. So what Whitehead had him do was write two one-hundred-thousand-dollar checks made out to Trump Plaza. He picks up the checks and calls Trump Plaza and says, 'This is Mr. Whitehead. I'm coming down with two hundred thousand that I want you to put in my account. I would like the helicopter to pick us up at the Thirty-Fourth Street Heliport.' We had Trump's jet helicopter pick us up right there. When we get to the casino he gives them the checks, but they wouldn't give him cash, just chips. So he has to take it all in chips and he'd play for ten or twenty minutes and then take two thousand in chips and go cash them. But he's down and it's late and we have to stop at four in the morning, so he decides to really start playing. He orders double-doubles of Dewar's and he's up like three hundred thousand. So now he has another bag of chips and he says, 'What do I do?' I said, 'You go right over there and cash the fucking things and give me my cut.'"

Billy took 20 percent, or $60,000.

They returned to New York on Sunday night, and the following morning Billy walked into the office, which was abuzz. Whitehead had been arrested.

"They go, 'Boy you missed it.' I said, 'What?' They said, 'Fucking nine cops came in and took Bob in handcuffs.' So I'm sitting there and Mal comes by and tells me that Bob's money he won in Atlantic City is in the safe by his desk and we should take it. Can you believe that fucking guy? Then, who comes walking in—the jeweler. I said, 'What are you doing here?' He said, 'Well, I know you told me, but Bob called me and it's his anniversary tonight and he wanted to surprise Joan Allen with this ring because he has a transfer coming tomorrow.' I just looked at him and said, 'How fucking stupid could you be.'"

After Whitehead was taken into custody on fraud charges, he called Billy's home seeking a favor: he needed someone to post bail.

But Ellen picked up the phone.

"I thought I had gotten rid of him," said Ellen. "He used to call our house—'My dear madam, my dear madam, I would need to speak to my friend.' But I didn't want anything to do with him and told him so. But then he called on our anniversary and said we had to bail him out. 'But, my dear madam, I need to speak to my friend right now!' I said, 'No, I threw him out. I'm divorcing him. I have nothing to do with him and I won't hear from him.' So he stopped calling me and bothering me. It was lies, I hadn't thrown Billy out. But he knew I was angry and I guess he thought I really did."

Whitehead eventually found Billy at the Helmsley and asked him to call a friend in Phoenix, Bill Falcon.

Falcon was another unwitting businessman taken in by Whitehead, who had the audacity to ask Billy to call Falcon to see if *he* would post his bail.

"I'm laughing inside thinking, 'Yeah, right,'" said Billy. "So I call Falcon and he says he doesn't like seeing anybody in jail. I told him I wasn't okaying it and this request wasn't coming from me, that it was between him and Whitehead. Would you believe that he not only bails him out, but Whitehead gets *another* hundred thousand dollars off him? Insane."

It was a couple of weeks later that Billy last saw his "dear friend." By then, he had already learned from the newspapers that Whitehead had been scamming people since the 1970s. So when Whitehead called him asking to come meet with him, Billy agreed. Sort of.

"He said I was his best buddy in his whole life and he had a briefcase with seventy thousand or something in it. I knew he had a red Mercedes convertible and he said he'd give that to me too. I'm thinking, 'Because I'll meet him?' I knew something wasn't right. He wanted to meet me at the Holiday Inn and I knew that the FBI always used the Holiday Inn when you're wired. So I'm supposed to meet him at noon there but I get in my car around ten and drive around the Holiday Inn. Sure enough, there was his fucking car in the back by the hotel. I never showed at noon. I knew it was a setup."

Whitehead pleaded guilty to brokering phony loans, but while awaiting sentencing he fled the country. Prosecutors followed him from Canada to Hong Kong to Greece and finally to Italy by tracking his credit card receipts. He was captured in Rome and spent eighteen months in prison there. Following his extradition he served more time in the United States.

Billy had told Russell about Whitehead and his crazy business dealings with him, but with each visit to Leavenworth, Russell appeared weaker and less interested. His health was waning and his mind didn't appear to be as sharp as it always had been. Russell had always been pleased to see Billy during his twice-a-month visits, but now, in his mideighties, the weight of wondering whether he'd die in prison was heavy. Russell wanted to be a free man again. Billy, as he always did, could only do his best to cheer him up and then get on a flight back home. But following this visit, tragedy awaited.

CHAPTER 13

Tookie

The police had set up a roadblock and were waiting for the dark green Buick sedan, which had raced through four boroughs with three police cars trailing it during a reckless fifteen-minute chase. It was around two A.M. when the car approached the roadblock at over seventy miles per hour. But instead of stopping, the car veered around to avoid the roadblock and the driver lost control. The car went off the side of the road and tumbled down a two-hundred-foot embankment. When it finally came to rest it had landed on its wheels but it was a wreck, the roof caved in on the passenger side. Inside were two occupants. The driver, Richard Amico, age thirty-six, was pronounced dead. His passenger, Shirley Osticco, forty-three, was rushed to the hospital in critical condition. She died there several hours later.

The death of Billy's sister Shirley devastated him. The only other time anyone had seen him cry was at his mother's funeral.

It was Shirley's marriage to Dave Osticco's son Anthony in 1966 that had led to Billy's first real introduction to Russell. But the marriage had disintegrated over time and the couple had divorced. Shirley and her sister, Peggy, moved into their own homes near Billy. Shirley's three sons moved in with her too, but one, Jimmy, suffered from a drug habit and had been missing.

The night of the crash, Shirley went to Anthony's restaurant in Old Forge, where she also worked part-time as a waitress. There, she bumped into Amico, whose family she had known for years.

They left together in his car, which matched the description of one that police were searching for as part of an investigation into the burning of several barns in the area. When an unmarked police car spotted them, Amico sped off for some reason and led police on a high-speed chase. When they searched the car after the crash, police found what they described as "drug residue," drug paraphernalia, and $450 in cash.

"Richie was giving her a ride home," said Billy. "He was a tough kid. They called him 'Richie Downtown.' But they decided to take a ride and look for her son Jimmy and they drove through the back mountain area, where someone was burning barns down. The police went to stop them and Richie took off and went over the cliff. Shirley really loved me, and she had her moments. She used to say, 'You're only who you are because of me!' or she'd go to Atlantic City and book a room and eat first-class and tell them to put it on my tab."

Shirley's death devastated Billy. But he didn't have much time to mourn.

In late February 1988 he received a call from a friend in Youngstown, Ohio, someone he had been building a personal and business relationship with for several years. Joey Naples was a soldier in the LaRocca Family in Pittsburgh, which had shared Youngstown with the Cleveland mob in an often-violent rivalry over the years filled with shootings, bombings, and dozens of murders.

A balding, slight man, "Little Joey" Naples owned the Youngstown Music and Vending Machine company and ran gambling operations in the city, among other things. He was the youngest of four brothers, of whom two had already met their untimely demises. The oldest, Sandy, had been shot to death with a girlfriend in 1960 on the front porch of her home. Two years later someone had placed dynamite in Billy Naples's car and blown him up.

Joey Naples had spent six months in prison on a gambling charge. As a repeat offender, it could have been a longer sentence, but his attorney Carmen Policy negotiated a plea deal. Naples's longtime attorney in Youngstown, Policy had headed west two years earlier to work as counsel for the San Francisco 49ers, which were owned by another Youngstown man and Policy friend, Edward DeBartolo.

Having traveled to Youngstown often, Billy had done business with Naples over the years. He liked Naples, and the two men became good friends. It was Naples whom Billy had called to help him collect a $200,000 gambling debt that DeBartolo owed to a Philadelphia bookie named Label.

"DeBartolo was a multimillionaire and a serious gambler, and Label calls and asks if I can get the money," said Billy. "So I call Joey and he makes a couple of calls and tells me to come meet him. So I go to Youngstown, pick up Joey, and we go to DeBartolo's offices. He and I go in the lobby and ask for so-and-so. They know who we are so they tell us to go to the money room. So we get in the elevator and go up and I get to see DeBartolo. He has a guy lead us into this room with guards and all this money in it. They come over with this brick of money wrapped in cellophane. It was like *this* big. We open it and there are two packages, each with one hundred thousand. We open those right there, count it, say goodbye, and I give it to Label."

But the matter didn't end there. Nicky Scarfo was the head of the Philadelphia family, having assumed control after the murder of Angelo Bruno and the turbulence that followed. A short, untrusting man who left a trail of bodies during his ascent to boss, Nicky had a problem, and he asked Billy to come to Philadelphia to help settle it.

"I got a message from Nicky and I'm sitting there with him and some of his guys and Label the bookie," said Billy, "and Nicky is saying that he's missing two hundred thousand from DeBartolo. I told him that I already picked it up. He was surprised and goes, '*You* got it? Where is it?' I look over at Label and I point to him and say, 'I gave it to *him*.' He never told Nicky I gave him the money."

Now Joey Naples called to say he needed Billy's help. He explained that he had a good friend who was Michael Jackson's manager. Everyone called him Tookie. His real name was Frank DiLeo, and he was a very successful music industry promotions executive who had worked with many of the top-selling bands and artists in the world, among them Jackson.

Tookie grew up in Pittsburgh, the son of a bookie, and was arrested himself for taking bets in the 1970s. He had been a senior executive at Epic Records and had worked with Jackson closely. So closely in fact that Tookie, who'd been given that name by his grandmother, left Epic to become Jackson's manager.

At just five feet two inches and over two hundred pounds, Tookie was a squat, heavyset man with slicked-back hair, a booming voice, boundless energy, and an ever-present cigar in his mouth. He had gotten his start in the music business in the 1960s and later became a promotions genius skilled at marketing as well as providing sufficient cash under the table to radio station executives and DJs to ensure his artists became stars. Tookie wore expensive suits and gaudy jewelry and intentionally gave off the distinct impression that he was "connected." Or at least he liked to tell people that. He had known Joey for years, and he used that friendship with the powerful Youngstown gangster as leverage in his career.

Billy already knew that Naples had some connection to Jackson. In 1984, Naples had secured twelve tickets for a Michael Jackson performance in Philadelphia by saying they were for his good friend Billy D'Elia, who was running the Bufalino Family while Russell was away. Tookie gladly obliged, and Billy used the tickets to celebrate his daughter Miriam's tenth birthday. He rented two limousines to take himself, Ellen, Miriam, and her friends to see the show.

During the 1980s there was no entertainer bigger than Michael Jackson. Tookie had guided his career into the stratosphere with the success in 1982 of his record-setting album *Thriller*. He followed that in 1987 with *Bad*, which included five number one singles.

Now at the height of his popularity, Jackson drew the interest of two threatening men from California, who called Tookie and told him in no uncertain terms that they were now his partners.

Tookie protested, saying he was already connected with a family back east, but their reply was swift and to the point.

"We don't give a fuck. You're with us now," they said.

Rattled, Tookie reached out to Naples, but neither Naples nor anyone in Pittsburgh had the stature to stop two high-ranking inter-lopers from California from demanding a share of the wealth from Tookie's relationship with Jackson.

So Naples reached out to Billy.

"Joey called me and said a couple of big, connected guys from the West Coast wanted a piece of Michael Jackson and were threatening Tookie," said Billy. "They told Tookie, 'From now on you're with us.' So Tookie got shaken up, called Joey, and Joey said the men were coming to New York for a meeting and he asked if I could step in and help him. He didn't know who the guys were, but I said sure."

Tookie was traveling to New York to attend the Grammy Awards, for which Jackson had received multiple nominations. Naples told him to book a suite at the Helmsley Palace. When Billy arrived, many of the staff stopped him to say hello, his several years there courtesy of Bob Whitehead still a fresh memory. When he arrived upstairs, Billy hugged and kissed Naples, who introduced him to Tookie. Despite the height difference—Billy was well over a foot taller—Billy liked Tookie immediately. He was successful, wasn't afraid to show it with the various gold and diamond rings on his fingers, and had that easy, familiar "street" persona that Billy clung to. But Tookie was nervous. These guys, he said, meant business, and there was no way he could have them involved with Jackson. Billy told him to relax. He'd handle it.

The men sat down to talk, but not long after the call came from downstairs that their guests had arrived. Billy picked up a newspaper and held it up to cover his face. When Tookie opened the door, the two men walked in and one yelled out, "My name is Mike Rizzi!"

Billy immediately recognized the voice and, with his head still buried in the newspaper, yelled out, "Didn't your name used to be Rizzitello?"

As Billy put the newspaper down to reveal himself, Rizzitello couldn't believe his eyes.

"Oh no, don't tell me it's you!" he yelled.

Mike Rizzitello hadn't seen Billy since 1981, when he was acquitted in the New York trial with Russell. He had immediately returned to Los Angeles, where he'd reassumed his position as a capo in the Milano Family and changed his name to Rizzi. He then sought permission to start his own family in California under the protection of the Gambinos in New York, but that idea was eventually dismissed and he ended up running his own crew under the Milanos and remained involved in a variety of entertainment-related schemes. He had just been let out of prison after violating his parole when he tried to extort money from the financier of the Mustang Club at the Santa Ana racetrack. That man was shot three times in the head but survived, and now Rizzi was attempting another bold shakedown, this time on Tookie.

After recovering from his shock at seeing Billy, Rizzi explained that Donald Trump had offered $1 million if he could get Jackson to perform at one of his casinos in Atlantic City. Tookie had already said no, explaining that Jackson never had and never would agree to perform at a casino anywhere. He said it again, this time emboldened by Rizzi's reaction to seeing Billy. Rizzi's posture immediately changed from demanding to begging.

"Mike was pleading with me to do the Trump casino," said Billy. "He kept saying, 'Please do me a favor. It's a million dollars.' But I said, 'How the fuck do you people think you can just grab somebody like that?' I told him that was never happening and to leave Tookie alone. He was with me."

Rizzi had brought another man with him, who was known as "Little Harry," a gangster who had once been shot seven times but survived the hit.

Dejected, Rizzi and Little Harry left the suite, and when the door closed behind them Tookie was ecstatic. He couldn't thank Billy enough. Billy said not to thank him yet.

"I told him and Joey to wait a little bit," said Billy. "Rizzi was just the front man. You watch. Someone else was going to come by, the guy that was really behind it. Sure enough, after about an hour there was another knock on the door, and I gotta say I was pretty surprised."

It was Eddie Sciandra, Russell's longtime consigliere, and he was accompanied by Little Harry.

Sciandra had served over a year in prison on the income tax charges and was now working several schemes within the entertainment business, which had always been his bread and butter. One involved MCA, the entertainment conglomerate. His 1981 tax conviction stemmed from his failure to report income from a company called North Star Graphics in New Jersey, which was involved in a false invoicing scheme, overbilling MCA for videocassette packaging.

"Eddie walked in and was all apologetic and said he didn't know that I was involved and he never would have sent Mike after Tookie if he did," said Billy. "But he said he had a guarantee from Trump of one million and he was begging me to get Jackson to do it. He said, 'Can you talk to him?' I told him the same thing I told Rizzi: There was no way. Michael Jackson will not play a casino. I said, 'Eddie, you can't get this guy.' He kept trying. He was a lot older than me and supposedly a lot smarter. And he was also fucking nasty, except for that day. Then he said there would be a nice piece in it for me. I said, 'No, he's not doing it. That's it.' Once Eddie realized it wasn't happening, he suddenly got more worried about me telling Russell. He knew what he did was wrong and he kept saying, 'Please don't tell Russell. Please don't tell him.' I said, 'Ed, don't worry about it, I won't. But don't ever come after Tookie and Michael Jackson again.'"

After Eddie left, Tookie was in awe of Billy. He had just told two powerful gangsters—Eddie Sciandra, the supposed acting head of the Bufalino Family, and Mike Rizzi, a leading member of the Los Angeles mob—to fuck off. But after witnessing Billy's exchange with Sciandra, Tookie realized who the acting head of the Bufalino Family really was. He cozied up to Billy and offered him a drink and a cigar, but Billy had something else in mind. It had been his plan all along.

"I told him to sit down, this wasn't over," said Billy. "I said, 'I just did you a favor, right? So now you're under my umbrella and I get a piece of what you make.' Tookie said fine and agreed to give me ten percent of everything he made with Jackson. Now Tookie could say he was with me and didn't have to worry about anyone else coming out of the woodwork, and I'm now Michael Jackson's co-manager."

The arrangement would prove to be lucrative.

As Jackson's manager, Tookie earned millions from a wide revenue stream that included record sales, live performances, and merchandising, legal and otherwise, as well as ticket scalping. And as Jackson's co-manager, Billy would get a piece of all of those revenues.

Jackson had just started the second leg of his *Bad* tour and after the Grammys was scheduled to play Madison Square Garden in New York, and then continue on to Kansas City and elsewhere.

Tookie already had a ticket-scalping operation in place in which he pulled a thousand choice seats from each concert and marked them up considerably, with people on the ground selling them at each venue.

But word quickly spread about what had happened in New York between Billy and Rizzi, and "friends" from around the country were calling Billy hoping to get in on the Jackson business.

One friend was Tony Civella from Kansas City, the son of the late boss Nick, who had passed away from cancer after spending a year with Russell in Leavenworth. Tony wanted one thousand tickets to an upcoming show in St. Louis, only he didn't want to pay for the tickets until after the concert. Tookie had a connected guy from Pittsburgh, Henry "Zebo" Zottola, who handled the ticket-scalping business for him, and Zebo told Tony that without any front money he'd need someone to vouch for him. So Tony called Billy.

"It was Nick Civella's kid," said Billy. "He said, 'Could you do me a favor?' I said, 'Get Zebo on the phone.' I knew him from Pittsburgh. He worked for Kelly Mannarino. I said, 'Zebo, give them the tickets. I'm responsible.' So he gave them the tickets."

Billy's first introduction to Michael Jackson was backstage at Madison Square Garden. Tookie introduced him as a security consultant, and they hit it off almost immediately. As the tour continued, Billy was a regular presence backstage, his fearsome appearance and jet-black hair casting a wide shadow of protection for Tookie, and for Michael. Michael would spend chunks of time talking to Billy, who could engage with anyone, including a superstar singer.

"We talked. He was a smart kid," said Billy. "He'd tell me about how he had been in show business all of his life and the fact that he never had a childhood. He said his father, Joe, would beat the fuck out of him. And he'd tell me how when he was growing up his father would put him on the stage, then take him in the back and beat him, and then put him back out there again. Want to talk about an abused kid? All he wanted was to be a kid again. So he wanted elephants or Ferris wheels or whatever. And he loved kids. He'd take maybe twenty kids from a hospital and take them someplace fun. He'd be like, 'Hey, kids, let's get a snow cone!' And all everyone did was wonder what he was doing. That kid was not—I'll bet five million dollars to one he did not abuse any kids and he was not a pedophile. He couldn't be. He was still a kid himself. Tookie did a good job for Jackson. They were like father and son. Tookie used to take him home and he'd stay at his house with him and his kids. Now, if you knew the guy was a pedophile, would you bring him home to play with your kids?"

Understandably, after spending time with Michael, Billy did not like his father, Joe Jackson. Billy thought he was nothing more than an opportunist who mooched off his own children.

"He was a real piece of shit," said Billy. "I chased him off along with Jackie Gordon, La Toya's boyfriend or agent or whatever the fuck he was. He owned strip malls in Vegas and strip joints there and in California. But his deal was he used to scam the credit card companies. Guys would come into his strip club and they'd juice up the bill by hundreds and even thousands. The trick was, who was going to complain? How are you going to explain to your company that you went to a strip joint? But he and Joe together were a terrible pair. Joe would criticize his kids, especially La Toya. He'd fuck with her head, just like he did with Janet Jackson and with Michael. Janet was absolutely fucking gorgeous. But Joe Jackson just fucked with them all. I had no use for him. He was always borrowing money from Michael. Joe was doing deals on the side, only he'd never pay anyone, so he went to Michael to bail him out. He'd come and say, 'Michael, I'm in trouble, I got to come up with two million.' So Michael would give him the money all the time. I told him, 'Don't bail him out anymore. Tell him to go fuck himself.' But he just couldn't do it. He didn't have it in him."

Since Russell's imprisonment in Leavenworth, the FBI had been paying more attention to Billy. They'd thought they had him with Bob Whitehead's arrest in New York, but Billy was never charged. When they learned about his new relationship with Michael Jackson, they began to search into Tookie's finances and questioned him about a $100,000 check he had given to Billy. Tookie told them that Billy was a "consultant."

"Tookie comes to meet me at the Woodlands and tells me about the FBI and that they told him that was a lot of money to pay a consultant. He tells me he agreed with them, that it was a lot of money," said Billy. "I take him out to the upper parking lot and I tell him, 'Tookie, I love you like a brother, but if you fell off this parking lot right now and died I'd go get a cheeseburger and sit on your dead body and eat it.' He got the message."

But Billy's tenure with Michael Jackson lasted only a year. In 1989, Michael fired Tookie. *Bad* sold twenty million copies, which would have been an incredible success for any artist, except for Michael Jackson, who thought it should have sold one hundred million copies. Despite their great success together, and close ties, Michael let him go.

"Michael was hanging out with David Geffen and Geffen was telling him he should act or some bullshit, which was what Michael wanted to do," said Billy. "So he didn't think Tookie could help him with that and that was it."

Tookie was devastated by the sudden betrayal, and his anger was amplified when he was told by Michael's representatives that he would not receive any of the millions owed to him. So Tookie again turned to Billy.

"Jackson's lawyer was giving Tookie the runaround," said Billy. "So I went to a hotel in Universal City with Tookie to meet with Jackson and one of his lawyers and I arranged for Tookie to get paid. They owed him five million and we got it all. And I got five hundred thousand out of that. But Tookie wasn't happy. He wanted him back, but then he got a call from Martin Scorsese, who wanted him to play a gangster in a film he was doing with Robert De Niro called *Goodfellas*, and Tookie said yes. So that took his mind off of Jackson for a while."

Russell Bufalino, circa 1930.

Russell (second from left) at the Volpe Coal Company, circa 1935.

Charles Bufalino (center, seated) and a balding Santo Volpe (rear, behind table) were the original "Men of Montedoro" who controlled organized crime in northeast Pennsylvania. Russell (right) would eventually gain control of the crime family and become one of the most powerful Mafia leaders in the nation. His friends Philip Medico (left, next to Charles) and Philip's brother William (behind Philip, with glasses) owned U.S. defense contractor Medico Industries but were said by the FBI to be capos in the Bufalino family.

Billy with his father, William, 1958. Their relationship never healed.

Russell's cousin and Teamsters general counsel William Bufalino with Jimmy Hoffa in 1962. Russell's placement of William with Hoffa in the 1940s was a masterstroke that for decades gave Russell immense influence within the Teamsters and control over its powerful Central States Pension Fund.

Billy (center) with Russell and garage owner Jimmy Aita (left), 1968. A former mechanic, Russell loved to work on cars.

Russell having a laugh at a banquet, circa 1970.

Angelo Bufalino with Billy at the first Italian American Civil Rights League, Chapter 34, Wilkes-Barre dinner, November 1971.

(Left) James Caan with actress Jackie Forrest and Russell. Caan, who portrayed Sonny Corleone, stayed with Russell and Billy throughout the filming of *The Godfather* in 1971 while Russell also tutored Marlon Brando on the finer points of being a don. (Right) Russell's outsized influence on the film also secured the coveted role of Johnny Fontaine for crooner Al Martino (with Carrie and Russell at their home in Kingston, Pennsylvania).

Russell arriving in Philadelphia for his deportation to Italy in 1973 with attorney Jim Moran (left), Angelo Bufalino (rear), and Billy (right). Russell had Billy pack the suitcase with forty pounds of toilet tissue to take to Italy, but he didn't need it after receiving a last-minute reprieve, when the Italian government refused to accept him.

Russell with Frank Sinatra and Colombo Family captain Andy Russo (left) during the filming of the TV movie *Contract on Cherry Street*. Sinatra paid proper respect to Russell, as did everyone else.

Russell ordered Frank Sheeran, enraged over Hoffa's murder, to promise Anthony "Tony Pro" Provenzano (left, with Jimmy Hoffa) and Anthony "Fat Tony" Salerno (right) he wouldn't harm them during a sit-down at the Vesuvio in New York City. But Billy knew Provenzano and Salerno wouldn't have moved on Hoffa without Russell's approval.

Andy Griffith with Billy in an Exeter, Pennsylvania, pizza shop following Griffith's appearance at an Italian American Civil Rights dinner in 1977.

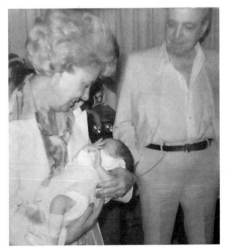

Carrie and Russell with Billy's son, Russell, at his christening, 1977. Childless, the couple doted on Billy's three children.

Billy with Russell at Leavenworth prison in 1986. Unbeknownst to law enforcement, Billy ran the Bufalino Family while Russell was imprisoned.

His health failing, Russell was transferred from Leavenworth to the medical center for federal prisoners at Springfield, Missouri, where he would meet up again with Frank Sheeran.

Russell with Ellen D'Elia and daughters Carolyn (left) and Miriam (right) after his return home from prison in 1989.

Billy backstage with Michael Jackson and manager Frank DiLeo ("Tookie") in Pittsburgh, 1988. Donald Trump offered the mob $1 million to lure Jackson to perform in Atlantic City, but Billy's intervention on behalf of DiLeo scuttled that effort and also earned him a lucrative role as Jackson's co-manager.

Billy with Bob Hope backstage at the Westchester Premier Theater, 1991. Billy had known the legendary Hope for many years and had his phone number in his personal address book.

Billy escorting his daughter Carolyn at her wedding in 1999. Firmly established as the head of the Bufalino Family, Billy threw a lavish affair with guests that included gangsters and judges alike.

Billy's son, Russell, (center) cared for Carrie Bufalino during the final years of her life. Carrie refused to read Frank Sheeran's 2004 book, and upon her death in 2006 she left her home and estate to Russell.

Father Joseph Sica with Russell and Billy (left) in the early 1980s, and with Louis DeNaples (right) attending a Pennsylvania gaming board hearing in 2006. Both Sica and DeNaples were charged with perjury for denying they knew Russell and Billy.

Billy with Detour (left), a member of the Mongols motorcycle club, at the federal prison in Tucson, Arizona, 2010. Angered after learning that Louis DeNaples put Billy's life in danger by alleging he was a government informant, Detour sought the contract to kill DeNaples, but Billy said no to him and to similar requests from several organized crime figures.

Billy sitting at Russell's old desk, December 2021. Furious over Russell's portrayal in Martin Scorsese's 2019 film *The Irishman*, and knowing the truth behind Frank Sheeran's claim that he killed Jimmy Hoffa, Billy finally decided to tell his story.

CHAPTER 14

Coming Home

For six years Billy had faithfully continued the twice-monthly trips to Leavenworth, and with each visit he could see that Russell was a little weaker and more feeble.

When he'd ask Russell how he felt, Russell would get angry, wave his hand, and tell him to mind his business. As far as Russell was concerned, he was still a bull.

But Billy knew that was far from the truth, and he wasn't surprised when he received an urgent phone call saying that Russell had had a stroke.

Deep into his eighties, Russell had endured the rigors of prison life. Leavenworth was no Danbury, where a few bucks to the guards provided a regular diet of good food and a comfortable existence. In Kansas, prison was prison, with no favors from the guards there. Other inmates stepped up to take care of him, getting Russell extra ice cream from the commissary, one of his favorite treats. But Russell spent weeks, months, and years in his cell reading books and magazines, whatever he could get his hands on, and calling Billy daily on the phone.

If there was anything remotely pleasant about Leavenworth, it was Billy's visits twice a month. But even that contact was limited.

Unlike Danbury, where they could sit next to each other unimpeded, at Leavenworth they sat across from each other under the observation of a guard. They'd share banalities until they thought no one was listening; then they would get into business.

"Russell was still Russell, even with the health issues," said Billy. "Who's doing what here, who did that there, who was paying this. Georgie Forrest, a big-time bookie under Russell's umbrella, was still providing him a thousand a week. And I always gave him a piece of whatever I made. But we'd go back and forth and he'd send me to New York for a couple of things, like pick up ten grand from a guy, or send me to Miami for some matter, or down the road to Kansas City to meet with Nick Civella's kid, Tony. And I'd fill Russell in on everything. He got a kick about Michael Jackson, but I never told him about Eddie Sciandra. Why aggravate him? But by then I was relying more on my guys, people like Wally and Kooch, and less on his."

Billy had always remained close to his childhood friends. Wally had become a bookie and, in the mid-1980s, a Pittston Township supervisor. Kooch was a successful business owner. Among his holdings were several strip clubs in the region. They were both Bufalino Family associates, men Billy brought closer to him as those in Russell's circle either were imprisoned or died.

Dave Osticco was officially "retired" following his release from prison after serving less than three of eight years for fixing Louis DeNaples's trial, while Guvy Guarnieri, Russell's capo in Binghamton, was serving two years on weapons and counterfeiting offenses.

But the biggest blows came with the deaths of Cappy Giumento and Carrie's cousin Angelo Sciandra. They both died in 1987, one month apart, of natural causes.

Cappy was awaiting trial following his indictment two years earlier by a federal grand jury in Scranton on forty-five counts of mail fraud. He was seventy-five and prosecutors said he had been collecting "black lung" benefits totaling nearly $20,000 over the past five years. He originally filed a claim in 1970 under the Coal Mine Health and Safety Act of 1969, which provided benefits to sickly miners. Cappy claimed he had worked underground for eleven years, but he never had the crippling black lung disease, which restricted breathing and in many cases caused death. He had actually collected over $40,000 in total, but the five-year statute of limitations prevented prosecutors from charging him on anything before 1980.

Angelo, the son of Carrie's cousin and the former boss John Sciandra, was a musician by trade, a trumpeter, and had his own orchestra. But he and Russell also went back many years, sharing ownership during the 1950s of several dress factories, and as a made member of the family, he'd attended and been arrested at the Apalachin meeting. A photo of Russell, Angelo, and Dave sitting and smiling at their arraignment had been featured in newspapers across the country.

As Russell's world got smaller, the power dynamic between him and Billy changed. Russell remained an influential figure, but in name only as the younger generation of gangsters rose to take their place in the world.

And while the government remained virtually clueless as to Billy's rising stature, he was already recognized by his peers as the acting boss of the Bufalino Family. Billy would never suggest it, but Russell was seen by many as his chief adviser.

"Over the years I'd go to Kansas City or L.A. or Philly, and there came a time when it wasn't about me being Russ's son doing his bidding anymore," said Billy. "Things started to change when Russell went away the second time and guys were comfortable dealing with me. I had their ears, and they had mine. And then when Russell got sick, it was pretty much all on me."

Russell had diabetes, and its crippling effects continued to worsen. By 1988 he was clearly suffering, and it did not go unnoticed.

"He had a stroke, but he wouldn't tell anybody," said Billy. "Tino Fiumara, he was the boss of the Genovese Family. He was doing time there and called me and said, 'Billy, you have to get him the fuck out of here.' He says he's limping and is slurring his words. He thinks he had a stroke. So my wife writes the prison system. She got the lady, a lady warden, and said, 'You get him to the hospital!' They moved him to Springfield, Missouri. He's eighty-five and sick but they put shackles on him and ran a chain wrapper around him, put a lock on it, and threw him in the back of a van and brought him to the hospital."

Billy and Ellen flew out to the federal medical facility in Springfield and immediately went to see Russell. He looked terrible. He had lost weight, his skin was a sickly white and pasty, and he had a large black-and-blue bruise on his forehead.

"They said he hit his head in the bus going there," said Billy.

Billy and Ellen remained in Springfield for a week. Before they left, Russell's attorneys filed paperwork seeking his early medical release from prison. As that request was considered, Russell's health improved. After a few weeks he was out of the hospital bed but relegated to a wheelchair. Still, it was a great improvement from Leavenworth. The food was better, as were the overall conditions. His spirits were also elevated when he learned that Anthony Salerno and Frank Sheeran were patients there too.

"He was using a wheelchair now to get around," said Billy. "It was better for him there at Springfield. He liked eating ice cream and playing bocce with some of the other guests that were there. Fat Tony was there. He had cancer. And Frank Sheeran was there. He had been somewhere in Minnesota where it was fifty below and his arthritis had kicked up and he couldn't move around, so he was reunited with Russell. They were always close, so it was good he had Frank there with him."

Their reunion would be short-lived. In May 1989, Russell's medical release was approved. After a seven-year incarceration, he was coming home.

Billy and Ellen made preparations to fly to Missouri, while Carrie remained home to prepare for Russell's homecoming. Aside from replenishing the house with food, she sought to insulate him from a prying press. That included extending all the window curtains and soaping the garage door windows so no one could see Russell when he arrived home and exited the car.

"We got the call that he was being released, so me and my wife and a kid from Pittsburgh, Panfilo Dicenzo, flew out there," said Billy. "We get a private jet and fly out to this little airport that was closed. There were no lights on but we landed anyway. We get to the hotel and Russell calls me and says to be here at seven A.M. sharp. I rented a Lincoln and we get there at seven in the morning and the guard says, 'State your business.' I say, 'I'm here to pick up a prisoner.' He tells me to come back at nine. I said, 'You don't understand, he told me to be here at seven.' The guard says, 'You don't understand. If you don't come back at nine, he'll stay here forever.'"

Billy did what he was told and returned at nine A.M. When he and Ellen entered the prison Russell was there sitting in his wheelchair accompanied by several prison guards. After he had served seven difficult years of a ten-year sentence, freedom was on the other side of the metal door. But Russell didn't want to go, not yet. He turned to Billy. "Tell them I want my walker."

"What?" said Billy, a bit taken aback.

"Tell them I want my fucking walker," said Russell.

An old friend from Philadelphia, Mike Marone, had been treated there, and before he was released, he had given Russell his walker.

"Tell them I want my fucking walker. Mike Marone gave me his walker," said Russell.

One of the guards told Russell that the walker belonged to the government, but Russell wouldn't have it.

"No, Mike gave it to me when he left. I'm taking that with me!" he insisted.

"They're going to ship you the walker," said Billy, who wanted to get Russell into the car and to the waiting jet.

"I'm telling you they took my fucking walker!" yelled Russell.

"You got nine walkers at home. And if you don't like them I'll get you a new one. What are you worried about?" said Billy.

Russell didn't want to hear it. He was too old and weak to punch Billy, so he grabbed his arm, leaned over, and tried to bite it.

Billy pulled his arm away. "Take it easy, Russ."

"If I don't get my fucking walker, I'm not leaving!" he yelled.

Ellen, watching and listening in disbelief, leaned into Russell's ear.

"Listen, you old fucker," she said. "Do you know how long we've been waiting for you to come home? You think I'm not going to leave here with you over a walker?"

Russell demurred. Ellen always did that to him. Even the guards were impressed. "This is the first time I ever had somebody say they didn't want to go home," said one.

Russell left the prison with twenty-seven dollars cash, a final parting gift from the government.

Once he was inside the Lincoln, Russell's mood changed for the better. He was finally free. He held Ellen's hand, and after they had boarded the plane, Ellen got him comfortable in his seat with a blanket over his lap.

"Russ, I have to go into the ladies' room and I'll be right out, okay?" she said softly.

Russell reached into his pants pocket and pulled out the twenty-seven dollars he had been given and handed it to Ellen.

"Don't forget to tip the attendant," he said.

The flight home was pleasant. Russell spoke Italian with Panfilo, an Italian crooner by trade. After landing at the Avoca airport between Scranton and Wilkes-Barre, the plane taxied into a newly built private hangar, where Billy's maroon Lincoln Town Car was waiting. Russell was placed in the rear next to Ellen with Panfilo in the front.

Russell turned to Ellen. "Guess who's showing up with his three bodyguards."

He gazed out the window at the familiar and not-so-familiar landscape as the car traveled down the highway. When they turned the corner to Russell's home they were met with a large contingent of reporters waiting across the street. Billy turned onto the short driveway and reporters ran up to the sides of the car barking out questions. Russell ignored them as the garage door opened.

After they pulled in, and once the garage door closed, Russell was slowly led out of his car and into his home, where he embraced Carrie and held Billy's children, Carolyn, Miriam, and Russell, who'd been brought there by their babysitter, Marianne. Russell barely recognized them.

He sat in his favorite lounging chair in the living room but remained quiet, perhaps morose. He had endured a terrible ordeal, something he'd never expected this late in his life. And whether he wanted to admit it or not, returning home would require an adjustment.

"After a few hours some people came to visit him. Angelo came, and then a couple of friends," said Billy. "[With] people he wanted to see, he turned on like a switch and was all excited, asking what was going on, how's the business, all of that. But if someone came in that he thought was a phony, he was comatose. He'd close his eyes and pretend he was sleeping. We had a couple of those."

Over the next few days the phone wouldn't stop ringing. Friends from New York, Philadelphia, Binghamton, and elsewhere called. But Carrie told them flat out they couldn't speak to or see him and to never call there again. As far as she was concerned, Russell's old life was dead.

"She was afraid he'd be arrested again," said Billy. "Georgie Forrest wanted to come see him. When Russell went away he would send her cash every week. I told her that Georgie wanted to come by and she said, 'Absolutely not! Are you crazy? He's a felon! I don't want felons in my house!' I said, 'What the fuck you think we are?'"

But Russell wanted to see certain people, a handful of men from

New York, so Billy quietly made arrangements for them to visit with Russell in the Poconos. The location was a breakfast place off Route 611 in Swiftwater.

"I told them we'd go to a pub for drinks but the only place that was open was a place called Ham and Eggs in a Pan," said Billy. "We all go in and Russell says, 'Let's have a drink.' Only the waitress says they don't serve liquor. Russell looks at me and yells out, 'What the fuck kind of place did you take me to?' He may have lost a bit physically, but there was nothing wrong with his mind or voice."

The visit with his old friends from New York was the last one he'd ever have with them. Carrie wasn't wrong in trying to keep her husband from talking to or seeing anyone who was a convicted felon. His probation demanded it. So moving forward, no matter how irascible Russell would be, after Swiftwater, Billy honored Carrie's wishes.

With no one to visit, Russell fell into semi-retirement and his thoughts soon diverted away from business. He even surprised everyone when he hinted that he wanted to attend Mass. At Leavenworth, whether it was the harsh nature of the prison or Russell's advanced age, he had sought out a priest. Instead he'd gotten a nun.

Sister Margaret Mary "Peg" Driscoll was from Brooklyn, and despite her best efforts, she could not get rid of her distinct accent. Russell, who had spent much of his adult life in New York, recognized it immediately.

Sister Peg worked as a deputy juvenile officer in Kansas City and then focused her work on child welfare and criminal justice, victims and offenders alike. At Leavenworth, she counseled prisoners. Drawn to her familiar accent and kind manner, Russell met regularly with Sister Peg, and it was through those conversations that he finally found religion.

"She was the nun in prison and Russell loved her," said Billy. "They talked about religion and spiritualism. He loved her so much he called me one day from prison and told me to buy her a car. So I went out and bought her a car."

Now that he was home, Carrie arranged for a parish priest to visit on occasion to give Russell Communion. On Saturday mornings Angelo drove Russell to Billy's house, where he'd have breakfast with Ellen and the kids, then go sit out back with Billy and talk business.

"I still filled him in on what I was doing, talked to him about situations, who I was meeting with, things like that," said Billy. "If I told him I was going to New York, he'd ask who I was going to see and then tell me to send them his regards."

Billy's children, now all teenagers, had looked forward to Russell's weekly visits years earlier after he left Danbury. Sometimes he'd be late for breakfast, to the consternation of Ellen, who prepared his cantaloupe and blueberries.

"The kids were saying they're not going to eat until Papa comes, and Ellen told the kids that if Papa didn't show up soon she was going to shove these blueberries up his ass," said Billy. "So as soon as he walked in they said, 'Papa, it's a good thing you're here. She's going to shove those blueberries right up your ass.'"

Now that the kids were older, sometimes Angelo would drive Russell just to see them. Russell would wait out in the car and they'd come to him. Or Miriam would pick him up in her Mustang and take him out to get some strawberry ice cream.

"He was supposed to cut down on the ice cream, but they'd come back and it would be on his shirt," said Billy.

Russell remained devoted to Billy's children. He and Carrie were there for each of their birthdays, and Billy and his family would go to Russell's house for occasions like Carrie's birthday. For Christmas, Russell and Carrie would stop by Billy's to exchange gifts, but they always had Christmas dinner at the home of her cousins, the Sciandras.

But one close friend Russell couldn't visit or speak with was Dave Osticco. His former underboss had been home for little more than two years after serving only two and a half years of the eight-year sentence he had received for tampering with the Louis DeNaples jury. Few people were closer to Russell. From their introduction after Dave's first arrest at seventeen for running beer for William Medico in 1930, Dave had been at Russell's side as he built the Bufalino empire. There were the trips to Cuba, their arrests at Apalachin, the arms sales from Medico Industries, and of course Dave's changing the course of Billy's life with the suggestion that he put an eight-track tape player in Russell's car.

"Don't let my *goombadi* ruin you!" Dave always said.

Russell couldn't even visit when Dave was being treated for chronic lung disease in Wilkes-Barre General Hospital.

Dave died January 25, 1990. Russell and Carrie sent flowers but didn't attend the funeral.

CHAPTER 15

Making Do

For the entirety of Russell's incarceration Billy had managed to keep much of the Bufalino Family business off the radar of the press and of law enforcement.

Every now and then there would be a news article, like the one in a Pittsburgh newspaper that said he was now considered a "key member" of the Bufalino Family who enjoyed a "comfortable relationship" with John LaRocca and the Pittsburgh family.

Or when he was subpoenaed by the Pennsylvania Crime Commission, which described Billy as a major link between at least two mob families, to testify about a prison project in Philadelphia at which he had a no-show job as a night watchman. It was part of a deal with the Scranton construction company GTI-Superior Inc., which had won the contract for the $6.5 million job. The firm sought to prevent threatened labor difficulties from a competitor. Billy had even had the construction superintendent go out to Leavenworth to talk to Russell personally.

Billy got involved as a favor to Philadelphia boss Nicky Scarfo. A commission inspector and former FBI agent said phone records showed that during the four months of the prison labor issue, there were 153 calls between Leavenworth prison and Billy's home. Prison records confirmed it was Russell who made those calls. Billy said there was another reason for all the chatter.

"He talked to Ellen and the kids half the time," said Billy.

Billy refused to testify and fought the subpoena all the way to the Pennsylvania Supreme Court, which, surprisingly, ruled in his favor in 1988. But the press coverage was by far the most he had ever received.

Video poker and gambling were among the mainstays of the family, and with those pursuits Billy had been spending more time in Atlantic City, New Jersey. The South Jersey shore town had fallen into neglect and hard times in the years after its pre–World War II heyday. To reverse the decline, state officials had legalized gambling in 1976 with the hope that it would bring wealth and opportunity.

The casinos soon followed. Resorts International, Caesars Boardwalk Regency, Bally's Park Place, Harrah's, and the Golden Nugget were among the first to open, and tourists and gamblers flocked to them.

Billy had already infiltrated the casinos by obtaining printing contracts for his friend Thomas Joseph's firm Markdata, and he had become a familiar figure on the casino floors. He had his own cabal of dealers, waitresses, security personnel, and others to tip him off to potential scores. He even brought Ellen down to join him for long weekends, and together they'd pick out a five-dollar slot machine and take turns playing it until it paid out. And it usually did; they'd often come home with thousands in winnings.

But Billy's hulking presence drew plenty of attention, and there were often requests for assistance. One came from Leonard Tose, a debonair former owner of the Philadelphia Eagles.

Often spotted at the baccarat table at Resorts, Tose, now in his seventies, was a trucking company magnate who had been a minority owner of the Eagles until he bought the team outright in 1969 for $16 million, then the highest amount ever paid for a professional sports franchise.

The team had little success until 1980, when it lost in the Super Bowl to the Oakland Raiders. But as much as Tose loved the Eagles, he loved to gamble even more. The only problem was, he wasn't any good at it. By the late 1980s he had lost his team, which he had sold in 1985 to pay off gambling debts. He then lost millions more in the New Jersey casinos. When he needed a boost, he turned to Billy.

"He used to walk around with an assistant who carried cash in a duffel bag," said Billy. "One time he was playing baccarat and was down four hundred thousand and said he had to go to the bathroom. But on his way to the bathroom there's a craps table and he loses four hundred thousand there before he comes back. He had a big gambling problem, but whenever he needed money he came to see me. He took me up to his room at the casino and he says, 'Here's my deal, Billy.' He got a million-dollar insurance policy when he sold the Eagles and he said he'd sign it over to me. I said, 'Yeah, okay, whatever.' He never had to. He'd lose his shirt, but he always paid me. One time when he gave me a big check he wanted to do a toast. Classy guy. Years earlier he met this girl. She was with the Eagles cheerleaders and she was gorgeous and half his age. So he sent her a yellow Rolls-Royce and two hundred dozen yellow roses and he proposed to her. They get married, but then she runs away on him and marries the president of Resorts, where he had lost a lot of his money. So he ended up broke with them and lost a wife there."

While Atlantic City was fertile ground, opportunities continued to come from elsewhere, including one deal to gain control of the multimillion-dollar fireworks market in New York City.

A business in Youngstown had been importing fireworks from China and selling them around each July Fourth holiday. Business was so good, the owner, known as Bruce, was forced to build a huge warehouse. But each state had different fireworks laws. They were legal in Pennsylvania but only available for sale to out-of-state residents. Since fireworks were illegal in New York and New Jersey, some of those residents would drive into Pennsylvania and visit places up and down the Delaware River, such as the Delaware Water Gap, Easton, and New Hope, and fill their cars and trucks.

But the vast majority of buyers in the New York metro purchased their fireworks from local street dealers who were given their merchandise by organized crime figures who drove trucks to Youngstown. The constant back-and-forth between Ohio and New York proved burdensome, so Joey Naples called Billy to see if he could find a facility in Pennsylvania to store them as a drop-off point.

"I went to New York and talked to John Gotti," said Billy. "He didn't think there was much there in fireworks, maybe ten grand here, ten grand there. I said, 'John, they purchase nine million every year.' I told him, 'We're going to do this, and I'm going to tell this guy Bruce in Ohio that he can't sell fireworks to New York or anywhere else unless they come directly through us.'"

Billy drove to Youngstown with Eddie Lino, a close friend and one of Gotti's capos, and Sally Scalzo, another Gotti soldier, and they told Bruce in no uncertain terms that they were taking over his fireworks business. From now on, they told him, he couldn't sell to anyone other than Scalzo, who would serve as point man.

"We cut out every other guy in New York," said Billy. "We made a lot of money on fireworks that year. It was better than being a banker. But then we found out that guy Bruce in Ohio was doing side deals. So we taxed him, told him he had to pay us three hundred thousand, and he did. I took half and Sally took the other half. It was a great business, and we made millions. But then those things with Eddie and Joey happened."

Eddie Lino had just been acquitted in a federal trial in which he had faced charges that he was a major heroin supplier. One of Gotti's closest confidants, he had struck up a friendship with Billy, and they socialized whenever Billy was in New York. In November 1990, they planned to meet for dinner in Brooklyn. Billy would meet him at the Mother Cabrini society, where Lino would pick him up and they'd go for dinner at Fiorentino's restaurant down on Avenue U in the Gravesend neighborhood near Sheepshead Bay. But it was Election Day in New York City, so Lino called Billy to suggest they meet the following day. Billy said fine. Lino got into his car and that night his Mercedes was found on the service road off the Belt Parkway in Brooklyn. Lino was in the driver's seat slumped over, shot multiple times in the head and chest.

"Eddie called me. He said, 'Billy, it's election night. Why don't we wait until tomorrow. Come here tomorrow,'" said Billy. "I said okay. I find out the next day that he was killed. I was supposed to be in the car with him."

Billy would learn that Lino had been killed by two New York City police detectives, Stephen Caracappa and Louis Eppolito. The so-called Mafia Cops had both been doing work, mostly hits, for various gangsters for years. They had forced Lino off the Belt Parkway; walked up to him, one on each side; and opened fire. Lino was shot nine times. His murder was in retaliation for Gotti's 1985 execution of Paul Castellano.

Lino and Billy had been doing a lot of business together. They had met years earlier during a meeting in New York with several of Gotti's crew over a union problem. Among those there was Sammy "the Bull" Gravano, whom Billy didn't warm to. He and Lino were close, and between Lino's murder and yet another federal prosecution against Gotti, Billy decided it would be healthier and wiser to spend less time in New York, which gave him more time to spend with Joey Naples.

Billy traveled to Youngstown at least twice a week, partly to conduct business for Russell, who still had old ties that produced thick envelopes, but mostly to visit with Naples. Between Michael Jackson, the Eddie DeBartolo gambling money, the fireworks business, and a host of other scams and scores, the two men did well together. Now Joey had another idea. He wanted to sell Billy's "Family Jewels."

Billy had kept a large, diamond-studded ruby necklace and diamond-studded ruby ring under his and Ellen's bed for years. They were such an ostentatious display, resembling the type of jewels a royal family would wear. So Billy's family dubbed them the "Family Jewels." Billy guessed they were worth close to $400,000, but Ellen thought they were so outrageously gaudy she didn't want them and tried for years to convince Billy to sell them. He wouldn't—until he received a call from Joey Naples.

"He says, 'You still have those things?' and I says yeah. I said, 'If you're going to sell them, then anything you get we split.' It was a good deal. So he said, 'Can you send them to me?' and I said, 'Absolutely.' So I put them in a box and I get one of the guys from around here and put him in the car and tell him to go to Youngstown. Go to the Ramada. You know the guy, the little guy, Joey. Go and see him and just give this to him. So he did. That was on a Friday. On Monday night I'm down at the Woodlands watching a game and I get a phone call and it's Tookie."

The release of *Goodfellas* in 1990 made Tookie a celebrity. He played the role of cab stand owner Tuddy Cicero, and with his background and knowledge of the various gangsters he knew in real life as well as his brash personality, he was a natural for the part. But Tookie wasn't calling about the movie. He was distressed and screaming into the phone.

"He's gone!" said Tookie.

"Gone?" said Billy. "Who's gone?"

"Joey."

"What?"

"Joey. He's gone."

"What the fuck are you talking about?"

"He's gone. Dead. They shot him."

Billy still didn't understand. "Shot who, Naples?"

"Yeah," said Tookie. "A sniper took him out on a road by his house."

Joey Naples was building a new home in a rural suburb of Youngstown. He had taken Billy to see it once. The palatial home was on a property that was across from a cornfield. Billy didn't think much of the cornfield.

Naples had emerged from the house about eight P.M. and as he approached his Ford Mustang, which belonged to Tookie, someone hiding in the distance among the cornstalks took aim with a high-powered rifle and shot him in the chest and lower back, killing him instantly.

"It was a sniper," said Tookie. "Someone took a contract out on Joey."

Naples had been with the Pittsburgh family since the early 1960s, and among all the friends that Billy claimed to be close with, aside from Wally and Kooch, there was no one closer than Naples.

"Joey was someone I really liked," said Billy. "They said it was from that old war Youngstown was having with Cleveland, that it was ordered by this guy Lenny Strollo. But the guy that shot him was close to Joey. So I also heard something else, that it had to do with Joey cheating with the guy's wife. Whatever the reason, I know they killed the guy that did it. He was on the highway getting off the Youngstown exit and a car stopped in front of him, another car stopped behind him, and when he got out to see what was going on they blazed him."

In the aftermath of Naples's murder, Billy was counseled by many in Pittsburgh and Youngstown and back home against attending the wake. The FBI would be watching from the outside, and gangsters eager to point fingers at the people responsible for Naples's death made it hostile and unsafe.

Billy wouldn't have it and put out the word that he was coming, but paying his respects to his dear friend wasn't the reason he drove to Youngstown.

"I'm thinking about the jewels," said Billy. "I don't know who got them. I'm thinking he must have sold them to somebody or gave them to somebody. So I go to the funeral parlor for the wake and there's a long line to get in. As I'm walking around outside I'm looking at everyone's neck to see who had them, and the same when I go inside. I never saw them again."

The following April, John Gotti stood trial in New York for five murders and was found guilty and put away for life, done in by the testimony of his once-loyal hit man Sammy Gravano. The fireworks business was over.

"Eddie got killed, then Joey got killed and John went to prison. That was it. No more fireworks," said Billy. "That was a tough year."

Billy dealt with the despair of losing two close friends to violent deaths and having another friend sent to prison for the rest of his life. But there was little feeling or sadness when his father passed away.

For nearly the entirety of his life, Billy's relationship with William P. D'Elia was distant and often nonexistent. From his earliest memories of his father killing his puppy, Billy had no use for him.

The elder D'Elia showed no warmth to his only son, provided no guidance, and rarely if ever engaged him in conversation, and they became so estranged the only way anyone knew they had any connection was through their names. Billy was immensely grateful he wasn't a junior. He was William J.

During the years after his mother's death, Billy had not spoken to his father. It took a chance sighting at a Kmart to change that. Billy had his family in tow and they saw his father buying fishing gear. William had always been pleasant to his grandchildren, and it was they and Ellen who said it was time to mend fences. The two men, father and son, would have brief conversations every now and then, which for them could be considered mending.

William P. D'Elia Sr. died on August 10, 1992, at the age of eighty-nine. He had been at the Valley Crest Nursing Home in Wilkes-Barre, and it was mostly out of a sense of duty that Billy held a one-day wake at the Recupero Funeral Home in West Pittston. Billy's stature drew a who's who of organized crime figures who came to pay their respects, dozens of them. Large floral arrangements, sent from all corners of the country, filled the room. In Billy's mind it was a far greater tribute than his father deserved. But they didn't come for William P., they came for Billy, and among those who shook Billy's hand and kissed him on the cheek were his newest acquaintance, Philadelphia boss John Stanfa, and an old friend who had just been released from prison, Frank Sheeran.

CHAPTER 16

The Wild, Wild West

After six years in prison in dreary, cold places like Minnesota, and after another four years at the medical prison in Springfield, Missouri, Frank Sheeran had been approved for release on a medical hardship.

He was seventy-one years old and could barely walk.

Unable to speak to Russell—Carrie wouldn't allow it—Frank called Billy to deliver the news that he was getting out. He also needed a favor.

Before his incarceration in 1982, Frank had put $28,000 on the street in Philadelphia. He knew who owed him, but his prison address prevented him from collecting. Now that he was soon to be a free man again, Frank wanted his money back, with interest. And he asked Billy to help him get it.

"Frank didn't have anything. Nothing," said Billy. "So he calls me from prison and says he was getting stuck, he started putting feelers out to people but they wouldn't pay him money he was owed and he wanted to see if I could help him collect. So I called Joe Scalleat in Hazleton."

Scalleat had gone back years with Russell and, like him, was politically connected, counting Pennsylvania State Senator Henry "Buddy" Cianfrani and another man, Pat Solano, as close friends.

Pennsylvania Crime Commission agents once followed Scalleat to the state capitol building in Harrisburg and watched Scalleat pull directly into Cianfani's senate parking spot, go into Cianfrani's office and ask the secretary for messages, and then go into Cianfrani's office and sit behind his desk. A convicted felon, Cianfrani had attended Frank Sheeran's "appreciation night" in 1974.

Solano, from Pittston, was known as a political "fixer" and one of the most powerful men in Pennsylvania. Crime commission agents nicknamed him "The Kingmaker." During one surveillance, Billy was followed to Scalleat's home in Hazleton. The agents later subpoenaed phone records for Billy, Scalleat, and Solano and found multiple phone calls between each of them that day.

"Russell and me had done business with Scalleat for many years but he was really with Philadelphia," said Billy. "Joe sets up a meeting for me with John Stanfa, who was the new boss down there. He was in the car when Angelo Bruno got killed. So I go see Stanfa at a restaurant in Philly called the Mona Lisa. It was his hangout, and we sit in the back. I tell him what's going on with Frank and how much he was owed. Stanfa said no problem and he'd take care of it and put out the word."

Billy thanked Stanfa, whom he liked immediately, and he told Frank it was getting done. But getting Frank's money didn't start off well.

Another war had begun for control of Philadelphia, this one between Stanfa and a younger faction of men, and the first victim was Felix Bocchino, who was seventy-two. Bocchino was a member of Stanfa's crew and was shot three times in his car. He was also one of the men who owed Sheeran.

"They killed him before we could get Frank's money, five thousand. It was my fucking luck," said Billy. "But after that we got it all straightened out in a week, maybe two, getting the money owed to Frank. I took a piece, gave a piece to Stanfa, and gave the rest to Frank, who just got out of prison. He was grateful. But from then on every single day he'd call me at six in the morning, and he'd wake up everybody in the house. Every day. He didn't have anybody. So when I went down to Philadelphia I'd pick him up and he'd pal around with me."

Frank hadn't seen Russell since they were at Springfield together and he wanted to sneak a visit with him, but Carrie repeated her edict: Russell would have no contact with felons. Besides, the diabetes had progressed and he couldn't walk at all and also had difficulty with his sight. Billy religiously brought him to the eye doctor every week, and during the rides Russell still asked about business. Billy told him about Frank and his difficulties, and his burgeoning relationship with John Stanfa in Philadelphia. Russell remembered Stanfa, the guy with the thick Italian accent who was with Angelo Bruno when he was killed.

During his reign as boss in Philadelphia from the 1950s until his violent end in 1980, Bruno had maintained relative peace among the ambitious gangsters in what was then America's fourth-largest city. But the environment in Philadelphia changed in 1976 with the birth of gambling in Atlantic City, which Bruno claimed as his territory. The casinos, as predicted, soon rose from the boardwalk, and now jealous eyes from New York were looking down, among them members of the Gambino and Genovese families.

Bruno always had strong ties with New York, and his friendship with Russell kept a lid on any potential trouble that might brew from there, and within Bruno's own family.

But when Russell went to prison in 1978, Bruno lost a key ally. He lost another one when Ralph Natale was sent to prison in 1979 following convictions for arson, mail fraud, and drugs. Natale was one of Bruno's point men in Atlantic City and his liaison to various casino unions. An enforcer, he once killed two Irish gangsters in a union dispute.

Natale's imprisonment for arson left Bruno exposed, and his subsequent murder in 1980 set off a war to determine his successor. His underboss Phil "Chicken Man" Testa assumed control, but his reign was short-lived, when he was killed by a nail bomb placed under his porch in 1981.

Testa's underboss Nicodemo "Little Nicky" Scarfo ascended to lead the family. At five feet five inches, Scarfo was a small man with a violent temper, and for months blood poured through the streets as he cemented his position, wiping out more than twenty men, many of them Bruno's supporters, while elevating those loyal to him.

But he was sentenced to fourteen years in prison in 1988 for extortion, and then another fifty-five years in prison in 1989 for murder and racketeering. He tried to lead the family from prison, but that proved futile.

So in 1991 he selected his replacement, John Stanfa.

A Sicilian immigrant, Stanfa had the prototypical background and family tree to lead an organized crime family in a major city. He had lived in New York with his brothers, who were tied to the Gambino Family, and with their help he left in 1967 for Philadelphia, where he was placed with Angelo Bruno. Stanfa remained under the radar until Bruno's death in 1980. Some thought that he was involved in Bruno's execution, given the fact that he was Bruno's driver and had close ties to the Gambino Family, which some believed was behind the shooting. But others pointed to the Genovese Family as the culprits, and since Stanfa was in the car with Bruno and nearly killed, he couldn't have been involved.

Stanfa went to prison for lying to a grand jury after Bruno's death. Following his release, he was tapped by Scarfo to lead the family at the urging of the Gambinos in New York.

The low-key Stanfa once listed his trade as bricklayer. But he was firm, tough, and not a man to take for granted. Most were pleased with Stanfa's ascension, but some weren't, among them a younger group led by a personable man still in his twenties.

Joseph Merlino was the son of Salvatore Merlino, a longtime

member of the Bruno Family. Known as "Skinny Joey" for his obvious thin physique, he had been in prison following a conviction for interstate theft and conspiracy involving the heist of an armored truck. In prison he met Ralph Natale, who had a few years remaining on his twelve-year sentence for arson. Together they plotted to kill Stanfa, and upon Natale's release he would become the boss in Philadelphia with Merlino as his underboss.

It was Merlino who struck the first blow by ordering the death of Felix Bocchino. Several other men close to Stanfa were also shot, and some were killed. Another war had begun.

Billy knew Philadelphia. During his first trips there with Russell in the 1960s he had formed his own friendships with soldiers and associates of the Bruno Family. And after Russell's imprisonment in 1978, Billy continued to visit there, usually on behalf of Russell, to meet with Bruno or his underlings. But after Bruno's death and Russell's second imprisonment, Billy began doing his own business there. While his primary focus remained New York City, he nourished his contacts in Philadelphia and visited the city when needed amid the ongoing bloodshed. The propensity for violence there reminded him of spoiled children with guns.

Billy had also deepened relationships with important men back home, among them Louis DeNaples. Billy served as a "waste broker" for DeNaples, steering trash-hauling contractors to the gruff businessman's Keystone landfill in Dunmore to dump their refuse. Billy received a percentage of each new contract, which he shared with Russell. With regulatory agencies eliminating available landfill space through the 1980s in New York, New Jersey, and Pennsylvania, Billy found many eager trash haulers, most with mob ties or owned outright by Mafia families willing to take their refuse to the Keystone landfill. And DeNaples took everything.

"I'd work it out to where, say, they paid Lou twenty dollars a ton, and I'd get four dollars a ton out of that," said Billy. "They'd pay Louie his money, and then they'd pay me separately."

Billy had also placed pay phones throughout the region for Bud-Tel, a Philadelphia telecommunications company owned by another friend, Barry Shapiro, with whom Billy did business in Atlantic City. The phones went up everywhere, including one outside of DeNaples's auto parts business. Billy met often with DeNaples at his massive auto parts complex in Dunmore. It was an indoor facility opened just a few years earlier that stretched five football fields. Thirty vehicles a day would arrive for disassembling, and the alternators, radiators, starters, and other parts were placed with the other one hundred thousand parts that were stored in the facility.

"I'd go visit him three, four days a week," said Billy. "If he had a problem, I'd help him take care of it. He became very, very rich. And he knew how to use his money with the politicians—congressmen, senators, governors—so that also made him very, very powerful."

But Billy would cast his gaze south again toward Philadelphia after receiving the call from Frank to help collect his money there. By then, Billy had all but given up on doing business in New York. Federal prosecutions in the mid-1980s led by Rudolph Giuliani, the U.S. attorney for the Southern District of New York, had virtually wiped out the leadership of New York's leading organized crime figures. Dozens of men, including Anthony Salerno, Carmine Persico, and eventually John Gotti, were among those imprisoned. Even Andy Russo, then the acting underboss of the Colombo Family, received fourteen years in 1986.

Billy had never been charged with a crime, and he didn't want his first arrest to be in New York, so he began a business relationship with John Stanfa, who sought out Billy for his counsel and his connections.

"After I helped out Frank, I started going to Philly a lot more and got close to John Stanfa," said Billy. "I liked him. He was tough and sincere. He was a stand-up motherfucker, and he'd ask me this and that and we ended up doing some business together."

Stanfa was lured by Billy's pedigree and his deep contacts across the country. Billy was a mob unicorn, someone who could pick up the phone and call anyone, anywhere, and the call would be answered. As a newly appointed boss, Stanfa knew that having close ties with someone like Billy, with his access and influence, could only help his effort to cement control in Philadelphia.

And Billy understood the importance of having strong ties in Philadelphia, like Russell had enjoyed years earlier. To impress Stanfa, Billy delivered an easy score.

It involved Alfred DiSipio, whom everyone knew as Freddie. DiSipio was a well-known record label promotion executive with a notorious reputation who had once been linked to a major payola scandal in the mid-1980s. As an independent promoter, he belonged to "the Network," a group of firms that received large fees from record labels to promote their artists and ensure they received radio airplay. DiSipio and the others then used that money to pay off radio station executives to play their records. It was cash under the table, payola, and DiSipio reaped millions in fees from the record companies, who looked the other way, knowing a single hit record could add tens of millions to their bottom lines.

A native Philadelphian from the south side with long-standing ties to the Gambino Family in New York, DiSipio denied the payola allegations and was never charged. He was forced to quit the business temporarily following an NBC News investigation, but he returned after a few years, and in 1993 he was hired as a consultant to the new chairman and chief executive of EMI Records, one of the largest labels in the world. And with him as EMI's consultant, everyone knew that the money would be flowing again under the table. It was illegal money, the kind of business Billy feasted on.

"DiSipio was based in Philly," said Billy. "And in the eighties, when some of my friends there found out how much money he was making, I said, 'Here's what you do. You go to him and tell him you want two hundred and fifty thousand and you want it now, and he'll run to me.' I said I knew Freddie, so trust me when I tell you he'd run to me. And he did. So I said, 'Freddie, you know how much money you made. You made millions. These are the only people in town. Take care of them and they will take care of you. Don't take care of them, and they won't take care of you.' So he gave me the two hundred and fifty, and I split it with Nicky Scarfo, one hundred and twenty-five thousand each. Then John Stanfa was boss and a new organization took over Philadelphia. So I went to Freddie again and said, 'Hey, there's a new sheriff in town. They know what you did for Nicky and they want the same deal.' Freddie said fine. So he met me at a bar at Franklin Mills Mall in Philly and gave me another two hundred fifty thousand, and I gave half to Stanfa."

DiSipio knew he was making illegal money in their city, and he also knew he'd have to pay them if they ever found out. They did. For guys like Billy, it was about keeping your ears open for any opportunity, something he learned early on from Russell.

"That's the way it worked," said Billy. "If you're legit, then you're legit. But if you're a scammer, then whatever. You're going to have to pay."

When Billy gave Stanfa his $125,000, Stanfa couldn't have been happier. And he asked Billy to stay close to him. But then came the swashbuckling Joey Merlino. Clean-cut and personable, Merlino was likable, and he wooed the media, making himself available for television interviews.

"Joey started the war there," said Billy. "I liked Joey Merlino. I liked him a lot. I liked his style and the way he acted. But his eyes would fucking burn a hole in you, like the devil."

Following Bocchino's murder and the shooting of Stanfa's underboss, who was shot in the head but survived, a furious Stanfa ordered a hit on Merlino, and in August 1993 a car pulled up to him and his associate Michael Ciancaglini. Two men jumped out and opened fire, killing Ciancaglini. Merlino survived.

Stanfa was so irate over the botched hit that he wanted to kill his own hit men. So he discussed with Billy a plan to have them lured to Wilkes-Barre and murdered there, and dispose of their bodies at Louis DeNaples's Keystone landfill. Billy nixed that idea. But as the violence became epidemic in Philadelphia, Billy was increasingly drawn to the city.

"I liked to be in the middle of it, the violence," said Billy. "It was like the fucking wild, wild West. Every week I was asked to solve a problem there, and I'd meet some sick people."

One of them was Harry J. Katz, a wealthy Philadelphia playboy and self-professed bon vivant who knew celebrities such as the television journalist Maria Shriver but who also developed relationships with members of Philadelphia's underbelly.

"I think his mother was the heir to the Singer sewing machines, or that's what he told everyone," said Billy. "I was at the Mona Lisa one night and he was badmouthing Frank Sheeran. So I told a guy to go hit that cocksucker, but he said he was just busting balls. So he and I became friends, sort of. He knew a lot of people in Philly. His driver's license listed 'the Mayor's Office, City Hall' as his address. I went to his house once and opened the refrigerator door and he had all these frozen dildos in there. He was a real pervert. He always hung out with beautiful women. There was one he was with at the Mona Lisa. She was gorgeous. He leaves with her, then later that night we hear she drowned in his hot tub."

One of the most disturbing people Billy met was John Veasey, who was one of the men whom Stanfa wanted Billy to bury at De-Naples's landfill up north for botching the Merlino hit.

"He was a tough-looking fucker, a really tough kid," said Billy. "I wore a ring with a seven-carat diamond. He says, 'Can I have that ring? That ring would make a nun fuck.' I told him to get the fuck away from me. He had tattoos of bullets of how many people he supposedly killed."

As the mob violence continued back and forth, it provided plenty of drama and large bold, black headlines for the local newspapers. The coverage was overwhelming and nonstop as reporters sought to publish one inside scoop after another. But the omnipresent coverage and so-called scoops enraged Stanfa, who soon came to believe that it was the press that stoked much of the bad blood.

"You sit there and you pick up the paper and on the front page it says, 'Who's the boss? John or Joey?,'" said Billy. "They'd say Joey's the new boss. He pushes Stanfa around and now Stanfa's trying to get even. It was the papers that created the feud."

Stanfa didn't believe much of what was being reported and thought a simple sit-down with Merlino would resolve their differences. But then another sensational headline would drop, and Stanfa knew there could be no peace. Stanfa was particularly angry with George Anastasia, the veteran, well-connected reporter with the *Philadelphia Inquirer,* who authored one story after another, often citing unnamed police and mob sources.

Stanfa became so angry with Anastasia, he wanted him to stop writing, permanently.

"Stanfa was really mad," said Billy. "Stanfa wanted to kill Anastasia. John said he was inciting people and getting them crazy and the press had started this war. So we're sitting in the back at the Mona Lisa and he told me that he was going to have someone throw a bomb into Anastasia's office, and what did I think. What did I think? I said, 'John, are you crazy? You can't go around killing reporters!' He wanted to kill him. If I didn't say anything to him he would have killed him, that's how mad he was."

As close as Billy was with Stanfa, he had also developed a similarly close relationship with Joey Merlino. It was one of the oddities of the ongoing war in Philadelphia, but they both knew that Billy was Mafia royalty.

"The reporters and cops couldn't understand it," said Billy. "I'm here with Joey one day, then Stanfa the next. They were my friends. I respected Stanfa and I really respected Joey, and they both respected me. Joey was a tough kid. But things were so crazy there. Stanfa got to hate Joey so much he wanted to cut his tongue out and send it to his wife."

Stanfa and Merlino weren't Billy's only interests in Philadelphia. His last real connection to New York was intermittent trips to the Diamond District. But that ended when he secured a new jewelry partnership with Bobby Stone, who had a store on Sansom Street and did business with everyone. Billy's first introduction to Stone was on behalf of someone who asked Billy to order a ring but not pay Stone.

"The guy said, 'What's he going to do?'" said Billy. "But when I met Bobby, I loved him. If I went to Philadelphia five days a week, the first place I ever stopped was Bobby Stone's jewelry store. It could be ten in the morning or three in the afternoon. I'd walk in and go, 'Bobby, I'm here!' and he'd tell his people to lock up, he was going out with his friend. He was a millionaire twice over. He went broke because he had lent money to every wise guy that was killed. But he was one of my best friends."

Billy's presence in Philadelphia didn't go unnoticed by the FBI, which had a task force that was closely monitoring the different factions in the war there. There was just too much violence and the government wanted to put the combatants away forever. The bureau used everything at its disposal, including wiretaps, photo reconnaissance, and informants. And along with Stanfa, Merlino, and their people, the FBI agents zeroed in on Billy.

For his part, Billy knew he was being trailed. It wasn't hard to spot the FBI agents following his car or walking behind him down the street. Sometimes he'd play with them and duck into one store, leave from the rear, and emerge on another block. But the surveillance was intense. During a dinner with Stanfa at the Mona Lisa, he couldn't keep his eyes away from a young couple.

"I met John there and we're sitting back at this little table and I'm watching this gorgeous, I mean fucking gorgeous, woman having dinner," said Billy. "When she and the guy she's with leave, the waitress comes over and says, 'Hey, Billy, can you come to the kitchen?' So I go back there and they give me a man purse and I open it up and inside was a nine-millimeter Ruger 85 handgun and an FBI badge and FBI credentials. That couple were feds and they must have left it at the table. So Stanfa says, 'Bill, what do you-a think we should-a do?' I said, 'We could take it over to the projects and let some people kill each other and they'd blame it on the FBI.' He laughed. But then the phone rang. The waitress goes, 'Billy, it's him. He's on the phone. He said he left his thing on the table and he wants it now.' She asked him to describe what was inside the purse and he wouldn't. Within seconds something like nine cars come screeching in front of the restaurant with their lights on. So I told the waitress to just give it back."

CHAPTER 17

The End of an Era

The Pennsylvania Crime Commission believed the Bufalino Family was in decline, and it said so in its lengthy 1990 report *A Decade of Change*.

It reported that the Bufalino Family's hold over labor racketeering, gambling, loan-sharking, extortion, counterfeiting, receiving stolen property, jury tampering, and infiltration of legitimate businesses was waning due to deaths and prosecutions.

The commission also said that the future of the family was uncertain, with indications it would be disbanded and its members would flee to other crime families, especially once Russell was gone.

But the report was wrong. The family was prosperous. Gambling, loan-sharking, and receiving stolen property were always mainstays, and there were plenty of associates on the streets handling that work.

Billy always thought the commission was a joke and, not that he cared, but a waste of taxpayer money that served as more of a nuisance than anything else. The commission had no statutory legal power, which Billy himself proved in 1988 when the state supreme court ruled that he did not have to answer its subpoena to testify. So aside from the annual headlines from some new report, Billy typically dismissed the commission.

"They were the dumbest fuckers on the face of the earth," said Billy. "They had this special agent, Steve Keller, and I'd see him hiding at the Halloween parade or if I was coming out of the Howard Johnson's with Russell. One day I have to go see my kids at a school and I'm in the parking lot and he's got a camera out. I yelled out, 'You're a pervert, taking pictures of my kids!' He runs back to his car and picks up the radio and starts yelling, 'Car one! Car one! We're in trouble!' They were idiots. They put out these big reports, but they knew nothing about what had really been going on. They were still calling Eddie Sciandra the acting boss, or [saying] that the family was in decline. They really didn't know. It shows you how dumb they were, but I guess that was a good thing. They didn't know that I was spending a lot of my time now in Philadelphia."

Billy had always kept Russell abreast of what was going on with family business, and Russell didn't object when Billy said he was expanding into Philadelphia. He was his own man now and had been for years. Russell had raised him, taught him, nurtured him, and in Russell's absence the family had survived and thrived under the man he had proudly called his son. And it was that son and his wife and children who helped Carrie care for Russell during his final months.

During the summer of 1993 Russell required constant attention, forcing Carrie to make arrangements for him to live at the Dorrance Manor nursing home, which was just a few blocks down the street from their home.

He was still well enough to go out on occasion, and he enjoyed his ninetieth birthday celebration that October. Billy, Ellen, and their children took him to Piledggi's, a local restaurant in Kingston, and Carrie glared when Russell and Billy ordered shots of Dewar's. Russell enjoyed it so much, he ordered another round. For old times' sake.

"He remembered that night at the Copa when he first brought

me there," said Billy. "I told him I hadn't drank anything else since. So we had a few. That little birthday dinner was probably the last good night we all had with him."

With the New Year, Russell's condition worsened, and in February he was transferred to Nesbitt Memorial Hospital, which also was just several blocks from his home. Carrie refused to allow anyone into Russell's room or even on his floor with the exception of Billy, Ellen, and their children. Tales that had begun circulating about lines of people coming to Russell's room and kissing his feet were just that, born from someone's rich imagination.

Billy sat next to him, and when Russell could, they'd talk. There were no mentions of how much they loved and meant to each other. They already knew it, just being there together, or when Billy wiped him down with a wet towel and changed his soiled clothes.

Ellen, the former nurse, also tried to make Russell comfortable. She doted on him, held and caressed his hand. He had warned her so many years earlier about the life she'd lead if she married Billy; if Russell had been anything to her, he had been honest, and she'd always loved him for it. Ellen had learned to compartmentalize her feelings when it came to Russell, choosing instead to see the goodness in the old man, the kindness and sweetness he showed her and her children over the years, and not the monster she read about in the papers.

As Russell's end approached, there were more calls from friends requesting to visit, and some even came to the hospital lobby. But Carrie shooed them all away with the exception of her family, the Sciandras, and his cousin Angelo. Like Billy, Angelo had remained one of the few constants in Russell's life.

"She didn't let any people get through," said Billy. "She'd be saying that no one's going on this floor and other bullshit. So there were no last goodbyes."

And there were no last words.

Russell died peacefully with Carrie by his side on February 26, 1994.

Later that evening Billy and Ellen drove to Russell's house and found Carrie sitting in the dark by herself at her small kitchen table with rosary beads in her hand. They hugged one another and joined her at the table and made small talk. The house felt empty, cold, quiet. Billy got up and walked downstairs to Russell's bar and grabbed the bottle of Dewar's and three glasses. He paused for a moment and took a mental snapshot of the room. There were so many memories. He went upstairs and poured the drinks, they toasted Russell, and then they sat there quietly through the night.

Word of Russell's death traveled quickly. The local papers ran front-page headlines while the national media gave its due attention, with nearly every story mentioning Jimmy Hoffa. Reporters called, but when they identified themselves and asked for comment or information on Russell's services, either Carrie or whoever else answered the phone hung up immediately. The press then waited for Russell's obituary to be posted and reveal the closely guarded details on the services.

But there was no obituary. There would also be no church Mass, no long procession of cars and limousines overflowing with gaudy floral arrangements, no burial service surrounded by mourners wearing black, and no law enforcement with their cameras spying from a distance. Carrie had planned a very small, private service with just a few close friends and family. No one, except for the few who were invited, knew that the wake and service would be at the Recupero Funeral Home in West Pittston, where Billy had waked his father. There was a brief service, and a priest offered Communion to the small group, which included Carrie; Billy, Ellen, and their children; Angelo Bufalino; and several of Carrie's cousins on the Sciandra side.

Billy found it ironic that his father had gotten the send-off that Russell should have had.

As they left the funeral home, a nephew pulled Carrie aside.

"You're no longer a Bufalino," he said. "You're a Sciandra again."

Several reporters were spotted the following morning standing in the cold outside the funeral home. They had somehow learned about the wake the night before, and that Russell's remains would be taken to Philadelphia, where a cousin had bought two plots for Russell and Carrie.

A black hearse carrying a coffin emerged from the back of the funeral home, and the reporters jumped into their cars and followed it onto the Pennsylvania Turnpike and down toward Philadelphia. Not long after, Billy and Angelo arrived at the funeral home and hurried inside. Within minutes they emerged in the rear with the owner, Tony Recupero, carrying another coffin, and they loaded it inside Recupero's station wagon. After making sure no one was out front, they pulled onto the street and drove to the Denison Cemetery in nearby Swoyersville Borough and pulled up to the mausoleum. Once there, they pulled the coffin out of the car and carried it to an open crypt up on the wall. They paused, took deep breaths, lifted the coffin, and slid it inside.

"The reporters somehow got wind of the funeral home, and Tony the funeral director said they were waiting outside," said Billy. "So we came up with a plan to get rid of them, and they followed the hearse all the way down to Philly. Then we took the real coffin to the cemetery. It wasn't easy. We almost dropped it trying to get it inside the wall. But we were able to get it up and slide it in, and that was it."

CHAPTER 18

The Boss

Just a week after Russell's death, John Stanfa learned he was going to be indicted, and likely imprisoned.

He asked Billy to come visit with him and explained that Ralph Natale was finally getting out of prison after fourteen years and he needed someone to fill in for him as acting boss to prevent Natale from taking control.

And that someone, said Stanfa, was Billy.

Following Russell's death, Billy had received calls from men in cities throughout the country expressing their sorrow over Russell's passing and giving their congratulations for something they had all known for a while—Billy was the boss of the Bufalino crime family.

It was a position he had held unofficially for years. Billy never hid from it, he just never publicly said it, and he never would while Russell was alive.

But now John Stanfa had asked him to become the boss of the Philadelphia family. Somehow that request leaked to a rabid press, which queried Billy's neighbors in Hughestown, asking if they knew he was a well-connected mob figure with strong ties to crime family leaders throughout the country, ran his own family, and could potentially be the boss in Philadelphia.

They said he was just Billy, the good neighbor who attended church and cut his lawn.

"John asked me if I'd be boss, and I thought about it and I just said no," said Billy. "I got along with Joey Merlino but I knew he and his people would never go for it. Besides, Ralph Natale was getting out, and it was Ralph that was behind Joey and his war with Stanfa. I didn't need a target on my back."

But he had one anyway. Billy had kept a gun on him ever since Russell gave him the pearl-handled handgun back in 1970. He even had a concealed weapons permit allowing him to carry as many guns as he wanted, or could. It had been issued back home by Luzerne County sheriff Frank Jagodinski. Billy also had personal references from Steve Rinaldi, Pittston's police chief, and his attorney Charles Gelso, who on Billy's recommendation had also been representing Stanfa.

Stanfa was arrested on March 17, 1994, in a major racketeering indictment that, if convicted, would likely put him away for life. The charges were the culmination of a three-year investigation that included microphones planted by the FBI in the law office of a Camden, New Jersey, attorney, Salvatore Avena, who had also been arrested with Stanfa and twenty-two other men.

For nearly two years beginning in 1991, FBI agents were just a block away and listened to every conversation in that office, including several involving Billy and Stanfa.

Stanfa had grown paranoid during his desperate, but failing, effort to reach a peace with Joey Merlino during their power struggle. At his wits' end, and knowing he was a target, Stanfa could be heard on the tapes saying in his broken English, "What it comes down to here is they fuck me or I fuck them. That's where we are." Stanfa was old-school and didn't like how business was conducted in Philadelphia, saying the Mafia there had lost its old codes of respect and loyalty.

"I was born and raised that way," said Stanfa. "Over here, it's like kindergarten."

The FBI tapes had also captured a conversation with Billy in December 1992. He had been brought in to mediate a prickly issue involving a lawsuit Avena had filed against Carmine Franco, his partner in a waste disposal business. Franco was the powerful figure in the carting industry with strong ties to the Genovese Family whom Billy had had to deal with on behalf of Louis DeNaples.

Avena alleged that Franco had stolen millions from him; the lawsuit was going to trial and it had drawn the wrath of the Genovese Family. Franco was among their top earners, and a trial was sure to spill family secrets.

Joining Billy and Stanfa were Stanfa's consigliere Anthony "Tony Buck" Piccolo, Avena, and Salvatore Profaci, a capo with New York's Colombo Family, who had driven down for the meeting on behalf of the Genovese Family.

They had all asked Billy to step in and convince Avena to drop his lawsuit and accept a $2 million payment. The FBI listened clearly as Billy spelled out to Avena his options.

"See, Sal, the difference is, [Franco] is a street guy. You're not a street guy . . . They're two different breeds. In other words, when this guy is making moves and you're doing it straight, you don't have a shot."

Profaci also said that the Genoveses and other New York families were angered by the constant turmoil in Philadelphia, and it had to stop.

"They're saying that [you] are the cause of destroying everything that they've created in Philadelphia. And by blowing Carmine out of the water, you are destroying their number one earner in the whole organization. Goodfellas don't sue goodfellas. Goodfellas kill goodfellas," said Profaci.

Billy seized on Profaci's argument. "The answer was that when [Franco] was standing by the trash trucks, somebody should have bumped him in and let them compact him," he said.

Profaci replied that killing Franco would have drawn the anger of the Genovese Family, but Billy said there was an answer.

"You know what they say in New York, don't you?" he asked.

"Accidents happen," said Profaci.

"Oops, we didn't know," said Billy, emphasizing the "oops."

"Oops is right. Shame on us," said Profaci.

Realizing the Genovese Family could wipe out everyone in Philadelphia, Stanfa told Avena to settle. "Better to win small than to lose big," he said.

Avena and Franco ended the matter three months later.

Stanfa's bail was revoked and he remained in custody awaiting trial. When asked by reporters about Stanfa's wanting Billy to be the acting boss, one Philadelphia organized crime unit investigator said, "That's the rumor."

A few months after Stanfa's arrest, Ralph Natale was released from prison and immediately proclaimed that he was the boss in Philadelphia and that Joey Merlino would serve as his underboss. Billy had known Natale back in the 1970s, their paths crossing during Billy's visits there with Russell, and he stayed neutral as Natale set up his headquarters at the Garden State Park racetrack in New Jersey, where he would host meetings at the restaurant upstairs.

The FBI knew Natale was doing business there, and like they had with Avena's office, they wired the racetrack restaurant as well as Natale's condo on the Delaware River. They recorded every conversation in each location, including one on October 5, 1995, at the racetrack in which Natale discussed killing Billy with Steven Mazzone, a newly made member who had grown up with Joey Merlino, and another associate, Martin Angelina. Natale gave them the contract.

After listening to the tapes, the FBI contacted Charles Gelso. From time to time, whenever the FBI heard through a wiretap of a pending act of violence, it would try to get word to the unsuspecting gangster in the crosshairs. Gelso was in his office in Wilkes-Barre when he received a call from an agent in Philadelphia about a life-and-death matter involving Billy. They had to speak to him immediately.

"Charlie called me at home and said I had to come to his office," said Billy. "When I got there he said the FBI was here and 'I want you to go upstairs and talk to them.' There were a couple of special agents and they go, 'You know there's a contract on you. Do you want to know who's going to kill you?' I'm just sitting there and looked at them and said I didn't care. He goes, 'Well, I'm going to tell you anyway. There's a contract on you by Ralph Natale and Joey Merlino. We have wiretaps and we picked up Natale talking and he plans on killing you coming out of the Saloon.' Now, the Saloon is my favorite hangout in Philadelphia, so I believe them. I got right into the car and went right to Philadelphia, over the bridge, and to the track in Jersey.

"There was a nightclub, and Ralph was sitting up there and I go right to him and said, 'Ralphie, do we have a problem?' He goes, 'What?' and I said, 'You're trying to fucking kill me? You and Joey put a contract out on me?' Ralph goes, 'Are you crazy! Are you crazy! I love you! I love you! You're my guy! No one would ever do that to you, not in this town!' I told him what the FBI said and that it was on tape and he denied it. Joey denied it too. So I don't know if it was true or not. For all I know the FBI was fucking with me. But there was all this talk in the papers about me being the boss down there, and Ralphie told me he heard I wanted Joey killed. He said I told John Stanfa we were going to have a sit-down with Joey and the zips—they were his greenhorns from Sicily—at a restaurant in North Philly and we'd tape guns under the table and when we all sat down we'd shoot the guy in front of us. I said, 'Are you fucking crazy?' He said that's what got Joey mad and now word's going around that he's trying to kill me and I'm trying to kill him. I never had a problem with Joey Merlino. They were my friends. But there was so much shit going on in Philly."

Billy was angry, but he remained quiet as Natale's status as boss in Philadelphia remained tenuous, even with Stanfa in jail for life. So Natale looked north to New York for allies, and despite their blowup over the alleged hit, he asked Billy if he could arrange a meeting for him with the Colombo Family in New York. Natale knew that recognition by the Colombos would certainly cement his position, and the Colombos were now led by Billy's old friend Andy Russo, who was out of prison. So Billy set up the meeting for January 18, 1996.

"Andy Russo was the acting boss," said Billy. "Ralph knew I had known Andy for over thirty years. I was still a little raw about the hit thing. But I was also still alive, so maybe it was all bullshit. Whatever. When Ralph asked me to set up the meeting I said sure. We knew the FBI was all over us, so me and Ralphie agree to meet in New York and I get a couple of rooms at the Helmsley Palace. We wait an hour or so and the Colombos send a car that takes us to a restaurant downtown. We have a couple of drinks, and then a van comes and takes us to Brooklyn. They wanted to see if anyone was following us. We get to a house in Brooklyn and Andy is there with a lot of his guys. We're all downstairs in this huge basement. I make the introductions and we all sit down. I think Ralph knew Andy before he went to prison. It was very cordial. They had dinner for us, and Ralphie explained why he should be boss in Philly. When it was over, Andy tells Ralph he has his support and the support from the other New York families and that's it. He's the top guy in Philadelphia. So he's happy, and Joey even invites me to his kid's christening. I liked Joey and had a lot of respect for him, so things with them from then on were good."

But Billy's instincts about the FBI were correct. Agents from Philadelphia had followed Natale and two of his men up the New Jersey Turnpike before handing them off to another surveillance team with agents from New York. They followed Natale to the Helmsley. Despite the cloak-and-dagger of switching from car to van, the FBI followed them to Brooklyn and watched them go inside the house. But they had no idea what the meeting was about.

After settling things for Natale, Billy flew to California to handle an emergency involving Fabio. The internationally recognized male model, whose herculean physique had been emblazoned on the covers of millions of romance novels and paperback books, was having a problem with his former manager. He required Billy's expertise.

Fabio and Billy had been friends for several years and Billy was called on for help every so often. Fabio said his current predicament involved a woman, and Billy flew out there and quietly convinced Paul to settle the matter.

Billy traveled to California often, sometimes two, three, four times a month, and he stayed at the Four Seasons in Beverly Hills. He had been going there for years on business for Russell, and he'd have breakfast or, at night, drinks there with gangsters, actors, managers, and film and record people.

After settling the problem for Fabio, he returned to Beverly Hills for a sit-down with two men looking to muscle their way into the management of Toni Braxton, a talented, rising young singer signed by the music industry legend Clive Davis. Billy took care of it but was so annoyed with the two men he demanded and received a case of expensive wine from the antagonists, who were just happy to walk out of the hotel unscathed.

Billy also intervened in a disagreement between the co-producers of the hit television show *Baywatch*, Henry and Paul Siegel, to help retrieve money they said they were owed by All American Television, the production company they had teamed up with. It was owned by the Scotti brothers, Tony and Benjamin, who had founded a successful record label in the 1970s. The Siegels owned the distribution rights to *Baywatch*, and Henry was named All American's president and Paul president of international markets. But the Scottis allegedly had long-standing mob ties, and when they rebuffed the Siegels' attempts to collect a large payment owed to them, the Siegels sought help and were introduced to Billy.

"The brothers were owed money and the wise guys said they'll pay it when they feel like it," said Billy. "So I go out there and they said the Scottis were doing stupid things and they wanted no part of it and wanted them to buy them out. One of the brothers said they didn't even want the money and just wanted out. I said, 'How much money are we talking about?' He said they didn't care about the money. I said, 'Oh yes you do. You have to care about the money.' It was two million. I knew the other guys, so I went in and within two or three days I got the money."

When he returned back east, yet another opportunity presented itself in Philadelphia with another artist, a rapper named Kurupt, a.k.a. Ricardo Emmanuel Brown. The Philadelphia native had been signed to Death Row Records, which was run by Suge Knight, a former college football player who'd joined the Los Angeles Rams as a replacement player during a player strike in 1987, and Dr. Dre, who was a member of the popular gangsta rap group N.W.A.

An internal rivalry had developed between East Coast and West Coast rap artists, stoked by Knight, who had a violent streak and considered himself a "real gangsta." The rivalry led to the murder of Knight's recording artist and friend Tupac Shakur, who was gunned down in a car in Las Vegas with Knight sitting next to him. Fearing Knight and the violence that seemed to always follow him, Dr. Dre left Death Row, followed by Kurupt, who was searching for a new record label.

"Kurupt's lawyer was one of our guys and he comes to me and says, 'Listen, we can probably do a deal with this guy,'" said Billy. "'He's in trouble, and he needs a new record deal.' So they came to me and I said we can get a record deal tomorrow. All I had to do was call Joel Katz. He was one of the top music industry lawyers. He had Michael Jackson. So we tell Suge Knight that Kurupt is with us now. He really couldn't say anything. He knew who we were, or someone told him. So we start up a company, Antra, and I ended up with three hundred thousand shares. I then call Joel and we got Kurupt a record deal with A&M Records and they put out the album on our Antra label. My partners didn't want to sell the shares yet. They were worth about three bucks apiece and they kept saying they were going to bring it up, which I knew was bullshit. So I sold the shares. It pissed some people off, but I made nearly a million."

CHAPTER 19

Frank

Frank Sheeran was writing a biography.

The untitled book, he said, would tell the true story of his life and reveal what really happened to his great friend Jimmy Hoffa.

The press release he issued on December 14, 1994, was written in the first person, and it recalled a meeting Frank had attended at Vesuvio with Anthony "Tony Pro" Provenzano, Salvatore Briguglio, and Russell Bufalino, where "a statement was made that Hoffa had been taken out. This came from a high political official via a New York contact."

Frank said that for twenty years he had been the object of conjecture about his role in Hoffa's 1975 disappearance, hurtful rumors perpetrated by the FBI and its scandalous investigation. He also said, in no uncertain terms, that he did not kill his friend, and that he had promised Russell he would not discuss Jimmy's disappearance until after Russell had passed away. And since Russell's death earlier that year, Frank said, he'd received numerous "calls and inquiries" to discuss Jimmy Hoffa.

Billy already knew about the book. Frank had told him he was working on a manuscript after his release from prison in 1992. Grateful to Billy for collecting his money after his imprisonment, Frank sought a closer relationship. All of his friends were dead, with the exception of Billy, and he missed his companionship.

"He'd call me every day," said Billy. "He would talk to my wife, my kids, and then get me on the phone. He had such a bad stutter it took a bit to get out what he wanted to say. He was lonely, so I told him I'd take him around with me. And I did."

Several days each week, Billy took Frank with him on his rounds throughout Philadelphia. He'd enter a restaurant with Frank in tow and get him settled at the bar and leave him there while he took a meeting. His white hair combed straight back, Frank walked with a slow gait and was hunched over. He even appeared to have lost a couple of inches in height. But even at seventy-three Frank remained a fearsome figure who could still easily kill a man if he had him cornered. And he could still drink most anyone under the table. When Billy parked him at a bar, Frank ordered his usual—a Heineken, a shot of sambuca, and a glass of champagne with strawberries—and he'd wash it all down at once and order another round.

Billy even invited Frank up to his son Russell's high school graduation party, which better resembled a wedding reception.

Billy had also taken him to meetings in New York and in New Jersey, and Frank's probation officer had accused him of violating his parole by leaving the Eastern District of Pennsylvania, which was prohibited. He also met with organized crime members and associates, which was also prohibited.

"Frank had a parole officer that terrorized him," said Billy. "I brought Frank around to some of my meetings with Stanfa, and to some others outside of Philly. I wasn't a convicted felon. I had never been arrested in my life, but they said I was someone he shouldn't be with, so they violated him. He stuttered to them, *'I knew that kid since he had pimples!'*"

When Frank told Billy about the book, he had two demands.

"I told him it was all right as long as you don't name anyone that's still alive, including me," said Billy. "And that you don't ever release it while Carrie is still alive."

Frank agreed. He and Billy were among the very few still breathing who knew the truth about Jimmy Hoffa. Frank also promised to give Billy 10 percent of any advance or royalties should his book be published.

Now, two years later, the manuscript was completed and Frank gave Billy a copy. Billy couldn't believe what he read.

The story, as told by Frank, was bizarre. Frank claimed that the weapon used to kill Hoffa came from the CIA and the killers were little Vietnamese hit men who were hiding in the rear seat of the car that had taken Hoffa from the restaurant where he was last seen alive. They were hired, said Frank, by former president Nixon.

The book would have been shocking if it weren't so laughable. Frank had a co-writer he'd met in prison, John Zeitts, who had been convicted of distributing child pornography.

"Frank had four different endings for that book," said Billy. "The guy he was working with was sitting in jail with him. He wrote the whole story. I had copies of each edition. One made less sense than the other. I told him he was fucking nuts. But he was looking to make some money. He had nothing left and wanted to leave something to his kids and grandchildren."

Despite his arrest for violating his probation, Frank held a party at the Copper Penny Restaurant in Philadelphia to celebrate his seventy-fourth birthday. About two dozen people were there, among them his biographer John Zeitts and Billy.

"I walk in there and I'm sitting next to him and this lady comes over and is talking to me for a while and leaves. I said, 'Frank, who was that?' and he said, 'Oh, that's Kitty Caparella.' I yelled, 'Are you fucking crazy! You had me talking to a reporter!' She was one of them writing up all those stories that got everyone crazy. I said, 'Why the fuck do you have a reporter here?' I told him I had to go."

Billy didn't know it then, but Frank was about to issue the press release announcing his book, and Caparella was invited to cover the party, which led to a story about Frank's book in January for the *Philadelphia Daily News*.

But while Frank had a manuscript, he didn't have a publisher or an agent, and he hoped the publicity would pave the way for not only a book deal but the sale of the film rights. Frank thought he'd rake in millions. It was wishful thinking. So were his letters to Hoffa's daughter, Barbara Ann Crancer, asking if she'd be willing to participate in the book project.

Barbara, who was fifty-six, was the eldest of Jimmy's two children, the other being his son, James P. Hoffa. She worked for years as an attorney in St. Louis before her appointment to associate circuit judge for St. Louis County in Missouri.

In his letter, Frank told Barbara about his book and what he planned to write, including his belief that the former Nixon administration was behind her father's murder. He also wrote that he was facing more time in prison and his health was generally poor.

Barbara replied on March 5, 1995. Her letter, which began with, "Dear Frank," said that she had discussed his request to participate in his book with her brother Jim, but they would decline. She urged him to contact the FBI if he had any information about her father's death, but also asked why he waited twenty years to say anything.

"It is my personal belief that there are many people who called themselves loyal friends who know what happened to James R. Hoffa, who did it and why," she wrote. "The fact that not one of them have ever told his family—even under a vow of secrecy, is painful to me. I believe you are one of those people."

Frank replied quickly, on March 15, 1995. He recognized, he wrote, that his "letter upset you and I am sorry about that. Truly sorry!" He went on to state in the two-page letter that he had "stood accused as a participant in your dad's disappearance for twenty years," and "the untrue allegations has had a horrible impact on my life Barbara . . .

and so has your letter which accuses me again of 'knowing' something about what happened for the last twenty years. For the record Barbara, I never knew what happened when it happened. I only knew that it could not have happened like the FBI theories put it."

The last time Frank had seen her father, he added, was in October 1974, at Frank Sheeran Appreciation Night. Frank also wrote that he was angry with the FBI for spreading lies and accused them of leaking false information to the authors of two bestselling books about the Hoffa case, *The Teamsters* and *The Hoffa Wars*. The truth, he wrote, was that Russell had told him while they were at the Springfield medical facility together in 1988 that her father had been "taken out."

Frank reported to prison for his parole violation, and after his release several months later he summoned Billy for another meeting. He had made no headway finding a publisher for his book, so he'd fired his coauthor, and he wanted to introduce Billy to his new writer, Charles Brandt, and work out percentages. Brandt was a former deputy attorney general in Delaware who had represented Frank in his successful application for his medical release.

"Frank calls me and says, 'You and Charlie Gelso have to come to Philadelphia,'" said Billy. "I used to hang out at Medora's Mecca there, so me and Gelso go there and Frank is there with this guy Charles Brandt and another lawyer and he starts talking about the book and he tells Brandt and the other lawyer to make sure that me and Gelso each get ten percent, and we signed papers. I didn't like Brandt, and he knew it. I thought the whole thing was nuts and that Frank was nuts. We both knew the Hoffa story. But after all these years he had nothing, and he really wanted to leave something behind. So after that meeting he sort of drifted off to work on his book and I didn't really see him much after that. When I did talk to him it was always, '*The book, gotta finish the booook. Gotta finish the booook.*' I just went about my business."

Billy had locked into another venture, one where he could tap his celebrity friends and business partners. It was long-distance phone cards.

Crime families across the country had widely distributed the cards and were selling them in cities to immigrants for ten or twenty dollars. Each card carried blocks of cheap minutes for immigrants to make international calls to their home countries. Some of the cards worked, others did not supply the promised block of minutes, while others got busy signals and didn't work at all. But the organized crime families involved in the scam were earning millions, in cash. Even better, the phone companies supplied the minutes on credit and were stuck with unpaid invoices. John Gotti Jr. was even involved and was partners in a deal with former Detroit Tigers pitcher Denny McLain. Their venture even drew the attention of the U.S. Secret Service.

For Billy, his contacts in the entertainment industry provided him with the rare opportunity of selling phone cards graced with photos of celebrities under his umbrella. So together with his old friend from Philadelphia Barry Shapiro, Billy had gotten into the phone card business.

"I knew Barry and his brother Larry from the 1980s in Atlantic City," said Billy. "Barry had a company, Bud-Tel, and I'd do some marketing for them, like I did for Markdata. I also got him phone contracts. It was easy money. People know me, I get the contract done and that's it. So me and Barry do the phone cards. Fabio owed me a favor so we do one with him, and we did one with Sandy Taylor; she was an actress, a beauty. Then we want to do one with Michael Jackson and fly out to L.A. for a meeting at Sony. We sit down and they say they want one hundred and fifty thousand up front and then maybe we'll talk about this and that. We went to lunch and as we leave and I run into this guy and he says, 'What are you doing here?' I tell him. Four weeks later he calls Barry and he says, 'Why the fuck didn't you call me first? We'll do the deal and you pay me.' So we did it. We sold a lot of phone cards."

The phone card business was profitable, and Billy considered partnering with others, including Donald Trump. Billy had known Trump for years, meeting the New York real estate czar before he opened his first Atlantic City casino, Trump Plaza, in 1984. Barry and Larry Shapiro, his partners in the phone cards, were associated with then–Philadelphia boss Nicky Scarfo, for whom Barry served as a so-called business agent. The brothers had made a deal with Trump to lease property across from his new casino that they were using for a parking lot and horse-and-buggy ride. The lease was for four years, after which Trump agreed he would buy the property for eight million. Trump did not use middlemen. He liked to negotiate directly, even with organized crime figures. When the lease expired, the Shapiros sought their money.

"Trump said he couldn't give him the eight million, that he only had seven. So either take the seven million or fuck it," said Billy. "So now what do you do, wait? So we're at this meeting with Trump and Barry said, 'Let's flip a coin for the other million.' Trump said fine, so they flipped the coin and Trump won. They took a picture of the coin and put it in their office. Trump got the coin and saved a million dollars. That's how he did business. He was smart."

Some years later, driven by the success of his other phone cards, Billy wanted to sell one featuring a photo of Trump's Taj Mahal casino, which he dubbed "the eighth wonder of the world" when he opened it in 1990. Billy enlisted Larry Shapiro to see Trump with him in Atlantic City.

For years Trump had denied doing business with or knowing organized crime figures. But Roy Cohn had been his attorney for many years, and before his death in 1986 of complications from AIDS, Cohn had schooled Trump on how to navigate the underbelly of business in America. And that included working with men such as the head of the Bufalino Family.

"I told him what we wanted to do and he liked it but said the only way he'd do phone cards is I had to pay him up front," said Billy. "He said he wanted cash and didn't want any records of it. I said absolutely not, but we kept talking about it."

They continued to negotiate on the phone cards when Billy went back to Trump soon after with another idea: selling time-shares. The idea was to use direct mail to offer a free weekend vacation at a re-sort, with the caveat that attendance at a time-share presentation was mandatory. Trump, after all, had the rooms. Trump liked that idea too, but he demanded that Billy offer another free gift: his 1987 book, *The Art of the Deal*.

"He said he'd do one or the other, the phone cards or the direct mail," said Billy. "But he'd do the direct mail on one condition, that we offered his book as another premium along with the trip. We would have to buy the books and then give them away. But he could say his sales went up five thousand copies. It would have cost us a hundred thousand. He was smart but he's also cocky. Of course we said no, but when we walked out of there we said, 'Yeah, that was fucking Roy Cohn's boy.'"

With business everywhere and revenue streams coming from a variety of sources, Billy continued to prosper, reaching a personal financial zenith that Russell would have been proud of. Now in his early fifties, Billy had followed Russell's road map on most every-thing, especially his talent for remaining in the shadows. And like Russell, he lived in a modest home, the same one he and Ellen had bought when they married.

He did once suggest to Ellen that they buy a six-bedroom man-sion about twenty minutes away in Bear Creek Village, but Ellen said no. She was comfortable in her smaller house and enjoyed living near her sister and close friends. And it wasn't the right time to buy a new house anyway since their marriage remained on shaky ground.

Billy had tried to be the devoted father who attended his kids' sporting events, school meetings, and other activities, but it was Ellen who'd remained at home to guide and nurture them, and insulate them as best she could from her husband's life and headlines.

Each of their children had graduated from college, and with clear career goals. Carolyn was a doctor of physical therapy, while Miriam had earned a law degree from Villanova, passed the bar exam, and become an attorney. Russell had just graduated from King's College and was embarking on a career as a health care executive.

Their success was due to Ellen, who kept their home free of any outside interference stemming from Billy's life. They all read the stories in the papers, and they knew what that life was. But Ellen and the children just went about their own lives as best they could. During the summers they went up north to the cabin she and Billy had bought in the early 1980s. She enjoyed it there, the peace and quiet. But she also knew better and carried a handgun. Ellen's life with Billy was often difficult. She knew Billy had girlfriends, and their arguments were fierce. A devout Catholic, Ellen prayed often. Like she had with Russell, she only saw the good in people. She knew her husband was a wonderful father. It was the rest of his life she prayed for.

By the end of the 1990s Billy was wealthy and, as the head of his own flourishing family, was among the most influential organized crime figures in the country. Nearly all of the old Bufalino Family soldiers had died off, but following Russell's death a new Bufalino Family had emerged.

Sam "Kooch" Marranca was now Billy's street boss, overseeing nearly one hundred associates involved in a variety of illegitimate and legitimate businesses. Billy had his arms around a variety of new industries, among them waste disposal and scrap metal, as well as gambling and jewelry and influence peddling. While the Teamsters connections were a thing of the past, Billy was called to settle a variety of problems across the country, often involving unions and the entertainment industry. He had been trained and tutored by the most powerful old-school don in the nation, and now he was exerting immense power himself.

Billy was at the peak of his success, and he wanted to celebrate.

And what better way to do that than to host his daughter's wedding.

Blessed Sacrament Church was filled on May 22, 1999, for the wedding of Carolyn D'Elia to Lance Moscatelli, and more than 350 people filled the Woodlands for the grand reception.

Outside looking on were members of various law enforcement

agencies, including FBI agents, cameras in hand, shooting from the street, with some even perched in and looking down from the trees. Billy's nephews, his late sister Shirley's sons, caused a bit of a ruckus when they blocked an unmarked FBI car.

"One of the agents came in and said they didn't want to interfere with the reception because I wasn't a bad guy, but they would unless I straightened out my nephews," said Billy. "I offered them some food and they said, 'Are you offering us a bribe?' I said, 'What the fuck? Where you guys from, Philly, the task force?' I offered them each a cigar. They took those."

Among the hundreds of guests enjoying the crab legs and shrimp during the cocktail hour, and the surf-and-turf entrée after, were several men who drove up from Philadelphia, among them Joey Merlino. He had assumed control of the Philadelphia family after Ralph Natale was jailed the year before for a parole violation. With Merlino was his underboss, Joseph "Uncle Joe" Ligambi, and a couple of their men. Any ill will between Billy and Merlino over old business had been forgotten long ago, and they considered each other good friends. Old friends from New York and elsewhere in the country were there, as well as close neighbors, among them the businessman Louis DeNaples, who was there with his wife, Betty Ann.

Billy enjoyed his daughter's wedding. Yet amid the handshakes and good humor, he knew, as he had since his first days with Russell, that there were always dangers lurking in the shadows. And from his own experience watching the government prosecute Russell over and over again, he knew hidden were the watchful eyes of the government.

Each day FBI agents from Scranton, Pittsburgh, and Philadelphia followed him everywhere, documenting his every move. So did the U.S. Secret Service and various task forces from other agencies.

But it wasn't the government that Billy had to worry about. Someone very close to him was already planning far into the future, and he had the time, money, and political power to make that future a reality.

And it did not include "Big Billy."

CHAPTER 20

The Beginning of the End

During the entirety of his twenty-eight years with Russell, and as the recognized head of the Bufalino Family following Russell's death, Billy D'Elia had never been convicted of a crime. Not even for jaywalking.

While some would credit it to extremely good luck, or circumstances, or both, in truth Billy was smart enough to avoid situations that he knew could lead to criminal charges. He also knew that for all these years, he'd had a great lawyer.

Charles Gelso had proved himself a brilliant defense attorney. Often combative in the best tradition of other Mafia attorneys, like Bruce Cutler, whose bombastic representation of John Gotti in New York was legendary, Gelso since the 1980s had defended Russell and members of his crime family against the full power and deep resources of the federal government and its Justice Department.

"He was better than Roy Cohn, he was better than Alan Dershowitz, he was better than Oscar Goodman in Las Vegas or Byron Fox in Kansas City," said Billy. "And I knew them all."

While Russell had often predicted that the government would get its grain of salt—his incarcerations during the twilight of his life were due to the overwhelming resources of a federal government determined to bring some sort of justice to the men it believed were responsible for the murder of Jimmy Hoffa, combined with a bit of stupidity on his own part—had he listened to Gelso and not testified on his own behalf, Russell would have spent the 1980s a free man.

And in his defense of Billy in 1988, Gelso had made mincemeat of the Pennsylvania Crime Commission after it subpoenaed him to testify about labor racketeering, taking the case all the way to the Pennsylvania Supreme Court, and winning.

So it was with the expectation that Gelso was going to break some news to him about some new government probe, or perhaps an upcoming indictment, that Billy drove to Perugino's Restaurant in Wilkes-Barre to meet with him. And after exchanging the usual kiss on the cheek and embrace and sharing some small talk, Gelso cut Billy short. He had some news.

"I'm dying," he said.

Unbeknownst to most everyone except for his own family, Gelso had battled lymphoma for years. Intermittent hospital stays had allowed him to keep the disease at bay. But his condition had worsened, and the most recent diagnosis was terminal.

"We're just talking and he stops me and goes, 'Oh, by the way, I should let you know I have cancer,'" said Billy. "He said, 'I'm going to die, and I'll be dead in about seventeen months.' I was shocked. He was still a young guy. But he got worse, and when he was in the hospital he sent for me. I didn't even know who he was. That's how fucked up he was."

Charles P. Gelso, fifty-two, died on May 21, 2000. News of his death traveled quickly throughout FBI field offices in Scranton and Philadelphia, and to headquarters in Washington, DC. Justice Department officials saw Gelso's demise as an opening. One year later, on the morning of May 31, 2001, Billy left his home and picked up Kooch, who wanted to drive.

"The driver pays all fines," said Kooch, oblivious to the flashing lights behind him.

"You better wake up, because this is more than a fine," said Billy, looking in the rearview mirror.

They pulled over on Route 315 and were immediately surrounded by roughly twenty vehicles from different law enforcement agencies, including the FBI, the Pennsylvania State Police, and the U.S. Postal Inspection Service. One agent from the Internal Revenue Service's criminal division stood outside the car door aiming a machine gun at them.

At the same time swarms of agents, including those from the U.S. Secret Service, cordoned off his block and, with search warrants in hand, raided his home.

They had watched and waited for Billy to leave before pouncing, and only Ellen was home when they barged in. Ellen, all of ninety-five pounds, was held there for hours while agents tore through every inch of her home. Downstairs, they removed all of Billy's office files.

Back on Route 315, the agents and officers searched Billy's car and found several guns in the trunk, including an AK-47 and a shotgun. In the backseat was a suitcase with a MAC-10 submachine gun inside.

When they searched Billy they found a nine-millimeter Beretta holstered to his side. But he produced permits for all his guns, and to his great surprise, they let him go. Billy turned around and raced home but stopped when he received a call from attorney Philip Gelso, Charles's cousin, who told him under no circumstance was he to go there.

"I just kept driving around, circling the neighborhood," said Billy. "I wanted to go in, but Phil kept telling me 'No! No! No!'"

Law enforcement raided six properties that day, including two owned by Kooch; another two owned by his friend Thomas Joseph, who ran Markdata; and one owned by Jeanne Stanton, a woman Billy had been seeing. It was at Stanton's house where they discovered Billy's black phone book, and among the many phone numbers was one for Louis DeNaples.

By the end of the day only Kooch had been arrested. A bookie and convicted felon from a previous gun possession charge, he was prohibited from having a firearm, and one was found in his home. The intent, however, had not been to arrest anyone. The aim of the overwhelming force was to search for evidence as part of a broader investigation.

When Billy finally returned home, Ellen was in tears. The morning after wasn't any better. Billy went outside to retrieve his newspaper from the delivery tube, and right there, along with the front-page stories about the raids with bold headlines, was a surveillance photo of Billy sitting casually at an outdoor restaurant having a beer with his arm around Stanton.

When Ellen saw it, she sat their adult children down in the kitchen and told them to ignore the papers. "You have a wonderful father," she said. But then she went into the bedroom and closed the door.

"Besides my kids, she knew there were three things I loved: my clothes, my car, and my jewelry," said Billy. "She took a scissors and cut off the collars of all my shirts. Then she carved a deep line in the dashboard of my car. I took her for a ride to a lake nearby to calm her down, but when we got there she pulled a seven-carat diamond ring off my hand and threw it out the window. There were geese everywhere, people were feeding them bread and popcorn, and they were running after the ring. I jumped out to get it but there were too many geese, and I had to kick them away like I was kicking extra points before I could pick it up."

The raid was the final act in a yearlong investigation of Billy by multiple federal, state, and local agencies. And they were helped along by his old friend from Philadelphia, Ralph Natale.

After receiving the blessing of the Colombo Family in New York, Natale didn't last long as the boss in Philadelphia. He had been indicted in 1999 on drug charges, and facing years in prison, he struck a deal with prosecutors and became a cooperator. He was the first sitting boss of an American Mafia family to turn government informant.

Natale was the prize witness in the ongoing federal trial of Joey Merlino, who had been charged with murder and racketeering. Natale told prosecutors a lot about Merlino, and about Billy, describing him not only as the head of the Bufalino Family but as a powerful figure with contacts throughout the country. Natale's cooperation led to Billy's banishment from Atlantic City. He claimed that for years Billy had run a multimillion-dollar money-laundering operation with runners bringing bags of cash from the family's gambling operation in Pennsylvania to Atlantic City. There they would buy chips at each casino, gamble a bit, and then cash the chips in. The laundering operation netted $2 million a year, said Natale. Billy wasn't charged criminally, but he was banned from entering any Atlantic City casino.

Nevertheless, the size and scope of the raid by the multiple law enforcement agencies led Billy to believe he would ultimately be charged with something, but an arrest would never come. Aside from headlines, the investigation produced little else, and it was eventually closed due to lack of evidence. It was a welcome surprise.

To celebrate, Billy took Ellen to Connecticut for a weekend of gambling. Since his banishment from Atlantic City, he'd been driving to the Foxwoods casino in the far eastern end of the state, a gleaming complex owned by the Mashantucket Pequot tribe. When he arrived with Ellen he took her to their room, she stepped inside, and her eyes widened. It was a suite, with a Jacuzzi, dining room, piano, and fully stocked bar with all of Billy's favorites, which meant a lot of Dewar's.

"The suite was almost as big as a house," said Billy. "I told them I needed a room, and we walked in and she's saying, 'Why are we here? Why are they giving us this stuff?' I told her don't worry about it. We're fine. But she was scared. This was right after they banned me from Atlantic City. I said, 'I can't go there, so fuck 'em.' So we made five or six trips to Foxwoods, then all of a sudden I got a letter. The Indian council is banning me from going there. Then I get another registered letter and it says I can't go to Delaware either. So now everyone is putting me on their list."

Around the same time came yet another surprise.

Frank Sheeran's book was finally published.

Big Frank had died on December 14, 2003. He was eighty-three and had been confined to a wheelchair and living in a nursing home in West Chester, Pennsylvania. Billy hadn't spent much time with Frank during his final few years. His health had been deteriorating and he was focused on his book.

"That's all he kept saying," said Billy. "'*Gotta do the book, gotta do the book, gotta take care of the kids, gotta take care of the kids.*' He had already written six versions, so I guess I really didn't take it seriously. What else was he going to say?" Apparently, a lot.

I Heard You Paint Houses was published in 2004, and in this version, Frank now claimed that *he* had killed Jimmy Hoffa.

In the book, touted as his "dying confession," Frank wrote that Hoffa was murdered as part of an elaborate scheme orchestrated by Russell, and it happened while Russell and Frank were driving with their wives to Detroit for the wedding of William Bufalino's daughter.

According to the book, Carrie and Irene Sheeran were dropped off at a diner in Ohio, and Russell and Frank then drove to a small, private airport off of Lake Erie. There, Frank boarded a small plane and was taken to Detroit while Russell waited in the car. The book claimed that once he was in Detroit, Frank was among the men who picked Hoffa up from the Machus Fox restaurant. They took him to a nearby house, and as soon as they stepped inside Frank shot Hoffa in the back of the head. He then returned to the airport, boarded the same plane, and rejoined Russell several hours later. It was a fantastic tale, and Billy had just one word to describe it.

"Fiction," said Billy. "It was worse than the others he had written. And in this one he said Russell waited three hours in a car while he flew to Detroit and back? Russell *never* would have done something like that. Russell never waited ten minutes for anybody. And he would never have let Carrie wait for him all that time. So now Carrie is an accomplice? It was insane. Frank did not kill Jimmy Hoffa. He knew that, and I knew that. We were both there at the meeting with the two Tonys. I saw and heard Russell tell Frank not to do anything. Frank wanted to kill them because they had Hoffa killed. His book was all bullshit. He even wrote that he killed Joey Gallo. He didn't. He wasn't there that night at the Copa, I was there with Angelo. That was all bullshit too. He wasn't there and Russell didn't call him.

"The only thing Frank did do right with the book was not include me. I told him not to mention me or anyone that was still alive, and he didn't. Don't get me wrong. Frank knew Russell long before me and was very close to him and to Jimmy. He was a scary man who could snap your neck in a heartbeat if he had to. But being with Russell all the time, I knew he tried to protect Jimmy. Russell loved the man. But then it just got to be too much with the Church Committee and the CIA and Cuba and all of that. They were all part of it, Jimmy, Giancana, Rosselli, the Kennedys, all that stuff. And who was the only one that was still alive? Russell. He never explained it to me and I never asked. You don't ask questions. He used to say that all the time. *Don't ask people questions.* But I knew when Jimmy was gone that Russell had to know. The Tonys would never have done it without Russell. I don't think Frank figured that out till much later. He said Russell told him in prison that Jimmy was taken out. But I knew Frank was just looking to make some money to leave behind for his kids, so when he couldn't sell the other crazy stories with his other writer, he came up with this. And it was just as nuts. And that little fucker he had write this book, Charles Brandt? I made Frank promise me that he would never publish the book as long as Carrie was alive. I told him again that day that me and Charlie Gelso met him and Brandt in Philadelphia. Brandt knew that, but Frank was dead, so Brandt didn't give a shit. I was really angry about that. I went to see Carrie about it. She didn't want to know about the book and didn't want to read it. She never did."

Frank had also promised Billy 10 percent of the proceeds and had papers drawn up. Billy had them in his office when the house was raided in 2001. But the contract was taken with everything else in his home and was never returned. Billy didn't care. Frank's claim that he'd killed Hoffa was such an overt fabrication, Billy thought he should have stuck with the Vietnamese hit men story. It was more entertaining.

But Billy's anger over the book quickly faded after he was called into a meeting with attorney John Moses, who was seeking Billy's signature. Moses, the former law partner of Charles Gelso, was representing Louis DeNaples.

"John Moses had become one of the biggest attorneys in the area," said Billy. "He came to Philip Gelso, Charlie's cousin, and said, 'Listen, Louie DeNaples wants Billy to sign this paper saying he was never associated with him.' Phil said no, but we meet and I said, 'John, are you out of your fucking mind? Why would he do that?' John goes, 'A million reasons.'"

The most powerful man in Pennsylvania wanted a casino, and he was about to do anything he could to get one.

CHAPTER 21

Take It to the Grave

In the summer of 2004, Louis DeNaples paid twenty-five million dollars for the shuttered Mount Airy Lodge in the Poconos.

Once a jewel that drew vacationers, honeymooners, and celebrities alike, it had fallen on hard times and gone bankrupt in 1999. It was finally closed in 2001 after its co-owner, Emil Wagner, committed suicide by shooting himself in the head.

The sprawling Mount Airy, with its eighteen-hole golf course and dilapidated facilities, fell into the hands of a private equity firm, Oaktree Capital Management, which sold it to DeNaples. When asked about his plans for the resort, DeNaples remained mum.

The onetime auto parts salesman, who once rebuilt a flooded car for Russell, was now a billionaire with over one hundred businesses, owned a bank, gave millions away to the University of Scranton and the Catholic diocese, and was the most powerful and influential man in the state whose reach extended to Washington, DC.

And now, he was eyeing a casino.

The plan had been years in the making and initially required the election of Edward Rendell as Pennsylvania governor in 2002. The former Philadelphia mayor and head of the Democratic National Committee ran on a platform that supported legislation to legalize casino gambling as a means to lower rising school property taxes. Rendell won as expected and the state legislature passed the new gambling legislation in July 2004.

After buying Mount Airy, DeNaples had every building on the vast property torn down before even applying for a gaming license.

DeNaples knew something, as did Billy.

"The fix was already in, that much I knew," said Billy. "We had talked about it before, him getting a casino. I tried to buy Mount Airy a few years earlier but couldn't put it together. Doc Mattioli, who owned Pocono Raceway, where they had the NASCAR races, he wanted one too. But now Louie wants a casino license and Mattioli backed down. But Louie figures he can't get approved for a license knowing me, and I'm not going to sign a paper that says I don't know him. There's a million ways that they know I knew Louis DeNaples. We were friends for years. The FBI had surveillance pictures and video of me going into his office four times a week. When I went to the auto shop they had an entrance in the front of the building and over here is a side door. This was Louis's private entrance. I'd use that entrance, and whenever I walked in we'd shake hands and he'd give me a kiss on the cheek. We'd go out with our wives. I had him at my daughter's wedding. After Moses wanted me to sign that letter I called his house and his wife, Betty Ann, picked up. She said, 'Bill, I'm so sorry. But he won't talk to you.' I knew the man for over thirty years. We did business together. I collected for him, kept other people away from him. He knew Russell. Dave fixed a trial for him. We helped him become a billionaire. Louie was one of us. He wasn't a made guy, but he was one of us. And now she says he won't talk to me? I'm thinking, 'How's he going to pull this off, trying to get a casino?' I figured that's the end of that."

But it was just the beginning.

For the first time in his life, on May 31, 2006, Billy was arrested. He had been charged in a five-count indictment alleging he helped two men launder drug money. Those men, Frank Pavlico and Louis

Pagnotti III, had been charged the previous year with laundering about $600,000 from drug sales. Billy stood accused of taking more than $460,000 of that money from Pavlico beginning in 2000 and putting it out on the street for him at 1 percent interest, with a payment to him once a week for over five years that totaled over $70,000.

Nearing sixty, Billy was arraigned and released. But his legal problems didn't end there. Over the summer he was called to the Woodlands to help resolve a dispute with "Johnny the Russian," who wasn't a Russian but a Serbian who claimed to have killed nine people. He had come to Hazleton a couple of years earlier and begun buying up real estate, including the local Veterans of Foreign Wars.

"He really stirred things up there," said Billy. "He was a tough guy. He had a rope that had to be ninety feet in the air and he'd climb it hand over hand in like forty seconds. He could sit next to you and put his leg over your head. All these Serbians were coming into Hazleton and he was the head guy."

Johnny asked Billy if he could set up a meeting for him with Luzerne County judge Michael Conahan. He was a close friend whom Billy had for years met several times a week for breakfast. Johnny wanted to see if Conahan would give him a license for a private detective agency.

"But then he says that he had this guy who took two girls from Serbia to come here and then he sent them somewhere," said Billy. "'But he's still here, and can I give you half a million dollars to get rid of him?' I said, 'Sure, no problem.' We agreed to meet again in Hazleton and I said, 'Here's the deal. If you want it, give me the names, I'll check them off the mat for half a million.' He says he'll give me one hundred thousand tomorrow. He has this guy with him, Big Earl, who had six or eight gold teeth. They were a fucking serious crew, so I said fine."

But Billy needed a favor from Johnny. After his May arrest, Billy learned that Frank Pavlico, whom he had known most of his life, was an FBI informant and the reason he had been charged. So he asked

Johnny to get rid of Pavlico and another man, Robert Kulick, a one-time close friend who had been an aide to Congressman Daniel Flood in the 1970s and who later married the daughter of Dr. Mattioli, the Pocono Raceway owner.

"But then I get arrested when Johnny tells the FBI that I tried to hire him to kill someone," said Billy. "It turns out Johnny was an informant too."

Agents from the FBI, U.S. Secret Service, Department of Homeland Security, IRS, Border Patrol, U.S. Immigration and Customs Enforcement, and the Pennsylvania State Police swarmed upon Billy and his home on October 17, 2006, and he was slapped with more charges, this time with money laundering, conspiracy, solicitation of murder, and witness tampering. He was immediately taken into custody. Following his arraignment he was transported to the Lackawanna County Prison in Scranton, and then to the Pike County prison. He would be taken back and forth between there and Scranton to meet with investigators. Billy was among the most valuable of prizes, and despite an onslaught of questioning over everything from Jimmy Hoffa to Middle Eastern terrorism, he remained mum. At his side was James Swetz, a well-known attorney from the Poconos who was appointed by the court after Phil Gelso was forced to recuse himself.

"So now I'm in jail," said Billy. "They would ask me questions—is this one in the New York family, is this guy in the Philadelphia family. I would say, 'Allegedly. This is what you people are saying.' They said I was mixed up in this kids-for-cash thing with Mike Conahan. They put that in the paper. I never knew about it until I got arrested."

The so-called kids-for-cash case involved allegations that Conahan and another judge, Mark Ciavarella, accepted nearly $3 million in bribes in exchange for sentencing hundreds of juveniles to a for-profit detention center. Phil Gelso had previously represented Conahan, which is why he had to step away.

"That whole deal, that wasn't Mike Conahan. I don't care what the fuck they tell me," said Billy. "I'd meet him every week at Perkins. The waitresses there knew our orders. Mike Conahan was the straightest judge I ever knew. Mike got eighteen years in prison. He was the president judge and knew about it, but he didn't need the fucking money and didn't take part in it. That I'm certain of. After that, they actually started from the early nineteen hundreds with the mob in this area and went from there. They thought I knew the history. I was with Russell, that's all I knew. And then they brought me in for Louie."

In December 2006, less than two months after Billy's arrest, the billionaire businessman Louis DeNaples was awarded a casino license. And accompanying him to the announcement in Harrisburg was Billy's old friend Father Joseph Sica.

Since his ordination in the early 1980s, Sica had remained in the area, serving at several different parishes and even authoring books on God and spirituality. But after DeNaples applied for his gaming license, Sica accompanied him to each public hearing. Dressed in his black cassock, he always stood so close to DeNaples he appeared to be a bodyguard rather than a spiritual adviser, clearing paths through reporters and other onlookers. It was a bizarre sight.

"Everyone was trying to figure out the relationship," said Billy. "All I can tell you is that they are supposed to be related."

DeNaples got his gaming license after interviews with the newly established gaming board and its investigators, during which he denied having any relationship with Russell Bufalino, Billy, or any organized crime figure. When asked about Billy, DeNaples said he was just some "guy from the neighborhood."

Billy knew his old friend had lied, but he also knew that it had already been preordained that DeNaples would get his license. DeNaples had his own fixer, Pat Solano, the Pittston native and powerful political insider who had served and advised nine Pennsylvania governors. After connecting Solano to Billy and Joe Scalleat of Hazleton, via surveillance and phone records, the crime commission was about to open an investigation of Solano in 1993. But the state House of Representatives passed a bill in December pulling the commission's funding, forcing its demise.

Billy knew for years that Solano had spread enough of DeNaples's money around to curry the political capital he always needed, whether for a business, for his bank, or even to pave the way for new legislation and a casino license. For the casino, it was money well spent, as Solano secured the cooperation of Governor Rendell, key figures within his administration, several state senators, and well-entrenched attorneys and lobbyists. The Pennsylvania Supreme Court was also on board, a necessity given the expected litigation from other casino hopefuls who, upon their rejection, would challenge the DeNaples license in court.

"I heard it was around four million, that's how much was paid out," said Billy. "They even put in the legislation that a felon whose conviction was older than fifteen years could get a license. Dave fixed his trial in 1977, and DeNaples pleaded no contest in 1978, so his felony was almost thirty years old. Who lets felons have casino licenses, no matter how old the felony? So the way they set it up it didn't count against him. But he needed me out of the way. He could never say how close we were, and he probably figured that me and Kooch would probably want something, like say the gift store. So after my first arrest in May, the next day I get a call from his bank, the First National Community Bank. They're pulling all my loans. Whenever I needed a loan or a mortgage I just went to see Louie and he'd sign his initials to the bottom of the page and that was it. Done. Now he doesn't want to know me. He already knew he was getting the casino license."

But DeNaples's license approval drew the scrutiny of the Dauphin County district attorney Ed Marsico, who empaneled a grand jury in Harrisburg, and Billy was among a host of people subpoenaed to testify in 2007. Others included his friend Barry Shapiro and several current and former Philadelphia city officials.

"I had to appear before the grand jury and I wasn't going to perjure myself," said Billy. "I told them Louie was a friend of mine, and we knew each other and did business for thirty years, that I knew his father, Patrick, and that I knew Father Sica from years ago. That was it. But when I saw what happened in Scranton with Tom Marino, the U.S. attorney and the guy that was prosecuting me there, it all came together. I realized then just how badly Louie wanted me off the streets."

Tom Marino was an unknown Lycoming County district attorney who had been unexpectedly nominated by Senator Arlen Specter in 2002 to become the next U.S. attorney for the Middle District of Pennsylvania, which included Scranton and Wilkes-Barre. Senator Rick Santorum gave his blessing, and Marino was appointed by President George W. Bush.

But in August 2007, following Billy's testimony before the grand jury in Harrisburg, he learned from newspaper reports that Marino was under investigation by the U.S. Department of Justice for providing a reference for DeNaples's gaming application. It was a shocking turn of events, and Marino was forced to resign two months later. He immediately took a job as an in-house attorney for DeNaples, who paid him $250,000 a year.

"I always knew the fix was in for DeNaples and that casino, but I didn't realize just how deep it went," said Billy. "Louie's money went far, all the way to Washington, and I knew he always had Pat Solano and Specter in his pocket, and he had Specter appoint Marino. Louie already controlled the state police, and now he had his own U.S. attorney to get me. But after Marino was forced to quit, Louie was arrested, and then he tried to have me killed."

DeNaples was charged in January 2008 with four counts of perjury for lying to the gaming board about his past and current ties to the hierarchy of the Bufalino crime family, specifically Russell and Billy. The charges filed were, in part, due to Billy's testimony before the grand jury.

DeNaples's preliminary hearing was set for February, and prosecutors planned to have Billy testify in public about their long-standing relationship. DeNaples was terrified at the prospect of such a spectacle, as were Rendell and the other political cronies who had supported DeNaples in his casino endeavor. But the hearing was suddenly postponed. The Pennsylvania Supreme Court, in a highly unusual and controversial action, stopped the proceeding after De-Naples claimed in a court filing there were illegal leaks to the press during the grand jury testimony. No one could remember when the court had ever stopped a criminal prosecution.

"Louie owned the supreme court too," said Billy. "He had it in his pocket. The only thing that could do him in was me. So he started telling people I was a government informant."

The claim was made by DeNaples's attorney Richard Sprague of Philadelphia. A former prosecutor who once worked for Senator Specter when he was the district attorney in Philadelphia in the 1970s, Sprague had risen to become one of the most powerful attorneys in Pennsylvania. In one court filing, he said Billy was reputedly a "longtime State Police Confidential Informant" who testified before the grand jury to earn favorable treatment.

"I was never an informant for anyone. Never," said Billy. "But you know what they do in prison to alleged informants. So they put that out there on purpose to put my life in danger, knowing it wasn't true. But they wanted me dead so I couldn't testify."

Fearing for Billy's safety, prison officials transferred him from one prison to another and kept him in isolation until his sentencing.

Along with DeNaples, Father Sica was also charged with perjury for lying to the grand jury about his relationship with Russell, which was also due to Billy's testimony. When two state police troopers arrested Sica the morning of January 3, 2008, they found $1,000 in cash on him and a loaded handgun. He was also heavily in debt, owing nearly $225,000 on credit cards, car loans, and a $148,000 bank loan from DeNaples's own First National Community Bank.

Billy had agreed to plead guilty when prosecutors dropped sixteen of the eighteen charges against him, including attempting to have a witness killed.

On November 24, 2008, his day of reckoning had finally come. Ellen was there, as were his children, Carolyn, Miriam, and Russell. He was sentenced to nine years in prison, less two years for time served.

"I would like to accept responsibility for my actions," Billy said before the court. "I hope I will soon be able to resume my life with my family."

Federal prosecutors, in agreeing to the reduced sentence, acknowledged Billy's cooperation in the DeNaples investigation. They also hailed Billy's conviction as a milestone. After more than a century, the Bufalino crime family, they said, was finally dead.

Six months later, Louis DeNaples agreed to a deal in which he'd relinquish his ownership of the Mount Airy Casino and turn over his interest to a trust to be run by his daughter, Lisa. In return, perjury charges against him and Father Sica were dropped.

The district attorney, Ed Marsico, said he had no choice given he couldn't continue to fight the Pennsylvania Supreme Court, which had delayed his prosecution for over a year.

For Billy, his federal prison experience had begun badly. He'd previously had surgery at a hospital near the Pike County prison to repair a ruptured hernia. It was awful. He had been brought back to his cell that same night and given the wrong medications, and he'd developed a severe infection.

"I was being transferred but first had to take a seventeen-hour bus ride to the Oklahoma City transfer station," said Billy. "The bandage was full of blood. They had given me a bag of milk and a bologna sandwich and I used the milk as a pillow. When we got there I was in the hospital for two months. I didn't know where I was; Ellen couldn't reach me. Then I was sent to Victorville prison in California, which was a hellhole, and then to Tucson, Arizona, where they shut the place down when they heard I was coming. They brought all the guards in and put my picture on the screen and said that I thought I was the godfather but I wasn't going to run things there."

Billy was placed in solitary confinement and remained in the cold and darkness for several weeks, given just one hour per day outside to stretch his legs. Once released to the general population, he was visited again by different investigatory agencies seeking information on one case or another. Among them were two FBI agents from yet another task force investigating Jimmy Hoffa's disappearance. Billy told them they were wasting their time.

Following his release from solitary, he was closely watched.

"They didn't think I'd settle in there but I had some moves," said Billy. "I got this little gambling thing going using tuna fish and stamps as money, and I knew a guy in the kitchen and we were making pizzas and selling them. Everyone knew who I was. Even the Aryan Brotherhood guys who celebrated Hitler's birthday gave me my space. So did the Spanish guys. And everyone knew I wasn't a snitch. Louie and Sprague and his people kept saying it, but no one in prison believed it. A lot of guys knew me, and there were other guys I had met. One was a biker, Detour. He was with the Mongols and I think he killed a few people. I liked him a lot. He was my best friend in prison. When he heard about Louie calling me an informant he was really angry and asked me if I wanted him killed. He wanted me to give him the contract. A lot of guys asked me that, in and out of prison, to give them the contract to kill Louie. That's how upset they were. I could have given the okay and that was that. But I said no. The way they all backed me, I knew I didn't have anything to worry about there. But I did worry about my family back home. I knew this was rough on them, especially Ellen."

The raids in 2001 and 2006 had taken their toll on Ellen. And then came the friends who suddenly disappeared and the financial distress that followed with Billy being away. Money was often tight, and at times she didn't have enough to pay for a flight to visit with Billy. She had also suffered a heart attack but didn't tell her husband. She didn't want to worry him.

"It was a difficult, terrible experience. A nightmare," said Ellen. "My blood pressure was really high and I got diabetes. I was a nurse, I thought I should have been strong enough to control it myself. But I couldn't. And I swore I had PTSD. To this day I still jump if I hear the front doorbell ring or helicopters overhead. There were a lot of people that we called friends, people we grew up with and knew for years, and a lot of people I met through Billy that I was very fond of and were always our friends, and then they weren't. And how about Louis? He doesn't know us? I was at your house the day your kids were going for their confirmation. I knew Betty Ann very well. And there were calls from people who said maybe it would be a good thing if we don't talk to each other for a while. I think the worst thing was that nobody cared what was happening to us."

Ellen didn't even have Carrie. She had passed away at the Wesley Village nursing home on December 30, 2006. She was ninety-five. Carrie left the home in Kingston she had with Russell to Billy's son, Russell, who helped care for her during her final years.

Aside from Ellen and the various law enforcement agencies, the only visitor Billy had was his childhood pal Wally. When he came out for a third visit, Wally was visibly thin and sickly.

"Whenever he flew out to see me we'd talk for hours," said Billy. "But that last time I knew he didn't look good and I told him he had to go to a doctor right away and he did. They told him he had cancer, and he died pretty quickly."

Billy served four years of his seven-year sentence and was released from prison in the fall of 2012. He returned home to Pennsylvania, and at sixty-six he took a job at a local ice-cream shop as part of his probation. He also had a lot of mending to do with Ellen, who stuck by him through it all. They started working on being thankful for what they had. Their children were doing well professionally, they had grandchildren, and they still had their home in Hughestown and the summer house they had bought years earlier up north on the Susquehanna River. They went up there each summer with their family, and it was peaceful and quiet, and each passing day was another day removed from the tumultuous life they had led.

"When I was in the hole in Arizona I had a lot of time to think," said Billy. "And I thought about my life and what it would have been like if I hadn't met Russell. Even sitting there all day and night in that dark, cold jail cell, or even being locked away for four years, I knew being there was part of the deal. I accepted that. Russell had introduced me to so much, good and bad, and I absolutely loved him for it. He'd say, 'Kid, this is the life we chose.' And it was. And I don't have any regrets. None."

EPILOGUE

Billy D'Elia and I met dozens of times inside the modest Kingston house that for many years Russell Bufalino called home with his wife, Carolyn.

The house is a literal museum. Much of the original furniture and gold (some might say gaudy) fixtures are still in place, including Russell's office, as is the downstairs, which was his sanctuary where he entertained and held many of his important meetings.

It took a few weeks for Billy and me to feel comfortable, maybe a couple of months, but we eventually got there. Of course, some of the big questions concerned Jimmy Hoffa. Billy is the last surviving member of the Bufalino Family, and law enforcement officials had waited many years for their chance to get to him. When they finally did in 2006, they believed they'd hit the jackpot.

Billy's reach was far and wide, yet when all was said and done, after the FBI, Secret Service, Homeland Security, IRS, various organized crime task forces, and a grand jury (among others) came and went, there were only two arrests—businessman Louis DeNaples and Father Joseph Sica. And those resulted not from Billy's telling a grand jury that he had been friends with both men, but from the men's perjuring themselves with their own denials that they had known him.

In the end, Billy gave them nothing. And that included Jimmy Hoffa.

Hoffa's disappearance has vexed the nation since 1975. And his possible burial sites (New Jersey swamps?) have been the butt of jokes since then.

Billy scoffed at it too, finding it ludicrous that anyone would think the most recognizable labor leader in America would be murdered and his body transported through several states just to be disposed of. Billy knew that world and how things were done, and he didn't hesitate when he said Hoffa had been "cooked," or cremated, likely within minutes of his death.

Yet after confirming the FBI's long-held suspicion that it was Anthony Provenzano and Anthony Salerno who carried out the plan, Billy was hesitant to involve Russell. He loved the man, more than anyone will ever know, and you could see it pained him when he admitted that Russell had to have approved it.

Russell had kept Hoffa out of harm's way for two years, but the U.S. Senate's Church Committee was the final straw, and the news stories of his involvement in the CIA/Mafia plots stoked Russell's fears that he and Hoffa would be subpoenaed to testify and further investigation could reveal the full breadth of Russell's secret alliance with the CIA. Those ties ran deep. How deep, no one may ever know.

But in an ironic twist, the committee wasn't investigating Russell or Hoffa, and both men were never in any danger of being subpoenaed to testify.

Karl Inderfurth, who served as an investigator on the Church Committee and was interviewed for this book, said the focus of the committee's investigation of the CIA/Mafia plots was Sam Giancana and Johnny Rosselli, who turned out to be the second group of Mafia members the CIA recruited for its operations in Cuba. Giancana was killed before he could testify, and Rosselli, who did testify during a closed session, was about to testify again when he was killed.

"The committee was very concerned to have a witness before the committee murdered," said Inderfurth. "We went down there and the police showed us photographs where Rosselli was chopped up and [of] the barrel that he was stuffed in. That was a sobering moment, to see all of that."

So if the committee wasn't investigating Russell, who leaked the information that he was one of the CIA recruits?

Denny Walsh, the former *Sacramento Bee* investigative reporter who broke the story about Russell's CIA ties in June 1975 (along with *Time* magazine), told me his source was Herbert Itkin, a former CIA agent who had operated among organized crime families for years and also served as a source for the FBI. Someone familiar with the inner workings of the committee was trying to get the word out about Russell's involvement, and it was Itkin who leaked it to the press. But even after Russell was outed publicly, Inderfurth said, the committee *still* didn't pursue Russell or Hoffa.

For its part, then–CIA director William Colby thought it important to deny any CIA involvement soon after Hoffa's disappearance.

And aside from confirming to Billy that he had been on a boat off the coast of Cuba during the Bay of Pigs invasion in 1961, Russell never shared anything with him about his CIA ties. Not a word.

"Russell never kept anything from me. Never. But I could see a couple of instances where he was trying to protect me, like a father would, and maybe this was one of those instances," said Billy. "Russell told me about the two Tonys and Frank, and I was there that day in New York with them, but that was pretty much it. I knew they wouldn't have done it, killed Jimmy, without Russell's approval. But were others involved? Jimmy was scaring a lot of people with his threats, even the government."

As for why Frank Sheeran later claimed to have killed Hoffa, Billy said it was all about money, and that Sheeran's children did benefit from the book and from the 2019 Martin Scorsese film based on the book *The Irishman*.

And finally, as to who actually pulled the trigger and killed Jimmy Hoffa, Billy said Russell never told him but that his gut said it was Salvatore "Sally Bugs" Briguglio. It appeared that Frank Sheeran shared that opinion.

This is my second book on the Bufalinos. The first, *The Quiet Don* in 2013, relied mostly on FBI files, government documents, prosecutors, my prior reporting, and several fringe sources. But no one knew the Bufalino story as well as Billy, and I jumped at the chance to immeasurably add to, and even correct, the known history of the Bufalino Family. During the nearly two years that I spent with Billy, I've never found an instance where he lied to me or led me astray. He was earnest, as was his wife, Ellen, who sat down with me for one session. Billy's memory was razor-sharp, and his encyclopedic knowledge of organized crime was something to marvel at. Each interview was recorded and fact-checked as best as possible—mostly dates and places and people. After sharing his stories about his dealings with Donald Trump, for example, I spoke with Barry Shapiro, who confirmed what Billy told me. And Hoffa's daughter, Barbara Crancer, a retired circuit court judge in St. Louis, told me she never believed Frank Sheeran's story, calling it "fantastical."

Billy didn't shy away from any topic, with the exception of his involvement in any violence. It was one area he wanted to stay away from.

He's pleasant, even funny, and his natural charm caught me off guard. He has the same disarming personality as Russell. But make no mistake: Billy D'Elia was a stone-cold gangster, a man of great influence, well respected and feared.

When he was in prison in 2009, he thought he'd caught a final score with his old friend Frank DiLeo (Tookie), who reunited with Michael Jackson and signed on again as his manager. But the reunion was brief. Jackson died just a few weeks later while preparing for his comeback concerts in London. Tookie died two years later, in 2011.

Since his release from prison in 2012, Billy has led a quiet life. He suffered a blow in 2018 when his childhood friend and former street boss Sam "Kooch" Marranca passed away. He spends his days with Ellen, who amazingly stayed with him through it all (they celebrated their fiftieth wedding anniversary in 2021).

During the summer they go up north to their home on the bank of the Susquehanna River, the one they've had since the early 1980s, where they often receive their children and grandchildren, and every now and then reminisce about Russell, who once gave Billy a choice—one that he made without hesitation.

Matt Birkbeck
August 2022

ACKNOWLEDGMENTS

This book was born from an email I received in August 2020 asking if I'd be interested in meeting Billy D'Elia. Five minutes later I wrote to Dave Mathis, a friend of Billy's who had sent the note, and thus began this journey.

Dave and Russell D'Elia were instrumental in bringing this book to life. Russell was kind enough to allow me to conduct my many hours of interviews with his father in the old Bufalino home. They also maintained the secrecy this project required, and I can't thank them enough for all their help.

Thanks also go to journalist extraordinaire Alex Napoliello, who researched several key story lines, particularly the Church Committee; to my longtime attorney, Jay Kenoff, who provided his usual good advice whenever I needed it, and to my friend and editor Don Armstrong, whom I've relied on for years.

Special thanks to my agent, Susan Canavan, who was invaluable in guiding this project along from an idea to a proposal to a book, and to my gifted editor Mauro DiPreta and his team at William Morrow, especially Andrew Yackira.

And, of course, there wouldn't have been a book without Billy D'Elia.

He had a hell of a story, and I'm glad he let me tell it.